Family Secrets and the Contemporary German Novel

This book focuses on representations of familial conflict in German and Austrian prose of the last twenty-five years. Some of the most prominent German and Austrian writers examine the theme of familial conflict that cannot be explained by traditional explanations: psychic hostilities, economic deprivation, or repressed experience. At the heart of these novels is the collision between the bonds of family and the events that form the decisive turning points of our age: National Socialism, the Second World War, and the Holocaust. Elizabeth Snyder Hook examines five novels in detail: Christa Wolf's *Kindheitsmuster*, Thomas Bernhard's *Auslöschung*, Peter Schneider's *Vati*, Elfriede Jelinek's *Die Ausgesperrten*, and Elisabeth Reichart's *Februarschatten*. Central to the discussions of each novel are questions of guilt, cultural identity, and atonement, and of the relocation of these ultimately unresolvable issues from the larger national and political arena to the realm of intimate relationships between parents and children.

Elizabeth Snyder Hook is assistant professor of German at the University of North Carolina-Asheville.

Studies in German Literature, Linguistics, and Culture

Edited by James Hardin
(*South Carolina*)

FAMILY SECRETS
AND THE
CONTEMPORARY GERMAN NOVEL

Literary Explorations in the
Aftermath of the Third Reich

Elizabeth Snyder Hook

CAMDEN HOUSE

First published 2001
by Camden House

Camden House is an imprint of Boydell & Brewer Inc.
PO Box 41026, Rochester, NY 14604–4126 USA
and of Boydell & Brewer Limited
PO Box 9, Woodbridge, Suffolk IP12 3DF, UK

ISBN: 1–57113–185–x

Library of Congress Cataloging-in-Publication Data

Snyder Hook, Elizabeth, 1963–
    Family secrets and the contemporary German novel: literary explorations
    in the aftermath of the Third Reich / Elizabeth Snyder Hook.
        p. cm. – (Studies in German literature, linguistics, and culture)
    Includes bibliographical references and index.
    ISBN 1–57113–185–X (alk. paper)
    1. German fiction—20th century—History and criticism. 2. Austrian fiction—
20th century—History and criticism. 3. Family in literature. I. Title. II. Studies
in German literature, linguistics, and culture (Unnumbered).

PT405.S56 2001
833'.91409355—dc21
                                                                    00–066754

A catalogue record for this title is available from the British Library.

This publication is printed on acid-free paper.
Printed in the United States of America

MACBETH   Canst thou not minister to a mind diseas'd,
Pluck from the memory a rooted sorrow,
Raze out the written troubles of the brain
And with some sweet oblivious antidote
Cleanse the stuff'd bosom of that perilous stuff
Which weighs upon the heart?

DOCTOR   Therein the patient
Must minister to himself.

Macbeth
Act V Scene III

Contents

Acknowledgments

THE SEED FOR THIS BOOK WAS PLANTED over a decade ago when, as an American student in Germany, I began to hear stories about life during the Third Reich. Some older Germans spoke of Allied air raids, the unforgettable sound of sirens, the widespread loss of life and property. Others talked about the years that followed; the lack of jobs, food, and shelter. Many focused on Germany's collective guilt and expressed a deep-felt sorrow about the victims of Nazi atrocities.

But it was not just the older generation — those who experienced National Socialism firsthand — that spoke out. Younger Germans had their own stories to tell. The university students with whom I studied vocally resisted the burden of their country's Nazi past. In conveying this resentment, they frequently contrasted the exuberant nationalism of the United States with their own beleaguered identity as Germans. You Americans, they'd say, are proud of your country; you feel no qualms about chanting pro-US slogans or flying the American flag whenever and wherever you like — from post offices to football games. But what about us Germans? How are we supposed to feel?

It was with these thoughts in mind that I entered graduate school and began to explore how German-speaking writers address this problematic, ever-present past. My curiosity led to seminar papers, a dissertation, and finally this book. Looking back, I realize just how long and circuitous my search for answers has been. And I am once again aware of the many colleagues, mentors, and friends without whom this journey would not have taken place.

First, I wish to thank the Fulbright Commission for awarding me a study grant to Germany. I also want to express my appreciation to Christoph Schweitzer and Alice Kuzniar of the University of North Carolina Chapel Hill for their mentorship and support. A special thanks to Michael Proterra and Barbara Braden of Creighton University, who believed in the importance of this book and generously supported its completion by awarding me a summer fellowship and a much-needed course remission.

I owe a special debt of gratitude to Maria Tatar, Judith Ryan, and Beatrice Hanssen at Harvard University, who read (and re-read) early versions of this project and offered both expert criticism and timely encouragement. I am also grateful to Peter Schneider, whose Harvard seminar on Contemporary German Literature encouraged me to explore generational differences regarding the Third Reich in the context of the postwar family.

I will always be grateful to Judith Gurewich for listening and speaking her mind. To Peter Fritzsche, Jill Kowalik, Bryan LeBeau, and Andreas Gommermann I offer my heart-felt appreciation. Their professional advice, sound judgment, and sustained support was invaluable.

I am particularly thankful to my cheerful and resourceful research assistant Yvonne Reher, and to the dedicated, indefatigable staff at Reinert Alumni Library: Gayle Crawford, Lynn Schneiderman, Chris LeBeau, and Geraldine Chase.

As is so often the case, I profited immensely from the insights of my students. *Herzlichen Dank* for your hard work and enthusiasm and for giving me a place to test my ideas.

A writerly thank-you to Jim Walker of Camden House for assisting me in the contractual aspects of this book. And to my editor James Hardin for patiently insisting on clarity and for keeping my feet to the fire.

Most of all, I thank my parents, Charles and Marjorie Snyder, and my husband, Brian S. Hook. You understood better than anyone my need to write this book and gave me the determination and confidence to see it through to the end. Thank you for your patience, your love, and your support.

E.S.H.
September 2000

Introduction

FAMILY CONFLICT IS AS OLD AS LITERATURE ITSELF. Adam blames
Eve. Cain kills Abel. In Hesiod's *Theogony*, even the history of the
heavens and the world is one of intergenerational strife. What has
changed is the way we explain it. The Bible calls it sin; for the Greeks, it
is desire for power. In the modern world, theories of domestic conflict
extend to include psychological and social explanations, many of which
are now entrenched in our cultural repertoire: Freud's notion of familial jealousy and rivalry; the repercussions of a parent's unresolved
trauma; the discord caused by poverty, absentee fathers, or abuse. Family conflict exists as a ubiquitous theme not only in our literary and religious heritage, but also in our daily experience.

This book is about how recent German and Austrian literature adds a
new dimension to this ancient theme. For the last quarter-century, novels produced by some of these countries' most prominent writers examine the theme of familial conflict in ways that exceed the traditional
categories of psychic hostilities, economic deprivation, or repressed experience. Their fiction remains rooted in the complex and often difficult
nature of domestic alliances. But the origins of familial conflict, dysfunc-
tion, or disintegration embedded in their plots are unique. At the heart
of these narratives is the collision between the bonds of family and events
which figure as the decisive turning points of our age: National Socialism, the Second World War, and the Holocaust.

In his landmark book *Schuldig geboren: Kinder aus Nazifamilien*
(Born Guilty: Children of Nazi Families, 1987), Viennese journalist
Peter Sichrovsky records the voices of men and women whose families
were involved in the Third Reich — as soldiers, as officers, as bureau-
crats, as guards in concentration camps. Sichrovsky states in the preface
to his work that having previously interviewed Jewish children of Holocaust survivors, it was now time to hear from "the others," the children
of the perpetrators. The son of Jewish parents who had spent the war
years abroad, Sichrovsky recalls the impenetrable silences of his non-
Jewish schoolmates, a silence which contrasted sharply with his own desire to tell his parents' story. He writes:

> My interest in the descendants of the perpetrators of the Third Reich
> took me into uncharted territory, and confronted me, as I was forced

to admit, with men and women who were largely unfamiliar. I knew little about their concerns, their fantasies and their burdens, which their parents' histories had foisted upon them, and which they carried around with them day after day.[1]

What Sichrovsky uncovers in these striking interviews reveals that the period of National Socialism left its mark not only on the children of the victims, but also on those of the victimizers. Sichrovsky's subjects speak of the dissonance between public images of "radiant, youthful" SS officers and the private memories they have of their parents — "fleeing for their lives, bombed out of their homes, without shelter or work, pursued by Allied police, arrested and sometimes indicted."[2] They speak of the moment when they realized that this was only part of the story; that their parents, through passive acquiescence or active participation, allowed Hitler's regime to flourish. They speak of their own feelings of victimization, their sense of being burdened by a history that is not their own. And they speak of the guilt that will follow them all their lives. For these children of Nazi parents, Sichrovsky discovered, the history of the Third Reich is more than a generic political past. Despite their differences in age and background, the Third Reich exists for each of them as an ever-present legacy, one that shapes their sense of personal and cultural identity and their perspective on a history in which their own parents played a part. In the words of thirty-nine-year-old Anna: "Is one generation enough to make sheep out of wolves? After all, the families remain the same."[3]

This study focuses on five German-speaking novelists who, in the years surrounding Sichrovsky's project, began a similar process of exploration, examination, and disclosure. The authors I will discuss are from West Germany (Peter Schneider), the former East Germany (Christa Wolf), and Austria (Thomas Bernhard, Elfriede Jelinek, Elisabeth Reichart), and represent two consecutive generations of writers who have explored the Nazi past within the context of the postwar family. Specifically, I will attempt to show how the Nazi years are depicted in each of the novels as a period that is not yet over, an era whose destructive consequences for the family are still being felt. Central to these novels are questions of individual complicity, collective guilt, and personal atonement, and the relocation of these issues from the larger national and political arena to the intimate relationships between parents and their children. It is this concept of the Third Reich as an ongoing destabilizing force — problematizing, undermining, and in some cases destroying the relations between spouses, parents, and their children — that lies at the core of each novel. As Christa Wolf states in the opening line of her 1976 novel *Kindheitsmuster* (Patterns of Childhood), "what is past is not dead; it is not even past."

Following the standard division of postwar German literature into those writers who were adults during the war, those who were children during the war, and those born either during or soon after the war, I have organized this book according to the years the authors were born rather than by the publication dates of their novels.[4] I have also elected to restrict my study to writers who were children during or after the war. Literary reflections on the Third Reich's impact on the family are not limited to German and Austrian writers who grew up under Hitler or during the so-called *Wirtschaftswunder* (economic miracle) of the 1950s. As early as 1945, writers who experienced National Socialism as adults began to provide vivid images of the war's devastating impact on individuals and their families. Their novels are replete with war-torn landscapes, shell-shocked husbands, grief-stricken widows, and father-less children.[5] What is conspicuously absent from these early novels, however, is Germany's causal role in the war, which left such personal and material ruin. Mirroring attitudes of the population at large (for whom the war's close proximity appears to have precluded an ade-quately critical assessment of its causes),[6] the novels of the immediate postwar era present the period of National Socialism not as a product of widespread individual corruption, but rather as an evil force residing beyond the control of the average citizen.[7] Families are shown to be at the mercy of a fate they can neither change nor even fully understand. Spouses and parents are, as one scholar asserts, "good but weak; and are not able to make their way through this world of violence, cruelty and deception."[8] For those writers who were adults during the Third Reich, familial traumas take precedence over moral accountability; per-sonal losses supplant questions of collective guilt.[9] What they and oth-ers of their generation were not yet willing (or able) to fully countenance was the voluntary, even enthusiastic, support that brought Hitler to power in the first place, nor the implications of such complic-ity for future generations.

Writers of the next two generations, including those represented in this study, no longer speak of National Socialism as a plague. Fueled by the Eichmann trial of 1961 and the trial of Auschwitz guards in 1963–65, there emerged within the literary and larger cultural sphere a growing opposition to the older generation's failed political awareness. Those born during and after the war informed themselves about the crimes committed under Hitler and became increasingly aware of the cover-ups and denials rampant among their elders. In the late 1960s, the war in Vietnam and the tensions of the Cold War gave rise to criticism of renewed political aggression and motivated students to question their parents and grandparents about their involvement in the authoritarian structures of Nazism. Opposition to the older generation grew and ultimately found expression not only in the student rebellions of 1968, but in a literature intent on exposing the truth. Proving that postwar literature did not occur in a vacuum,[10] these novels mark the evolution of the postwar novel from accounts of defeated and hungry citizens to depictions of an economically secure population haunted by inescapable guilt.[11]

Judith Ryan writes that much of recent German literature is characterized by the tendency of Germans born after the war to confront "with very mixed emotions the idea that their parents may have been involved in criminal actions during the Third Reich."[12] Moving away from the New Subjectivism of the early 1970s, when private reflection and the search for identity often took precedence over political engagement, novelists began in the latter part of the decade to examine the more subtle and complex issues affecting the relationship between the older and younger generations. First among these novels of generational conflict were the so-called *Vaterbücher* (father books), largely autobiographical works that posed questions about the past to the older generation[13] and instigated a search into the "lost period of their fathers during the Third Reich."[14] It was in the 1980s that German authors shifted from writing about their own private experiences and began instead to compose "imaginative projections" into the minds of the children of Nazis.[15] Although these novels, like the father books, are steeped in an awareness of National Socialism and of its continuing impact on contemporary German life, their authors are less intent on assigning blame for the Third Reich to their parents than on investigating the more personal question of inherited guilt. Did their generation, as declared in the Old Testament, share in the sins of their fathers?[16] And if so, were its members fated to perpetuate a legacy they themselves despised?

For contemporary German and Austrian writers, this incriminating, destabilizing aspect of the Third Reich finds expression not only in the content of their stories, but in the structure and language of their narratives. In contrast to what Bahktin terms the "word of the fathers," an authoritative discourse that dictates our relationship to past and present,[17] the authors contained in this study employ a new kind of language to reflect the dislocations of their time. They consciously avoid the direct, "photographic" representations of suffering typical of early postwar writers[18] and prioritize the complexities of memory and testimony over realistic depictions of social experience. Their novels seek to tell the truth of history; but they also expose the difficulties inherent in the articulation of subjective experience and reveal the emotional and linguistic obstacles faced by those who seek to bear witness. The novelists presented in this study make use of multiple and competing voices, fragmented and illogical speech, contradictory and conflicted protagonists, and characters who seek refuge in silence.

The authors presented in this study are unified by a central dilemma — the troubled search for *Heimat*. This term, German for home or homeland, carries with it a wealth of romantic associations: the place of one's birth, the people and customs of one's childhood, the sights and sounds that animate one's memory. But is it possible to feel nostalgic about a country that killed millions? Is it permissible to remember fondly a hometown that facilitated such murder through complicity or cowardice? The Third Reich altered, perhaps permanently, the ability of German-speaking authors to speak of *Heimat* in unambivalent terms. What was once a simple declaration of personal and cultural identity is now, for new generations of writers, an enterprise "carried out under the cloud of Germany's history."[19] As one scholar succinctly observes, "there is not a single aspect of German life and letters that remains unaffected by Auschwitz."[20]

In the following chapters, I will attempt to show how, for each of the writers contained in this book, the complexities of memory, truth-telling, and *Heimat* become inextricable from investigations of the family. Common to these novels is the conviction that the German and Austrian family did not serve as a defense against corrupt political ideology, but rather laid the groundwork for political manipulation through the perversion of individual identity and the devaluation of a humane connection to others. The family was not simply the recipient of Nazism but its instrument. Similarly, patterns of familial rigidity, passivity, and denial are not considered isolated cases. They are depicted as traits embedded in the structure of the traditional authoritarian home and are seen to have furnished fuel for the National Socialist cause. The novels' narrators likewise share many key features. Their investigations of the Nazi past include an analysis of their own identity and provoke attempts to distance themselves from the attitudes and behaviors of their parents. Frequently, it is the death of a mother or father (or both) that serves as the catalyst for the narrator's journey into the past. In examining his or her familial history, each narrator engages in a kind of

Selbsttherapie, refining both an understanding of self and the actions of earlier generations.[21]

For those writers who were children during the Third Reich, this negative assessment of the German and Austrian family combines with painful memories of their own childhood. Although too young to have fully comprehended the import of their actions, their participation in Nazi youth groups or their indifference to Hitler's victims leads to a lifelong sense of complicity. Any examination of the Nazi past, any attempt to tell the truth, is for these writers the excavation of one's childhood and, in some cases, the re-opening of childhood wounds. Writers born in the 1940s and 1950s are no less haunted by their countries' crimes. Although few can personally recall the period of National Socialism, their novels are overshadowed by the guilt of their parents. Explicit in much of this writing is a persistent ambivalence toward those family members who are considered accomplices, either by committing actual brutalities or by failing to intervene. Filial love and acceptance are mixed with equal measures of anger and scorn. Of central concern to this third generation of writers is the question of inherited guilt. In learning the details of their parents' wartime lives, those born during or after the war confront the implications of this parentage and increasingly fear that they have somehow been corrupted. Perhaps such fears are warranted. As the writers of this study bear out, those who vehemently reject their parents' attitudes and behaviors are often driven to repeat them.

The five novels discussed in this book allow for a diverse exploration of familial conflict in the wake of Nazism, genocide, and war. The first chapter examines Christa Wolf's *Kindheitsmuster* (Patterns of Childhood, 1976), a novel which chronicles the narrator's return to the site of her war-torn adolescence and her attempts to share the memory of this experience with her own family. Chapter two is a study of Thomas Bernhard's *Auslöschung* (Extinction, 1986), the last of Bernhard's novels. It presents the confessions of Franz-Josef Murau, an Austrian expatriate whose parents' death establishes him not only as master of their estate, but as inheritor of a sinister familial legacy. Peter Schneider's *Vati* (Papa, 1987) is the story of how the son of an Auschwitz physician struggles to free himself from his father's Nazi past. *Die Ausgesperrten* (The Outsiders, 1980) by Elfriede Jelinek highlights the damaging repercussions of fascism upon three separate families in 1950s Vienna. The book concludes with Elisabeth Reichart's *Februarschatten* (February Shadows, 1984), the story of a woman haunted by her childhood devotion to Nazism. My decision to use these particular works is twofold: first, because of their incisive depictions of the continued impact of National Socialism upon the postwar German and Austrian family; second, because their location in the chronology of German literary history shows persuasively and distinctly how the lingering burden of the Third Reich intrudes not only upon the German and Austrian psyche, but upon its literature as well.

In *Kindheitsmuster*, described by one critic as a novel "of participants for participants,"[22] the narrator openly acknowledges her personal complicity in the Third Reich and turns her attention to the many forms of passive acquiescence that allowed Hitler's regime to thrive. Christa Wolf does not attempt to rescue the family from its role in the construction of fascist attitudes and behaviors, but rather explores the ways in which the German family can be considered the breeding ground for political oppression. The narrator's investigation exposes, for example, how the emotional vacuum of her childhood environment made her susceptible to the camaraderie promised by Hitler's youth groups and how the virtues glorified at home were the same as those espoused by National Socialism: obedience to authority, the denial of spontaneous emotion, and strict adherence to the status quo. In addition, the speaking subject of *Kindheitsmuster* places special emphasis on the next generation and feels it is her duty to educate Germany's youth about what happened in the past and what must be prevented in the future. The narrator's role as mother serves as the catalyst for coming to terms with her own family history; and it is through the narrator's discussions with her teenage daughter Lenka that the legacy of Auschwitz remains at the forefront of her analysis.

Thomas Bernhard's *Auslöschung* is similar to *Kindheitsmuster* in that the narrator's autobiographical project is imbued with an unrelenting examination of the self. Although Bernhard's protagonist does not share the same sense of personal complicity in National Socialism, he is intensely aware of the ways in which he is shaped by his parents' ideology and finds it necessary to leave his homeland in order to avoid further contamination. Murau likewise shares with Wolf's narrator the conviction that to write one's personal history is to place oneself in danger. Similar to the narrator's description of herself in *Kindheitsmuster* as a paleontologist or grand inquisitor, Murau announces that in taking his family apart he is dissecting, annihilating, and extinguishing himself. Bernhard's narrator ultimately surrenders the notion that he has remained untainted. Although he avoids such concepts as collective or inherited guilt to explain the impact of his childhood, he must finally concede that his worst traits — his deceitfulness, cynicism, and desire for revenge — indelibly mark him as his parents' son.

The novels of Peter Schneider, Elfriede Jelinek, and Elisabeth Reichart show that even as late as the 1980s neither German nor Austrian writers were finished with this theme. In *Vati*, coming to terms with the Nazi past is represented as an attempt to construct a separate identity in the wake of a devastating family legacy. Branded by the sins of his father and surrounded by those who either dismiss the past or displace it onto an earlier generation, Schneider's narrator must simultaneously seek out the truth of his father's activities and devise a means of coping with a history in which he played no part. The son suffers psychologically from the burden of his father's guilt and fears that he is himself a criminal. He also reacts to this sense of victimization by victimizing others, thereby perpetuating the legacy he consciously despises.

Die Ausgesperrten offers an even bleaker vision of the continued familial repercussions of National Socialism. For Jelinek, the attempts made by those of her generation to break with the past and usher in a more humane age have failed. In her novel, the ideological structures that gave rise to fascism remain inextricably bound to everyday postwar life, and the patterns of abuse condoned or deployed by the parents' generation are recreated in the violent and destructive behavior of their children. Thus, while it is possible to conclude that Schneider's narrator and Jelinek's Viennese teenagers are portrayed as the belated victims of a traumatic historical legacy, both novelists set out to remind their readers that acts committed by earlier agents still bind or burden the contemporary community and that younger generations can in no way claim the "blessing of being born too late."[23]

Elisabeth Reichart's *Februarschatten* is in many ways the ultimate fusion of the familial and historical. In Reichart's novel, the dysfunctional relationship between mother and daughter is set against the backdrop of the infamous Mühlviertler Hasenjagd (Mill District Rabbit Hunt) of 1945, when 500 escaped prisoners from the concentration camp at Mauthausen were hunted down and killed by the inhabitants of a nearby village. Christa Wolf's use of the term *Ausgrabung* (literally, "digging out" or "bringing to the surface") to describe Reichart's novel hints at the similarities between her own project in *Kindheitsmuster* and that of the young Austrian writer almost twenty-five years her junior. Reichart's protagonist, like that of *Kindheitsmuster,* is a woman haunted by memories of a childhood spent under National Socialism. Her youthful attraction to Nazi ideology produces feelings of complicity and guilt, as well as a lifelong struggle to keep certain memories at bay. The intensity of the narrator's inner conflict is borne out in the structure of the novel itself. Reminiscent of *Kindheitsmuster*, Reichart's speaker-subject does not present a unified, linear account. Her story shifts continually between past and present and alternates between first-, second-, and third-person forms of address. In her afterword to *Februarschatten* Wolf admits that such a narrative style is not easy. The "chopped off, breathless sentences" of Reichart's heroine frustrate our ability to piece together her life story and ultimately require us to "participate in the convulsions of a woman who needs to cough up something terrible."[24] What is at stake, Wolf implies, is not only the disclosure of a secret, but our own willingness to accompany a woman who indeed has something to hide.

* * * * *

For writers born during or after National Socialism, the burden of the crimes committed during the Third Reich gives rise to questions which cannot — and moreover should not — be conclusively answered. The reluctance of writers in the last twenty-five years to simply render the "facts" of the Nazi past, or provide a definitive outcome to their own ambivalence, underscores the wariness of recent generations to pronounce a final judgment on their country's fascist past. As Judith Ryan proposes, the slighter forms employed by the third generation of authors (*Vati* being a mere eighty-two pages; *Februarschatten* weighing in at just over one hundred) undermine by their very size the idea that a writer has claim to the whole truth of history.[25] Because of this, it is misleading to read their novels as examples of *Vergangenheitsbewältigung;* that is, as a type of literature that seeks to overcome, master, or resolve the past. The novels presented in the following chapters suggest that a genuine confrontation with the Third Reich entails the loss of easy answers and clear distinctions. The specific forms these newer literary projects take will vary and appear as novels, autobiographies, partial documentaries, or a creative combination of all three. The basic questions they elicit, however, are remarkably similar: In what ways are the events of the Third Reich re-experienced or re-invented in the lives of the authors' fictional subjects? What are the attitudes of those characters who experienced National Socialism first-hand? How do such attitudes differ from those of their children? What is it about the memory of the Third Reich that makes its conversion into language so difficult? What are the authorial techniques employed by each novelist in portraying the eruption of a painful past into the postwar familial sphere? And finally, what are his or her strategies for approaching Germany and Austria's dual role as victim and aggressor?[26]

In seeking to make sense of this uneasy union between private familial histories and the burden of a murderous past, writers of the last twenty-five years have engaged in an arduous and often incriminating process of questioning that collapses distinctions between traditional opposites: guilt and innocence, victimization and participation, prosecution and defense. Caught between the bonds of family and the harsh realities of dictatorship, genocide, and war, contemporary German and Austrian writers can no longer pretend to a harmony that seems wholly absent from their world. Their writings expose the power of the Third Reich to disrupt previous categories of emotional attachment, personal identity, or moral evaluation and present a new form of literature plagued by ambiguity, ambivalence, and self-doubt. To quote Peter Demetz, the books of the past two generations have emerged from a "tortured process of questioning," and lay the groundwork "on which future generations of writers will stand."[27]

Notes

[1]Peter Sichrovsky, *Schuldig geboren: Kinder aus Nazifamilien* (Cologne: Kiepenheuer & Witsch, 1987) 14–15. Translations from the German are my own. Other books which address the subject of children of perpetrators include Dan Bar-On, *Legacy of Silence: Encounters with Children of the Third Reich* (Cambridge: Harvard UP, 1989) and Dörte von Westernhagen, *Die Kinder der Täter* (Munich: Kösel, 1987).

[2]Sichrovsky 17.

[3]Sichrovsky 39.

[4]Similar chronological divisions are found in Judith Ryan, "Postoccupation Literary Movements and Developments in West Germany," *Legacies and Ambiguities: Postwar Fiction and Culture in West Germany and Japan*, eds. Ernestine Schlant and J. Thomas Rimer (Baltimore: The Johns Hopkins UP, 1991); Ursula Mahlendorf, "Confronting the Fascist Past and Coming to Terms with It," *World Literature Today* 55. 4 (Autumn 1991) Reiko Tachibana, *Narrative as Counter-Memory: A Half-Century of Postwar Writing in Germany and Japan*. Albany: State U of New York P, 1998.

[5]This is primarily a German phenomenon. In Austria, as Demetz suggests, "the deepest wounds and the most incisive shocks were not felt until twenty, if not thirty, years later." The protracted discussions concerning the fate of literature that took place in West Germany (and with a different ideological impetus in East Germany) immediately following the war are largely absent from Austria's literary scene. Young Austrian writers put off by the dullness, clichés, or traditionalism rampant among their country's postwar writings were more likely to sell their manuscripts to West German publishers than fight to establish their own markets at home. Peter Demetz, *Postwar German Literature: A Critical Introduction* (New York: Schocken Books, 1972) 26–29.

[6]Judith Ryan, *The Uncompleted Past: Postwar German Novels and the Third Reich* (Detroit: Wayne State UP, 1983) 15.

[7]Examples of this type of literature include Wolfgang Borchert's radio play *Draußen vor der Tür* (1947), the story of a soldier returning to a Germany in ruins; Heinrich Böll's *Und sagte kein einziges Wort*, a moving portrait of postwar married life; Hans Erich Nossack's *Der Untergang* (1949), which chronicles the fire burning of Hamburg; Elisabeth Langgässer's *Märkische Argonautenfahrt* (1950), a novel that traces the journey of Berlin refugees to the convent of Anastasiendorf; and Hans Werner Richter's *Sie fielen aus Gottes Hand* (1951), which recounts the adventures of twelve people, differing in nationality, class, and religion, from the outbreak of the war to their internment in a camp for displaced persons.

[8]Horst Daemmerich and Diether Haenicke, eds., *The Challenge of German Literature* (Detroit: Wayne State UP, 1971) 385.

[9]The early activities of Germany's Gruppe 47 (which awarded its literary prize to Böll in 1951) is further evidence that the most pressing concern for many young writers in the immediate postwar period was not the production of narratives exposing German guilt and responsibility, but rather the restoration of German culture from the corrupting influence of Nazism. While participants in this informal gathering of writers were clearly politically astute, and mostly left of center, their creative energies were primarily invested in the redemption of German literature. The initial goal of Gruppe 47 was to remove all fascist terminology and style from the German language — displayed most blatantly in the bombast of Hitlerian oratory — and included the following suggestions: reducing the German vocabulary to three-hundred words, prioritizing the production of sober and straightforward narratives, and the use of factual reportage popularized by the American writer Ernest Hemingway.

[10]Ryan, *The Uncompleted Past* 15.

[11]For recent treatments of postwar literary developments see Ernestine Schlant, *The Language of Silence: West German Literature and the Holocaust* (New York: Routledge, 1999) and Reiko Tachibana, *Narrative as Counter-Memory: A Half-Century of Writing in Germany and Japan.*

[12]Ryan, "Postoccupation Literary Movements and Developments in West Germany" 200.

[13]Walter Hinderer, "The Challenge of the Past: Turning Points in the Intellectual and Literary Reflections of West Germany, 1945–1985," *Legacies and Ambiguities* 95.

[14]Michael Schneider, *Den Kopf verkehrt aufgesetzt oder die melancholische Linke: Aspekte des Kulturzerfalls in den siebziger Jahren* (Darmstadt: Luchterhand Verlag, 1981) 8.

[15]Ryan, "Postoccupation Literary Movements and Developments in West Germany" 200.

[16]"For I the Lord your God am a jealous God, visiting the iniquity of the fathers upon the children to the third and fourth generation of those that hate me, but showing steadfast love to thousands of those who love me and keep my commandments." Exodus 20:5.

[17]Mikhail Bahktin, *The Dialogic Imagination*, trans. Caryl Emerson and Michael Holquist (Austin: U of Texas P, 1981) 342.

[18]Tachibana 27.

[19]Marilyn Fries, "Problems of Narrating the *Heimat*: Christa Wolf and Johannes Bobrowski," *Cross Currents* 9 (1990) 221.

[20]Demetz, *After the Fires: Recent Writing in the Germanies, Austria and Switzerland* (New York: Harcourt Brace Jovanovich, 1986) 29.

[21]Maria-Regina Kecht, "Faschistische Familienidyllen: Schatten der Vergangenheit in Henisch, Schwaiger und Reichart," *Austrian Writers and the Anschluss: Understanding the Past — Overcoming the Past*, ed. Donald G. Daviau (Riverside, CA: Ariadne Press, 1991) 315–16.

[22]Mahlendorf 554.

[23]This expression was first used by former German chancellor Helmut Kohl (born 1930) during a state trip to Israel in 1984. Kohl's suggestion that those of his generation experienced National Socialism firsthand but were too young to be guilty has since become, in the words of Anton Kaes, a "proverbial cliché." *From Hitler to Heimat: The Return of History as Film* (Cambridge: Harvard UP, 1989) 239.

[24]Christa Wolf, "Struktur von Erinnerung," afterword to *Februarschatten* (Berlin: Aufbau Taschenbuch Verlag, 1997) 117.

[25]Ryan, "Postoccupation Literary Movements" 203.

[26]Maria-Regina Kecht, in her discussion of Peter Henisch, Brigitte Schwaiger, and Elisabeth Reichart, poses similar questions in the context of contemporary Austrian depictions of the family. See "Faschistische Familienidyllen" 316ff.

[27]Demetz, *After the Fires* 392.

The Trouble with Memory:
Christa Wolf's *Kindheitsmuster*

> You weren't prepared for this. . . . Where Nelly's in-
> volvement was deepest, where she showed devotion,
> self-sacrifice, these are the details that have been
> erased. . . . Because it is unbearable to think the tiny
> word "I" in connection with the word "Auschwitz."
> "I" in the past conditional. I would have. I might have.
> I could have. Participated. Obeyed.[1]

> The secret that we are looking for is the blatant lack of
> any secret. Which is perhaps why it can't be revealed.[2]

IN HIS DISCUSSION OF CHRISTA WOLF'S *Kindheitsmuster* (Patterns of
Childhood, 1976), Heinrich Böll reminds his readers that the dictatorship shaping the heroine Nelly Jordan's childhood was dismantled
not by Germans but by their enemies. He charges that the transition
from fascism to democracy did not result from an inner conversion; it
was imposed upon his country from without. For Böll, Germany's failure during the Second World War to denounce National Socialism was
followed by a postwar failure to accept responsibility. In the West, the
Federal Republic touted its constitution as a model of progressive government. In the East, socialism was trumpeted as the advent of an en-
lightened political age. In neither East nor West, however, did one hear
about the twelve years of Hitler's Reich. According to Böll, the years of
National Socialism were banished with few painful memories to speak
of.[3] The title of Böll's essay on *Kindheitsmuster* is taken from the novel
itself and underscores how Germany's amnesia long preceded the Allied
occupation. It is a question asked of Nelly's mother Charlotte by a recently liberated concentration camp victim. This man, dumbfounded
by Charlotte's belief that communists had somehow been spared, asks
more out of incredulity than reproach: "Where on earth have you all
been living?"

In selecting this question to introduce his remarks, Böll highlights
an inquiry central to Wolf's investigation of Germany's fascist past, one
which summarizes the dilemma her novel seeks to unravel more than

thirty years after Hitler's death: How could human beings have been physically present during the Third Reich and, at the same time, oddly absent? This paradox arises early in *Kindheitsmuster* and weaves its way as a virtual leitmotif throughout Wolf's text. It is first introduced by the narrator, who attempts to explain her father's feelings of victimization to her teenage daughter Lenka. Lenka rejects her grandfather's position as naive, as irresponsible, and "does not wish . . . to hear how one could be there and not be there at the same time" (60). The narrator will later claim that Nelly lived for twelve years under a dictatorship "apparently without noticing it" (530) and in a further passage describes the inhabitants of Germany as "a nation of sleepers."

> You imagine a nation full of sleepers; a group of people whose brains dreamily obey the orders given to them: Delete. Delete. Delete. You imagine an unsuspecting population, which when taken to task will later declare with one voice: we don't remember. (204)

What Wolf refers to as "the horrible secret of human beings in our century" (60), this ability to live through overwhelming or catastrophic events and to emerge with no apparent knowledge of them, informs not only the content of *Kindheitsmuster*, but lays the foundation for the novel's narrative structure. While Wolf, like Lenka, defies the notion that Germans were themselves the primary victims of National Socialism, and because of her own childhood involvement includes herself among the perpetrators, her novel offers striking parallels to the narratives of trauma survivors. In the same way that trauma victims do not register the catastrophe as it occurs, but only later emerge from a state of frozen watchfulness to speak of their encounter, *Kindheitsmuster* traces Wolf's search for a history which has yet to be experienced. The author's task is not so much to remember or reconstruct her past, but, through the process of writing, to live it for the first time.

Cathy Caruth suggests that the concept of trauma challenges traditional models of historical analysis in that it undermines our ability to know, to contain, and to define. The phenomenon of trauma "brings us to the limits of our understanding," and presents the possibility that an awareness of history can emerge not only from a strict correlation between experience and its historical referent, but from the gaps and disruptions that often delay our comprehension of such events.

> I would propose that it is here, in the equally widespread and bewildering encounter with trauma — both in its occurrence, and in the attempt to understand it — that we can begin to recognize the possibility of a history which is no longer straightforwardly referential (that

is, no longer based on simple models of experience and reference). Through the notion of trauma ... we can understand that a re-thinking of reference is not aimed at eliminating history, but at resitu-ating it in our understanding, that is, of precisely permitting *history* to arise where *immediate understanding* may not.[4]

Borrowing from Freud's analysis of trauma in *Moses and Monotheism*, Caruth proposes that the pathology of trauma rests in the structure of its reception. She draws upon Freud's example of an accident victim who escapes seemingly unscathed from his ordeal, but is later haunted by mental and physical symptoms indicative of a psychologically over-whelming experience. Caruth locates the central enigma of Freud's il-lustration not in the period of forgetting which succeeds the accident, but in the fact that the victim was never fully conscious when the event took place. Inherent in the traumatic event, Caruth maintains, is the survivor's inability to assimilate it at the moment it occurs. It is only belatedly, in its repeated intrusion into the victim's life, that the trauma is fully realized. In Caruth's words, "to be traumatized is precisely to be possessed by an image or event."[5]

This idea of possession is borne out in *Kindheitsmuster* by the nar-rator's conviction that contemporary German society, both East and West, continues to bear the imprint of a history whose details have not been fully explored and whose impact has yet to be adequately assessed. She acknowledges the "rows of books" written about the Nazi era but rejects the idea that coming to terms with National Socialism can be judged successful based on the sheer quantity of literature. In spite of a mass of material on the subject, the narrator remains convinced that the war has been insufficiently discussed. And she charges that those who have written about the war limit their analyses to a prescribed or agreed upon agenda, and tacitly avoid those issues that "shake up the soul anew" (232).

Wolf attributes her impetus for writing about the period of National Socialism to a sense of duty, to herself as well as to society. In a 1975 discussion of *Kindheitsmuster*, Wolf describes how she had long sensed something missing in her work to date, and had known, without real-izing the exact nature of the book's content, that she would someday write of her childhood. She speaks of her desire to come closer to a past that, even after the completion of the novel, remains very difficult to elucidate. Yet, despite this difficulty in communicating events that elude her full comprehension, Wolf insists that she — indeed all those who lived under National Socialism — must convey these experiences to others. To reject the past, Wolf maintains, is to deny one's moral accountability in the present and, ultimately, to halt all progress towards the future.[6]

This notion of personal and civic obligation lies at the center of *Kindheitsmuster*. As one critic writes, Wolf's novel is not only about history, but about the relationship between history and the moral activity of writing.[7] For Wolf, to "historicize" Germany's fascist past is to personalize it, to treat it as a product of human agency, and to take responsibility for it. *Kindheitsmuster* argues that even the most innocent submitted to the Third Reich; that those who did not understand the import of their actions, who themselves committed no acts of violence, were an integral part of Hitler's regime. Responsibility for National Socialism, Wolf proposes, touches everyone; if not as a juridical guilt then as a moral one.[8] In using the term *Vergangenheitsbewältigung* (to come to terms with the past), Wolf claims to speak not of collective absolution, but of the individual's painstaking examination of an unresolved and deeply personal past.

In attempting to take responsibility for the Nazi past and in placing her own childhood at the center of her analysis, Wolf begins a process of remembering which she terms a "cross-examination" (*Kreuzverhör*). She compares her method to that of a paleontologist; as the paleontologist uncovers layers of earth in order to discover the fossilized remains of previous life forms, Wolf seeks to expose historically constructed layers of human personality in order to make transparent the factors which determine her current self. Her narrator seeks to untangle the "chronic blindness" of her generation by asking not how they live with the burden of history, but rather what kind of circumstances could have caused their collective loss of conscience. As critic Marie-Luise Gättens suggests, the speaking subject of *Kindheitsmuster* does not so much encounter history as learn how her generation is produced *by* it.[9]

Such an investigation is not without risks. To examine the past is to confront events largely unknown; to uncover these "petrified remains" is to expose oneself to shock, disappointment, and possible despair. Wolf confesses in the opening pages of *Kindheitsmuster* her fear in writing the novel. She declares that "previous drafts had started . . . with the attempt to describe the working process of memory, a crab's walk, a painful backward motion, like falling into a time shaft" (13). Wolf has no delusions about the difficulty of her task, and makes no attempt to hide her anxiety from her readers. Rather, she openly records these moments of hesitation and self-doubt.

What compels you, you asked yourself — not with words (you seldom used words) but with headaches — what compels you to climb back? To confront a child . . . to expose yourself again: to the gaze of this child; to the offended resistance of all those involved; to the total lack of comprehension; but above all, to your own strategies of conceal-ment and your doubt. To isolate oneself — which means nothing less than opposition. (206)

Or again,

To what end? The question is as eerie as it is justified. (Let the dead bury the dead!) The feeling that grasps every living being when the earth begins to move under his feet: fear. (39)

Wolf's fear in narrating her childhood years is intensified by the very proximity of these experiences. While on the one hand, her narrator expresses the elusiveness of a history that hides "beyond the mountains, the chasms, the deserts of the years" (70), Wolf feels neither safe nor distant enough to write a straightforwardly autobiographical work. The author chooses the fictional name Nelly to address her heroine, and in the preliminary statements of *Kindheitsmuster* has her narrator proffer two possibilities: either to remain speechless or to re-experience herself in the third person. *Kindheitsmuster* presents history not as a series of completed events, but as a continuing, integral part of the present. "The present pushes in upon one's memory; today is already the last day of the past" (12). Margarete Mitscherlich highlights Wolf's atten-tion to a history that both shapes and undermines the subject's identity. She concludes that *Kindheitsmuster* is more than the author's confron-tation with her estranged childhood; it is a novel about the intrusion of a living past into the author's present life.[10] The trip to L. reveals just how many parts of the narrator's current self have their origins in a fas-cist past. And while Wolf herself feels estranged from these years, de-claring a *Fremdheitsgefühl* (feeling of estrangement)[11] toward the way she thought and behaved as a child, her novel exposes a period haunt-ing in its very immediacy. In her oft-cited interview with Hans Kauf-mann, for example, Wolf maintains that the experiences of her early years "cascade in waves" over her and that no one can escape the effects of one's own childhood, "even when this childhood took place under circumstances . . . one would prefer to forget."[12]

The history Wolf depicts in *Kindheitsmuster* is the history of a trauma both personal and historic. The narrator's crisis in returning to L. arises from the re-enactment of personally painful events: the fear of being raped by Russian soldiers, the lack of adequate food and shelter, the desperate flight westward, the sudden separation from her mother. Central to Wolf's narrative, however, is the conviction that others suffered more. Unlike Freud's accident victim, the narrator of *Kindheitsmuster* acknowledges that, although traumatic, the events of the Third Reich did not occur by chance but by design. In the course of the novel, the narrator is reminded of her own participatory status and becomes increasingly convinced that her childhood allegiance to Hitler implicates her in the traumatization of entire ethnic and religious groups, indeed of entire nations. The narrator of *Kindheitsmuster* can no longer separate her private recollections of National Socialism from its devastating public realities. Her investigation of the past involves a confrontation with death — the death of friends and relatives as well as those persecuted under Nazism. Although Nelly survived her premature encounter with death, others did not. The narrator's experiences under Hitler erupt in waves of personal and historic detail and, because of their painful implications, are met by a defensive urge to forget. Margarete Mitscherlich suggests that Wolf's decision to use "she" instead of "I" signals an effort at self-protection; more than an artistic device, it is a shield without which the information the author discloses would be "ungraspable and unbearable."[13]

The author's experience of fascism thus initiates an ongoing and problematic relationship with history. Similar to Caruth's assessment of the trauma survivor, Wolf carries an "impossible history" within her[14] and may at any time become the symptom of events she herself cannot entirely possess. In her 1968 essay "Reading and Writing," Wolf explains her attempts to take hold of a past that, because of its incriminating content, is continually subject to distortion. She writes that, in an effort to make history more palatable, society converts it into individual "medallions," which are then used to promote a clear conscience.[15] Wolf contrasts this safe reliance on neatly packaged and organized pieces of one's past with the more difficult and authentic process of remembering. For Wolf, to re-open the past is to challenge one's identity, to deconstruct a fixed conception of the self based on a falsification of historical reality. She suggests that to remember is to "swim against the current." To articulate these memories involves, to use Benjamin's phrase, "brushing history against the grain," an exhausting process of writing "against the ostensibly natural process of forgetting."[16]

Memory forms one of the central patterns under investigation in *Kindheitsmuster*. The narrator states that without memory we would be in continuous estrangement from ourselves; it is memory that reminds us "of the things we have done [and] the things that have happened to us" (12). Together with assessing patterns of childhood and perception, Wolf explores the act of remembering by testing a variety of mental processes. One finds in *Kindheitsmuster* the memories of the traveler to L. who recoups and redefines Nelly's childlike impression of events. There are the memories of the novelist, who one year later writes of this forty-six-hour journey. The novelist persona places the narrator's more spontaneous recollections under careful scrutiny. The narrator's reminiscences are problematized by the writer, are reordered, and finally are put to paper. The reader likewise hears the memories of Lutz and H., whose versions of the past appear intermittently throughout *Kindheitsmuster* to challenge or revise those of Wolf's protagonist.[17]

In contrast to the postwar tendency to shore up the ego by diverting energy away from memory,[18] Wolf's subject engages memory to deconstruct her moral and political development. The narrator claims that man is now living in "the age of universal loss of memory" (209) and suggests that if the past remains banished from awareness, society's access to it may vanish forever. Wolf's remarks are similar to those of Alexander and Margarete Mitscherlich, who state that memory, when not subjected to continued inspection and critique, runs the danger of dying out. In their words, an investigation into the past "is associated with the weakest part of man's psychic organization; that is, his capacity for critical thinking."[19] Wolf seeks to counteract Germany's waning capacity for critical thinking by employing what she considers the most important — and most often omitted — type of memory: moral memory. She refers to memory as a process of constant revision and insight. It is, in sum, "a repeated moral act" (195).

This "moralisches Gedächtnis" (moral memory) constitutes the driving force of *Kindheitsmuster*.[20] Moral memory exceeds the simple re-presentation of Germany's Nazi past, and involves an analytic, step-by-step investigation of the past from the vantage point of the present. Memory, which gathers up *what* happened, gains meaning by being subjected to consciousness, which seeks to answer *how* and *why*. At the center of Wolf's memory work are not so much her individual experiences of fascism, but rather the intellectual and emotional impact of this early socialization. And although Wolf avoids the application of interpretative models (Marxist, psychoanalytic, sociopolitical) to explain previous events, she does not react impartially to the information she uncovers. The author communicates her memories as material brought into awareness, reflected upon, and integrated into the progressive development of her life and current self. As Gerhart Pickerodt explains, the question posed in the ninth chapter of the novel — "How did we become what we are today?" — concerns both the historical dimension of the narrator as well as her present-day identity.[21]

Subtitled a novel, *Kindheitsmuster* is more correctly a fictional autobiography. As an autobiography, it reproduces the historical and personal details of a childhood spent under National Socialism; as a work of fiction it tests the facts of this childhood world against the author's own inner processes and fantasies.[22] *Kindheitsmuster* conveys a conceptualization of *Erfahrung* (experience) that deconstructs the strict separation between objective reality and author-subject. What remains inaccessible to Wolf concerning her childhood experiences is conjured up into the present through a variety of approaches and on a number of different levels. In addition to mediating between autobiography and novel, *Kindheitsmuster* shifts between past and present, between external events and private details, between publicly recorded information and personal recollections. The public realities of National Socialism (as revealed through newspaper articles, songs, poems, etc.) combine with the private reception of these events. These fluctuations are an extension of the investigatory project of Wolf's novel[23] and trace the narrator's attempt to move beyond speechlessness by recovering, through a multiplicity of sources, the emotions and experiences she was forced to conceal as a child. For Wolf, experience is not understood in terms of a philosophical empiricism, but rather as events which can be interpreted only through personal reflection and analysis. Subject and object are freed from their opposition as fixed and separate entities. As Margarete Mitscherlich maintains, what is most "factual" about *Kindheitsmuster* is Wolf's disclosure of her inner world, the product of her search for "the history of her feelings."[24]

In his essay "Wo habt ihr bloß gelebt," Böll underscores the congruity between the unmasterability of National Socialism and Wolf's refusal to feign a strictly autobiographical analysis. He considers the author's choice of genre a sign of her inner confusion, her helplessness in the face of a theme "that one single author can never completely tackle."[25] Judith Ryan draws similar attention to Wolf's inclusion of internal and external perspectives. She argues that Wolf's treatment of personal as well as objective realities reveals not only an attempt to balance her private experiences with historical truth, but exposes the fundamental contradictions inherent to her childhood world. Ryan maintains that while *Kindheitsmuster* is comparable to a number of West German autobiographies of the period, in that it "present[s] the past through the eyes of an ordinary person," Wolf's novel goes beyond these works "in its recognition that straightforward . . . autobiography cannot adequately reproduce the discontinuity experienced by the individual in the transition from Nazism to the present."[26]

Wolf's abandonment of traditional modes of narration and her combination of narrative genres mirrors the gaps and inconsistencies embedded in her experience of National Socialism. She embraces a relationship with history that is essentially problematic, both morally and aesthetically. Having experienced the trauma of National Socialism and been a contributor to its execution, the author finds it difficult to speak of this period from a secure and integrated position. At the outset of *Kindheitsmuster*, the narrator questions whether she will be able to record events accurately, stating that she is hampered by an "unreliable memory" (16). She is compelled to tell her story as it really happened, but simultaneously feels threatened by an inability to speak. The narrator fears she may at any moment become tongue-tied or, worse yet, willfully distort the truth.

> When it comes to personal matters we either fictionalize or we become tongue-tied. We may have good reason to profess our ignorance of events (or to censor out certain aspects, which amounts to the same thing). But even if there is little hope of an eventual acquittal . . . this small hope is still enough to defy the temptation to be silent and to conceal. (18)

In order to escape this lure of silence and concealment, Wolf undertakes an examination of the past that entails not only the re-witnessing of events, but a painful witnessing of the self. As Cathy Caruth proposes, "the inability to fully witness the event as it occurs, or the ability to witness the event fully only at the cost of witnessing oneself, seems to inhabit all traumatic experience."[27] Wolf's attempt to understand the trauma of National Socialism leads her to re-create this trauma in the structure of her narrative. The narrator of *Kindheitsmuster* feels compelled to seek out the truth, even if during this search her former existence collapses. And her fear is not unwarranted. The act of testimony confronts the narrator neither with a monolithic view of history nor of the self. Rather, she is brought face to face with the bits and pieces of her existence and seeks, through the process of writing, to find her way back to "I."

Such *Wahrheitsfindung* (truth-seeking) can easily become *Selbstvernichtung* (self-destruction).[28] It is a process during which the subject's understanding of self is placed in question and runs the risk of being destroyed. What were once valued systems of beliefs prove themselves not only untenable but despised. In *Kindheitsmuster*, the narrator does more than reconstruct the events of her childhood, she re-experiences its physical and emotional impact. In addition to the anxiety and guilt produced by her cross-examination, the events of the Third Reich elicit in Wolf's subject a powerful, visceral response. Just as Nelly's break-down coincides with the collapse of her country and the loss of her cherished ego-ideal, so the writer's exposure of these political and emotional attachments thirty years later induces a severe stomach illness for which she is eventually hospitalized.[29] The narrator states in chapter six of the novel that the road she has taken is "barred with taboos"; it is a path into the self "that no one travels unscathed" (165).

During a public discussion of her novel, Wolf explains her employ-ment of a third person address first in terms of an emotional safeguard, and second as a result of her "eerie estrangement" vis-à-vis the past. The author maintains that during the composition of *Kindheitsmuster* her sense of alienation was so strong, that to use "I" would have been to deceive not merely herself, but her readers.

> What I wanted to convey with this third person address, which re-sulted from my essentially fragmented biography, was that the ghosts of many persons exist in us simultaneously; and finding access to them is no easy task.[30]

This fragmented persona replicates the trauma survivor's inability to se-cure a simple, believable historical referent. The author's moral and temporal separation from a childhood spent under National Socialism, combined with the almost hallucinatory immediacy of these events, ini-tiates a crisis of truth to which there is no simple access. As Judith Ryan perceptively observes, "the many interruptions and asides and the in-terweaving of various time planes are part of [Wolf's] attempt to dis-cern a pattern in what appears fragmentary, chaotic, and discontin-uous."[31] The narrator's mode of address dramatizes this disruption. The author gives the name Nelly to herself before and directly following the war, "you" (*du*) to herself in the present, and "I" to the self who repre-sents a re-union of those disparate selves on the last pages of the novel.[32] As Wolf explains to her audience, Nelly is just one of the sev-eral people "wandering around inside her."[33]

Social historian Robert Jay Lifton observes that such dissociation or "splitting" is common to survivors of trauma, especially in situations where the victim is simultaneously connected with the aggressor. He states that during a traumatic incident there is a traumatized self that begins to take shape, a self which is brought into the trauma and is affected by that trauma. Lifton refers to this creation of a second self as a form of "doubling" in the traumatized person and maintains that the two co-existent identities are contradictory, even incompatible. They are two halves that remain ethically at odds and are especially prevalent among people "who doubled in order to adapt to evil."[34] In *Kindheitsmuster*, the narrator's sense of fragmentation results from a combination of socialization, exposure to traumatic events, and guilt. These different selves are created in reaction to the subject's shifting social and emotional environment and are borne out in the novel by the multi-layered composition of Wolf's narrative.

Nelly's first awareness of "I" is accompanied in *Kindheitsmuster* by shock, excitement, and a fierce awareness of self. The narrator recalls a scene in front of her father's store, in which the child, three years old, sits on the step chanting "I . . . I . . . I . . . I . . . I, each time with a thrilled shock that had to be kept a secret" (14). This first-person position comes under fire, however, when it does not conform to social norms or parental wishes. Again and again, Nelly is alienated from her initial sense of autonomy and is forced to displace, in the service of obedience and self-protection, her feelings and behavior away from herself and onto an outside other.[35] Nelly's doubling takes place before the onset of traumatic events. Nelly first assumes a separate persona in order to salvage her authentic, autonomous "I" and at the same yield to the unrelenting social pressure to conform. Several years later, this initial doubling is split into a third, adolescent Nelly, who hides the child both abandoned by her mother and forced to flee her home. The disruption of the speaking subject's "I" extends, therefore, beyond Nelly's experiences before and during the war. Nelly's adolescent years are characterized by "forced ideological and emotional reassessment" and are described by Wolf as a violent rupture in the young girl's life. It is, as one critic suggests, "a period of profound alienation and emotional stasis."[36]

The challenge to Nelly's identity and self-awareness is further compounded in the latter postwar period. As an adult, the narrator is faced with the terrible truths of Hitler's Reich, a regime which — estranged from "I" and seeking inclusion into "we" — Nelly readily and enthusiastically supported. The narrator's problematic search for self is not limited, however, to the distant past. Her self-interrogation encompasses those things which Nelly suppressed in her enthusiasm for National Socialism, but also those that the narrator has for years suppressed in her enthusiastic support for socialism. Wolf's adult subject finds her identity again confused by postwar GDR policy. In shifting the blame for Nazism onto the West, i.e. away from "us" and onto "them," the Communist Party inhibits a process of historical integration and perpetuates the narrator's fractured view of self.

Lifton maintains that recovery from trauma cannot occur until the traumatized self is re-integrated.[37] Critics of *Kindheitsmuster* disagree as to whether, for Wolf's narrator, this re-union ever takes place. One scholar contends that after working through those patterns of thinking and behavior that made her susceptible to Nazism, Wolf's subject emerges "as a person who calls herself 'I.'"[38] Another proposes, by contrast, that the narrator not only fails to achieve, but *should* fail to achieve, a final re-union of her multiple selves. According to this opposing view, the fragmentation or "breaks" articulated by Wolf's narrator exist as an essential part of the writer subject; they create the impetus for Wolf's narrative, and "cannot and should not be repaired."[39] The narrator of *Kindheitsmuster* suggests in the concluding pages of the novel that the endpoint of her account would be reached if "the second and the third person were to meet again in the first." She looks forward to a time when she is no longer "you" and "she" but a "candid, unreserved 'I.'" At the same time, the narrator voices her uncertainty as to whether such unity can be achieved: "It seemed very doubtful to you whether you could, in fact, reach this point; whether the road you had taken would ever lead to it" (468). The speaking subject of *Kindheitsmuster* does, in fact, end her account with "I." But she also announces that this harmony may not last. The past, whose hegemony "can still split the first person into the second and the third" (549), might or might not let her separate voices be still.

The narrator's failure to secure a stable and fixed identity should not be seen as a fault in the novel. As one critic suggests, the end of the book "attests more to a change in the narrator's goals and perspective than to a failure to achieve stability through closure." The real accomplishment of *Kindheitsmuster* is less the resolution of contradiction (the teleological quest for an integrated selfhood), than the ability to live with the tension between past and present. It can be argued that it is precisely the narrator's inability to effect a single, unified self that enables her to evaluate and mourn the component pieces of her National Socialist past. In failing to effect a recovery from her experiences, Wolf's narrator continues to inquire, to learn, to re-evaluate what is learned, and to change. The tentative nature of the narrator's secure "I" is congruous with the difficult questions of morality that arise during the investigation of her childhood.[40] In order to understand the trauma of National Socialism, to firmly situate it within her awareness, Wolf's narrator must ultimately relinquish her claim to a unity she can no longer perfectly achieve.

Wolf's disruption of traditional divisions — between the alien and familiar, exteriority and interiority, self and others, presence and absence — finds further expression in the shifting moral and geographical boundaries of Nelly's world. Central to the narrator's investigation of the past is the political transformation of her German town into a Polish one. The notion of *Heimat,* the romantic memories of one's childhood home, is undermined in *Kindheitsmuster* by geographical displacement. L. is no longer L. but G. New borders have been established; a new language is spoken. Equally painful, however, is the adult writer's moral remove from the world of her childhood. In addition to her choice of a third-person address, the narrator's fragmentation vis-à-vis her former self is manifested in her ongoing ambivalence toward the site of her childhood and in her inability to establish a single, consistent attitude toward it. The concept of *Heimat* in *Kindheitsmuster* is essentially a destabilizing one; it is bound not to a sense of security, but to a sense of alienation and loss.

The narrator's visit to the Polish town G. (along with her husband H., brother Lutz, and daughter Lenka) stands in sharp contrast to a sentimental voyage into the past. At one point in the novel, Lenka asks her mother if she feels a sense of nostalgia toward her childhood home. The narrator confesses that she is touched by her daughter's concern for her feelings. But as for nostalgia, "you responded with a clear and convincing 'no'" (369–70).[41] The current occupation of L. by Polish inhabitants is matched by the narrator's struggle to integrate memories of the elusive Nelly into her present concept of self. Her loss of *Heimat* is signified by the replacing of L. by G. but, more importantly, by a childhood which now appears so alien, so "unheimlich," that it seems to have transpired not merely in a different city but in a different world. The narrator's estrangement from her youth is defined largely by her sense of disconnection from, and painful disappointment with, her childhood self. Wolf's adult subject is separated not only temporally from Nelly but psychologically and emotionally. In pronouncing *Kindheitsmuster* "a documentary of the ruins,"[42] critic Evelyn Juers refers to a sense of alienation that began with Wolf's abandonment of her early home and her forced migration from East to West. Juers draws as evidence of Wolf's continued inner homelessness her later autobiographical work *Was Bleibt.* Published in 1990, the brief yet candid narrative reveals Wolf's lingering feeling of "not being at home in her own place."[43]

An essential component of the narrator's estranged *Heimat*, one uncomfortably situated under the cloud of National Socialism, is Nelly's family. While Wolf's earlier works are marked by an absence of family,[44] *Kindheitsmuster* is a narrative "embedded in familial affiliations."[45] The narrator is daughter to Charlotte and Bruno Jordan, sister to Lutz, mother to Lenka, and wife to H. The author's investigation of her past hinges upon the familial relations that shape Nelly's personality. And, in examining her childhood complicity in Nazism, Wolf exposes an arsenal of traditional family values that served to facilitate the transmission of fascist ideology. The narrator of *Kindheitsmuster* depicts her parents as largely unpolitical *Kleinbürger*, whose chief concerns are their children, their business, and their new home. Although Bruno and Charlotte Jordan do not directly promote fascist ideals, neither do they offer Nelly any counterbalance to the authority of local youth organizations and school.[46] The familial order of the Jordan household is founded upon secrecy and silence. Nothing can be talked about that is in any way "peinlich" (embarrassing), and what is not spoken of is treated as though it doesn't exist. This holds true for personal and familial issues as well as for events connected to the public, political sphere. Just as sexuality, miscarriages, marital conflict, and alcoholism are banished to secrecy, so too is the Nazis' treatment of the Jews, Tante Jette's death in Hitler's eugenics program, and the presence of concentration camps.

In chapter seven of *Kindheitsmuster*, the narrator offers an analysis of her family in which their failed awareness of Nazi crimes stems more from a willing and self-imposed ignorance than from fear of political reprisals.

> Curiosity was not their weakness, although no slogan such as 'Beware of Curiosity' was ever drummed into their heads. . . . Ignorance is bliss. Their ignorance made them lukewarm. . . . Trapped into being what they weren't, all that was required was that they remained nobodies. And for us that seems easy to accomplish. Ignore, overlook, neglect, deny, unlearn, obliterate, forget. (203–4)

It has been argued that such "amorality of non-perception" is indistinguishable from other forms of political and moral failure, whether based on "opportunistic thinking, cowardice, or lack of scruples."[47] What Wolf makes clear in *Kindheitsmuster* is that this parental mandate to remain uninvolved is drilled into Nelly and those like her at a very early age. The narrator comments, for instance, that it is "unbelievable and inexplicable" that Nelly visited the burning remnants of a local synagogue destroyed during *Kristallnacht*. How had Nelly known that the synagogue existed, she inquires. How had she found its smoldering remains? One thing seems certain: "She didn't ask anybody" (217).

The case of Tante Jette marks what is perhaps the most vivid inter-section of the political and familial. The mystery surrounding her death, resulting from the government's cover-up of its euthanasia program, is matched by the secrecy within Jette's own family. The Jordans do not wish to acknowledge that a member of their family could be mentally ill, and therefore refuse to discuss this "embarrassing" matter. The narrator's reference to "the many gradations between knowing and not knowing" (267) applies equally to the murder of her aunt as to the myriad of forbidden topics banned from polite conversation. In her words, family life is conducted "in an atmosphere of Let's-Not-Talk-About-It." Similarly, what her parents consider tact is "simply knowing what one should not do" (219).

The most notable exception to this secrecy is Charlotte's angry out-bursts about the incompetence of the Führer and the insanity of the war. Unlike Bruno, Nelly's mother does engage in small acts of defi-ance.[48] It is important to note, however, that Charlotte's critical obser-vations come only after the negative impact of National Socialism has hit home and are uttered at a time when Hitler's repressive measures have made such opinions not only infrequent but largely ineffectual. While such criticisms are testimony to Charlotte's intermittent acts of courage and resistance — and her partial rejection of a call to silence — hers is unfortunately a case of too little too late. The narrator states that Hitler's 1933 curtailment of civic freedoms was virtually ignored by both parents. Because such laws hardly affected the Jordan's private lives, they received no serious attention. For Charlotte and her hus-band, the Nazis' abridgment of political liberties "really didn't concern them" (57).

In contrast to Lenka, who is allowed to disagree with and even re-fuse her parents' wishes, Nelly's childhood is "scarred by the myth of the happy family."[49] This myth requires the suppression of Nelly's curi-osity and negative emotions and forces her to live her life virtually in disguise. The pressure Nelly feels to conform is rooted in her mother's insistent emphasis on happiness. The narrator declares that words such as sad and lonely "are not part of a happy child's vocabulary" (38). In chapter seven of *Kindheitsmuster*, Wolf's subject combines her own thoughts on family with those of her mother Charlotte. What results is an illustration of the awesome responsibility exacted by Nelly's tribute to obedience.

> Happy marriage, happy family. At any rate, my children had a happy childhood. Only she feared this happiness was far too fragile. Happiness and glass, how each breaks fast. So her children began to cure themselves when they were sick, in order to spare their mother any anxiety. (207)

Nelly learns that to transgress time-honored standards of well-being and compliance means not only to violate social expectations, but to shatter her mother's illusions of familial perfection. To be "normal" is to be orderly, patriotic, and submissive. To stray from the limits of good breeding is to become an outsider, an outcast; it also imposes unhappiness on those closest to her by betraying their desire for a "model" child.

In exposing the rigidity, passivity, and denial embedded in the Jordan family, Wolf offers what she believes is an example representative of the German lower middle class. Her narrator does not consider Nelly an isolated case, but rather presents the child's training, experiences, and responses as typical of a generation, as essentially commonplace. As Elaine Martin suggests, "the very ordinariness of the lives and the people described is a reminder of how fragile the boundary is between reason and irrationality, between normalcy and monstrosity, between legality and crime, and between legitimacy and usurpation."[50] The author employs Nelly not only as a shield against personally painful discoveries, but because, as a child, Nelly provides a privileged glimpse into "the breeding ground of fascism," the German petit-bourgeois family.[51] *Kindheitsmuster* reveals, therefore, how the dissatisfactions, resentments, and repressions characteristic of the German family furnished fuel for the National Socialist cause. Nelly is trained to be nothing but the responses conditioned by her environment, and it is this emotional vacuum that leaves her susceptible to the ideological enthusiasms of the Nazi movement.[52] Ironically, while Nelly joins a Nazi youth group in order to assert her identity and flee the oppressive restrictions of familial life, she enters a community that divests her of any remaining autonomy. The central paradox in Nelly's choice is that, believing herself to be a subject of fascism — that is, an individual, self-determined participant in a national cause — she submits to an enterprise which transforms her into the mere object of mass psychology.

Nelly's decision to join the *Bund deutscher Mädel* (League of German Girls) haunts the narrator during the excavation of her former

Heimat. That Nelly longs to escape the hold of her family is natural. What is unnatural are the external circumstances under which this desire is played out.[53] Nelly may have fled to the Nazi organization because of her unhappiness at home, or to enjoy the physical activities and freedoms traditionally available only to boys;[54] yet it is she who chooses to run away and she who picks this particular alliance to fulfill her needs. The fact that both decisions were made voluntarily, indeed willingly, intensifies the narrator's sense of personal culpability and aggravates her feelings of profound guilt.[55] The realization that Nelly embraced an organization dedicated to racial purity and hate effectively robs Wolf's subject of any remaining claim to a "normal" and innocent childhood. In the words of Evelyn Juers, "if innocence is guilty, if normal is abnormal . . . the innocent past is a taboo, a sheer impossibility."[56]

Nelly's sense of being constantly watched and judged according to the rigid principles of conformity comes close to Michel Foucault's discussion of the transformation of visibility into the exercise of power.[57] Just as the prisoner acknowledges the constant if unseen power of his captors, so Nelly internalizes the surveillance instituted by familial, social, and religious norms — thus providing her own correction. In Nelly's world, happiness is defined as *Übereinstimmungsglück* (the pleasure of conformity). She is taught from an early age that happiness and conformity are mutually dependent, that a sense of contentment is produced by being in agreement with prevailing norms.[58] Nelly's socialization leaves behind deep traces in the speaking subject's psyche. Even as an adult, the narrator is prey to the myth of familial bliss. She feels compelled to believe its veracity despite her knowledge to the contrary, and also senses the danger inherent in its deconstruction.

> Who wouldn't want a happy childhood? Anyone who probes into his childhood should not expect quick results. . . . But one thing is certain: acting contrary to nature produces guilt. It is natural for children to thank their parents all their lives for the happy childhood they provided. It is also natural to leave that childhood alone. (40)

Along with the myth of the happy family, the narrator inherits a fundamentally problematic relationship with language. She discovers that while Bruno and Charlotte Jordan operate with partial truths and silences, Nelly is told she is "transparent as glass" (82) and is ordered to withhold no secrets from her elders. When in response to this injunction, Nelly attempts to tell her mother the truth, Charlotte imposes upon her daughter the strictest censorship and punishes her for being a tattle-tale. It can be argued that it is precisely such confusing and contradictory messages that fuel the narrator's desire to tell the complete truth of her childhood. At the same time, Wolf's subject acquires a similarly contentious relationship between language and secrecy, and is herself "complicitous with the disciplinary powers that enforce silence and speech."[59] Although the narrator expresses considerable reluctance in forcing Nelly to divulge information, her stance towards the child frequently assumes a detective-like quality. Nelly is, in effect, ferreted out of hiding and is forced to speak. It should be noted, however, that unlike the authority figures of her own childhood, the narrator openly acknowledges the pressure her investigation places upon Nelly. She voices a desire to forge a new relationship with her former self and announces that if she cannot come to like the child, she hopes to respect her autonomy. It is the narrator's wish to understand Nelly and to free her from the manipulative power of adults: "Let's hope that whoever catches up with her will not exploit her helplessness" (70).

Because Nelly's fantasies and feelings must remain unconscious, she never acquires a language to speak of them. She learns to respond to the spoken (and unspoken) demands of authority and does so even when these pronouncements conflict with how she experiences herself and the world around her. To voice her desire is to disobey and to incur punishment — both from within and from without. The linguistic censorship imposed upon Nelly forms a central tension in *Kindheitsmuster*. During her investigation of the past, the narrator realizes that silence is as complicitous as speech. She discovers that in becoming an obedient subject of family and Reich, Nelly not only ignored her own pain and unhappiness, but became increasingly insensitive to the misery of others. The narrator's access to language is therefore made doubly difficult — first by the guilt-inducing nature of her memories; second by her early socialization within German petit-bourgeois society. Nelly begins to lose her authenticity when she assumes the role of the happy child. She becomes obedient to the demands of others and rejects her own feelings in order to spare those of her parents. What becomes a series of external and self-imposed restrictions takes place on a linguistic as well as on an ideological and behavioral level. In one passage, the narrator describes her family environment as one void of verbal communication. It is a world in which "silent films" take the place of speech; where having a good command of language was not only undesirable but grounds for punishment. As Ursula Mahlendorf concludes, "the silence in [Nelly's] family is deafening."[60]

It is the recovery of this access to the language of her emotions that Wolf's narrator considers the most essential and arduous part of her self-examination. The inhibitions Nelly learned as a child are linked to the narrator's political and moral development; they also form a stumbling-block to the narrator's current artistic project. By putting the past into language and by expressing the emotions she was forced to conceal as a child, the narrator of *Kindheitsmuster* hopes to integrate her childhood experiences into her current conception of self. Towards the end of the novel, Wolf's protagonist voices her hope for liberation (*Befreiung*); and she describes the gradual elimination, through writing, of her paralyzing fear of the past. It is the narrator's hope of speaking herself free that motivates her struggle to overcome silence. And it is her desire to tell history truthfully that enables her to face her insecurities.

In the end, *Kindheitsmuster* illustrates the writer's inability to narrate *Heimat* as an entity which can be completely known. The events of her childhood leave only vague traces in her psyche; and their painful, overwhelming content seem encased in a void.[61] Wolf's narrator openly acknowledges these gaps in consciousness. Comparing the absence of certain memories to black holes in the universe, she relates these empty spaces to man's limited knowledge of, and partial access to, the past. The narrator confesses, for example, that while the sight of her old school and playground conjures up bodies and faces she "could paint to this day" (312), those memories associated with Nelly's zealous devotion to National Socialism have been virtually obliterated. Faced with the finality of Germany's defeat, and with the harsh reality of her own homelessness, the adolescent Nelly wishes to escape into the "black hole" of failed consciousness and hopes beyond hope that history will somehow be reversed.

By contrast, the narrator's brother Lutz adamantly rejects a cosmic or human order that defies man's ability to understand and to define. He takes it upon himself to protect his teenage niece Lenka from such "nonsensical speculations" and is disdainful of any attempt to "reduce the mystery of [one's personal] origin to stupid coincidence" (396). Wolf's narrator differs sharply from Lutz in that she values contradiction and confusion as the catalysts for society's continued search for clues.[62] This discussion of black holes is a key moment in *Kindheitsmuster*. The scene dramatizes Wolf's departure from the psychological climate of the postwar era and represents an experiential and moral turning point.[63] By disowning a rational and unified vision of human history, the narrator reveals the mechanisms of repression and denial embedded in Germany's response to National Socialism and ultimately challenges the GDR's declaration of an unbroken chain of moral and political correctness. Wolf has her protagonist focus not on the certainties of man's existence, but on inaccessibility, doubt, empty spaces, and silence. And because there are no easy or formulaic answers, her project encourages, indeed demands, participatory thinking.[64] The intellectual and emotional crisis incited by the narrator's voyage into history's "black hole" arises both from her exposure of Germany's guilty past and from her transgression of current personal and cultural taboos.[65] Wolf portrays history, in other words, as a crucial component of contemporary reality. *Kindheitsmuster* begins by pronouncing man's tendency to disregard earlier periods ("We cut ourselves off from it and pretend to be strangers"). But the immediacy of the past remains unquestioned: "The past is not dead; it is not even past" (11).

Wolf argues that Germany's repression of the past arises from the fact that its experience of Nazism cannot be mastered. Like radioactive material, the twelve years of Hitler's Reich continue to have destructive, long-term effects.[66] Wolf likewise proposes in her essays and interviews that this historical contaminant is impervious to Germany's competing postwar economies. Becoming in the 1970s more critical and skeptical of GDR politics, Wolf actively confronts her government's deliberate attempts to absolve itself from any involvement in National Socialism. In her 1973 discussion with Hans Kaufmann, for example, Wolf exposes the fallaciousness of her country's "anti-fascist" tradition and criticizes its continued efforts to place the blame for Hitler elsewhere.[67] *Kindheitsmuster*, completed only two years after Wolf's statements to Kaufmann, provides further ammunition against the GDR's official version of history. Wolf refers only briefly in her novel to Hitler's opponents and adamantly contests the idea of an East German resistance heritage.[68] For Wolf, National Socialism is a topic for which social and economic analyses prove utterly inadequate. The Nazi era is viewed in relation to a historical continuum whereby fascism is seen as a contemporary problem and as the legacy of both East and West. Wolf insists that the current reliance of the two Germanies on different political systems has neither eliminated their common history, nor altered former patterns of behavior and thought. The author observes on both sides of the border a continued faith in authority, oppressive intolerance, and a tenacious disregard for historical reality. *Kindheitsmuster* overturns accepted notions of East-West cultural/historical difference and, in effect, undermines the very cornerstone of the GDR's claim to power. The author's call for a personal and collective examination of National Socialism threatens the State's assertion that its policies represent society's best interests. And by uncovering within postwar politics deeply embedded patterns of social and moral behavior, Wolf challenges the Socialist Party's own authoritarian rule.[69]

The author's focus on the generational transmission of ideologies and behaviors and on the lasting, if unacknowledged, residue of fascist ideals has not gone uncensured. Critics have challenged Wolf's connections between historical and contemporary events. In *Kindheitsmuster*, for example, the reader finds Wolf's investigation of Nazi Germany combined with commentaries on the failed political policies of the postwar East and West, on the war in Vietnam, and on Pinochet's takeover of Chile. The question most often raised by critics is whether Wolf draws important, illuminating parallels between past and present or diverts focus away from Germany. Does she underscore dangerous historical repetitions or imply that because atrocities continue to be perpetrated around the globe, her country is no more guilty than any other?

By interspersing different eras and different conflicts, Wolf signals an attempt to understand current society in light of historic developments. The author's decision to combine in *Kindheitsmuster* past and present events is inseparable from the novel's message. Although the past is full of politically motivated violence, genocide and imperialism have in no way been erased from the international scene.[70] The political present is placed as a horizon against which to investigate the transitions of Wolf's speaking subject; it is also a vantage point for viewing the development of society as a whole. For Wolf, the present does not distance itself from the past or declare the past invalid, but rather incorporates the past within itself. It is this disregard for fixed boundaries — between past and present, memory and conscience, self and other — that enables Wolf to write of an evolving history and of the centrality of human agency.[71] Her repeated references to the political abuse of power reject her country's rigid adherence to a humane and anti-fascist tradition and, at the same time, expose the barbarity of the West's battle against communism. Wolf undermines the illusory and irresponsible separation of ally and enemy. She reveals that at any moment the one can easily become the other.

In response to her conviction that the past is inextricably tied to the present, Wolf avoids a plot-centered narrative that separates her from her reader or from the material at hand. *Kindheitsmuster* deconstructs the myth that history can be written from a detached or disinterested perspective. The speaking subject of Wolf's novel is, as one critic suggests, "entangled in a history that still powerfully affects her and because of this requires her active intervention."[72] Such intervention into her own text is a distinguishing feature of Wolf's artistic project. Described in an interview with Hans Kaufmann as "subjective authenticity," Wolf sees the writer as a participant, not as an objective observer. Her program of aesthetics rejects the notion that narrative material should be presented only after it has been thoroughly scrutinized and resolved. Rather, Wolf makes the interaction of writing subject and written content an essential aspect of her text. This is nowhere more apparent than in *Kindheitsmuster*. By casting her experiences in the third person, the author makes herself as much the subject of her writing as are her characters.[73]

For Wolf, participation implies relationship — with herself, her reader, and her material. It also entails vulnerability. The author is committed to the belief that her reader will not be changed by what she writes if she herself remains exactly the same.[74] This "self-experiment" (*Selbstversuch*) is reported in *Kindheitsmuster* as a process instituted by and during the process of writing. There is no attempt to exclude the possibility that the experiment might fail, that the subject may not find her way back to Nelly or forward to a more integrated understanding of "I." This sense of risk is mirrored by the narrator's choice of provisional statements over definite assertions and by the multiplicity of perspectives that challenge her own narrative authority. The fact that the narrator informs her audience of her fear and vulnerability creates an intimacy with the reader;[75] it establishes a dialogic structure which includes not only the narrator with herself, her family, and the figures from her past, but with the reader of her written account. Wolf has expressed an appreciation for those readers who are co-workers versus consumers of her texts. She prizes readers that see literature as "invitations to work," that "add something of themselves to her novels."[76] Such reader participation is one of the author's most important achievements in *Kindheitsmuster*. As the novel progresses, the reader is urged to make sense of his own past, "the history of his coming-into-being."[77]

Many critics regard this dialogic and self-critical approach as evidence of Wolf's ambivalence. They criticize what they consider her faulty grasp of history and her lack of self-awareness. It can be argued, however, that it is Wolf's understanding of the historical ruptures marked by National Socialism and the divisive postwar restructuring of Germany that find expression in the breaks and fragmentation of her personal history, as well as in her narrative style. As Marianne Hirsch contends, the author's connection to the world is based upon "multiple fractures and rifts": between the ideology of National Socialism and the values of her postwar adolescence, between East and West Germany, between Poland and Germany, between capitalism and Soviet communism.[78] By employing a non-unified, splintered subject and a multiplicity of values and ideologies, the author avoids a rigid and immutable narrative stance. *Kindheitsmuster* deconstructs the traditional conflation of authorial with authoritarian, suggesting that after Hitler such intellectual certainty is no longer possible. For Wolf, to effect a genuine confrontation with the Third Reich means to relinquish time-honored yet dangerous monolithic and monologic assessments of oneself and the world.[79] In short, she can no longer pretend to a uniformity "that seems forever to have vanished from the universe in which she lives and writes."[80]

What the narrator terms in *Kindheitsmuster* her "preliminary work" (200) refers to the progressive, piecemeal nature of her self-examination. It describes her gradual, individual recognition of a childhood spent under Hitler. These words also convey a desire to initiate among contemporary German youth an understanding of National Socialism and an awareness of the "psychological ballast handed to them by the older generation."[81] Wolf's feeling of responsibility — toward herself, her children, mankind, and history — is borne out in *Kindheitsmuster* by the narrator's unsentimental tone as well as in the frequently didactic content of her observations. In contrast to what the Mitscherlichs term an unwillingness "to incorporate the past into the stock experiences of German young people,"[82] the novel actively embarks upon a mission to inform and hopefully protect the next generation.

Wolf's commitment to educating Germany's future adults finds expression in the narrator's relationship to Lenka and Ruth. The narrator concludes toward the end of *Kindheitsmuster* that her daughters are dealing with parents who themselves were never young. Ruth and Lenka reportedly "enlighten their mother about the foreign word 'youth'" (455–56) and ease her feelings of loss and envy by giving her the opportunity for joy. The narrator's daughters offer her a vision of youth she never possessed and challenge her to reassess the tenets and experiences of her own childhood. Throughout the novel, Wolf's subject communicates the changes in perception brought on by her teenagers' differing perspectives and focuses considerable attention on Lenka's reaction to G. Yet the narrator's relationship to her daughters is not as harmonious as it first appears; nor is the younger generation made synonymous with greater maturity and insight. Wolf offers no totalizing view of Germany's progressive moral and political development. If anything is passed down from one generation to the next, it is a legacy of paradox and contradiction.

Lenka is critical of her mother's childhood association with National Socialism. The narrator communicates her daughter's distress upon finding racist illustrations in her old biology book and confesses that after this episode Lenka looks at her with "different eyes" (17). At the same time, Lenka's moral rigor blocks her awareness of history. Unlike the narrator, Lenka substitutes moral and ethical judgments for analysis and insight. Lenka "equates explanation with excuse" (60) and responds by rejecting both.[83] In her indignation over the "idiocy" of fascism, Lenka refuses to consider the possible reasons for its occurrence.[84] What most clearly distinguishes the narrator of *Kindheitsmuster* from her daughter is the narrator's understanding of the interconnectedness of past and present. Because Lenka has been able to live out her youth free from the traumas faced by her mother, she lacks both an awareness of, and sense of connectedness to, Germany's recent history. Lenka is described as a "child of this century" (215). But in contrast to her mother (who experienced a greater portion of the century firsthand), Lenka is more concerned with the individual's current level of social engagement than with the broader cultural or global implications of historical events. The narrator comments that her daughter demands from each citizen unconditional involvement. What Lenka considers important are not the attenuating circumstances surrounding events, but simply a person's decision or failure to act responsibly. When these civic and moral standards are not met, Lenka refuses to contemplate the reason for man's inhumanity or cowardice. Rather, she succumbs to anger, frustration, and disgust and, in the end, responds by turning away.

Lenka's moral outrage is representative of her generation's disavowal of its disturbing cultural legacy. Lenka claims that, unlike her mother, she is impervious to the seductions of authority. Disdainful of the "Pseudo-Menschen" who yield to any propaganda, Lenka feels capable of seeing through would-be demagogues and prides herself on her political savvy. Yet Lenka's commitment to political and moral correctness is matched by a frequent indifference toward her country's fascist past, an attitude shared by others her own age. Lenka tells her mother, for example, that upon seeing a map of concentration camps in a school textbook, neither she nor the rest of her class felt the map "concerned them more than any other documents in the book" (318–19).[85] The narrator of *Kindheitsmuster* is shocked by the younger generation's sense of uninvolvement in Germany's National Socialist past.

She attempts to explain their behavior as an effort towards freedom. Should, after all, those of Lenka's generation carry the guilt of their parents' misdeeds? Is it necessary for them to heed the "horrible dictum" that demands that responsibility for Hitler be passed "unto the third and fourth generation" (319)?

> What do you expect from Lenka's history book? That it stop the passage of time? That it transfer the unhappy conscience of one generation onto another? That it hinder the fading away of everything, including the horror? (325)

Wolf's protagonist would like to answer no to such questions. She ultimately finds that she cannot. During her conversation with Lenka, the narrator is reminded of the tourist industry's current efforts to transform former SS barracks into guest hotels. She tries to sympathize with teenage Germany's noncommittal attitude yet envisions hordes of visitors eating, drinking, and chatting as they pass through government-operated concentration camps. These images fill the narrator not only with amazement but with fear. It is with considerable sadness that she reaches her final conclusion: that freedom from guilt can never, for Lenka or for any other German, be the point of history's painful lesson.

Böll concludes in his essay on *Kindheitsmuster* that an erasure of personal complicity and the onset of self-delusion go hand in hand. He proposes that while individual absolution or *Amnestie* means to forget what one has done, *Amnesie* (amnesia) is an illness defined by a loss of memory, and asserts that "a person or society without memory is sick."[86] What Wolf begins in *Kindheitsmuster* is a process of recovery from this self-perpetuating affliction. As Evelyn Juers maintains, "Wolf's writing is always in the service of memory, as a recognition of one's responsibility for the past."[87] *Kindheitsmuster* is an act of engagement with history and the self. It is less a reconstruction of the past than the author's effort to re-live, through the process of writing, the formative cultural, psychological, and emotional experiences of her generation. To abandon the memory of National Socialism signals not only a betrayal of one's responsibility for the past but a dangerous alienation from oneself.

Cathy Caruth suggests that, in attempting to understand trauma, one is brought repeatedly to one peculiar paradox: that trauma's most awesome power may occur as an absolute numbing to it; that immediacy "may take the form of belatedness."[88] The period of latency that follows Wolf's childhood under National Socialism effects a movement from the traumatic events of the Third Reich, to their absence from the author's awareness, to their gradual and painful return. In *Kindheits-muster*, it is the narrator's survival of a trauma, her act of escape, which initiates her crisis. Nelly's flight westward brings her face to face with the many victims of Nazism; and she encounters suffering which greatly outweighs her own. Nelly hears firsthand German denials of Nazi crimes and sees the many opportunities for intervention that her countrymen ignored. The question posed by one of Hitler's victims — "Where on earth have you all been living?" — presents a question central to Wolf's novel. It is also a question Nelly can never forget. Only later, "years later, did it become for her a kind of motto" (445).

Critics of *Kindheitsmuster* argue that at no point in the novel does Wolf come to terms with her childhood under fascism. They point out that in order to work through her experiences, the author would have to master them — an action she categorically rejects. According to some, the parallel between Wolf's novel and psychoanalysis breaks down at a crucial point. There exists no sovereign or unbiased analyst who remains uninvolved in the material Wolf presents. There is no narrative perspective that maintains an objective distance. In the words of one critic, the novel constitutes a "risky self-experiment" not a therapeutic analysis.[89] For another, neither Nelly nor the events of her childhood can be brought into consciousness and worked through in a psychoanalytic manner. Nelly is and remains a "discrete personality," separate from that of the narrator.[90]

Kindheitsmuster is not an effort at mastering the past. The narrator's integration of her disparate selves is at best only tentatively achieved. What Wolf accomplishes in her novel, however, are the two processes crucial to both an understanding of National Socialism and the capacity to bear its mental and emotional burden: remembrance and mourning. Mourning is defined in *The Inability to Mourn* as "the psychic process by which an individual copes with a loss."[91] In *Kindheitsmuster*, Wolf acknowledges not one loss but many. She mourns Nelly's loss of autonomy and integrity, her parents' stolen hope and vitality, the sacrifice of her early *Heimat*, and most importantly, the innocent victims of Nazism. The process of mourning initiated by Wolf's narrator begins with those emotions that her socialization, traumatization, and guilt have forced her to repress. As the author herself has admitted, "the intellectual realization that one has made a mistake is easier to bear than the emotion of shame."[92] Her attempt to lay bare Germany's fascist past is inextricably bound to her acknowledgment of her own childhood complicity. And in order to speak of history as a social phenomenon, she must first find access to her own personal experience.

Although Wolf's aesthetic project does not attempt to master or overcome the past, her intellectual and emotional acknowledgment of the trauma of National Socialism serves as the prerequisite to her experience of guilt and remorse. Alexander and Margarete Mitscherlich pronounce, as does Wolf, that the murder of millions can never be mastered. But, like Wolf, they also insist that Germany can, indeed must, subject its past to a "sequence of steps in self-knowledge."[93] *Kindheitsmuster* is in many ways a response to the Mitscherlich's diagnosis of Germany's narcissistic failure to confront the crimes of the past. Following Freud's tripartite process of remembering, repeating, and working through, the novel enacts a critical analysis of National Socialism needed to overcome the self-protective urge to forget and to deny. Wolf views this process of remembrance and mourning as an ongoing individual and collective activity and shares with Böll the conviction that no one can "come to terms" with the past. For both authors, Germany must engage in a process of "permanent discomfiture,"[94] whereby the past is held in continual scrutiny by the present. *Kindheitsmuster* begins this work of examination and critique in its conjunction of past and present, but also in the alliance of the historical with the personal. The novel's tone is one of sorrow versus resignation. For Christa Wolf, memory and mourning are not synonymous with a loss of hope, but rather offer each individual the possibility of acknowledging the past and shaping the future.

Notes

[1]Christa Wolf, *Kindheitsmuster* (Berlin and Weimar: Aufbau Verlag, 1976) 312. All further references correspond to the 1979 Luchterhand edition and will be indicated parenthetically. Translations from the German are my own.

[2]Wolf, *Kindheitsmuster* 336.

[3]Heinrich Böll, "Wo habt ihr bloß gelebt?," *Christa Wolf: Materialienbuch*, ed. Klaus Sauer (Darmstadt: Hermann Luchterhand Verlag, 1990) 8.

[4]Cathy Caruth, "Unclaimed Experience: Trauma and the Possibility of History," *Yale French Studies* 79 (January 1991) 182.

[5]Cathy Caruth, Introduction to *American Imago* 48 (Spring 1991) 3.

[6]Christa Wolf, "Erfahrungsmuster: Diskussion zu *Kindheitsmuster*," *Die Dimension des Autors* (Darmstadt: Hermann Luchterhand Verlag, 1987) 806–7.

[7]Myra Love, *Christa Wolf: Literature and the Conscience of History* (New York: Peter Lang Publishing, 1991) 97.

[8]Stanislaw Roshnowski, "Der Roman als Form des historischen Bewußtseins: *Kindheitsmuster* von Christa Wolf und *Der Aufenthalt* von Hermann Kant," *Literatur im Wandel: Entwicklungen in europäischen sozialistischen Ländern 1944/5 bis 1980* (Berlin: Aufbau Verlag, 1986) 442.

[9]Marie-Luise Gättens, "Language, Gender, and Fascism: Reconstructing Histories in *Three Guineas, Der Mann auf der Kanzel,* and *Kindheitsmuster,*" *Gender, Patriarchy and Fascism in the Third Reich: The Response of Women Writers,* ed. Elaine Martin (Detroit: Wayne State UP, 1993) 43.

[10]Margarete Mitscherlich, "Die Frage der Selbstdarstellung: Überlegungen zu den Autobiographien von Helene Deutsch, Margaret Mead und Christa Wolf," *Neue Rundschau* 91 (1980) 310.

[11]In a public discussion of *Kindheitsmuster*, Christa Wolf describes her sense of alienation from her childhood self. Conceding that the novel "is related to my autobiography," the author declares that *Kindheitsmuster* is best termed a "so-called autobiography" because of her feeling of "no longer being this person." Wolf, "Erfahrungsmuster" 814.

[12]Christa Wolf, "Subjektive Authentizität: Gespräch mit Hans Kaufmann," *Die Dimension des Autors* 785.

[13]M. Mitscherlich, "Die Frage der Selbstdarstellung" 294.

[14]Caruth, Introduction 4.

[15]Christa Wolf, "Lesen und Schreiben," *Die Dimension des Autors* 478–79.

[16]Wolf, "Lesen und Schreiben" 480.

[17]Judith Ryan is correct to point out that the changes in perception that Nelly undergoes are very different from the ones experienced by the narrator and writer. Nelly's transformations do not result from gradual insight, but rather erupt as sudden reversals brought on by external circumstances. The narrator's progressive awareness stems, on the other hand, from sustained reflection and critique. It is the narrator's mature and self-critical viewpoint that corrects and contextualizes Nelly's more limited judgments. Judith Ryan, *The Uncompleted Past: Postwar German Novels and the Third Reich* (Detroit: Wayne State UP, 1983) 149–51.

[18]Central to the Mitscherlichs' analysis of post-1945 Germany is the belief that all events in which Germans were guiltily implicated have been either denied or re-interpreted. They argue that in order to maintain a separation between acceptable and unacceptable memories, Germans have summoned up a "considerable expenditure of psychic energy." In protecting the self, they have sacrificed an honest engagement with the past, and, paradoxically, have diminished their vitality in the present. Margarete and Alexander Mitscher-

lich, *Die Unfähigkeit zu trauern: Grundlagen kollektiven Verhaltens* (Munich: R. Piper & Co. Verlag, 1967) 26.

[19]Mitscherlichs, *Die Unfähigkeit zu trauern* 8.

[20]Roshnowski 437.

[21]Gerhart Pickerodt, "Christa Wolfs Roman *Kindheitsmuster*. Ein Beitrag zur 'Vergangenheitsbewältigung'?," *Exil: Wirkung und Wertung. Ausgewählte Beiträge zum fünften Symposium über deutsche und österreichische Exilliteratur,* eds. Donald Daviau and Ludwig Fischer (Columbia, SC: Camden House, 1985) 304.

[22]M. Mitscherlich, "Die Frage der Selbstdarstellung" 292.

[23]Per Øhrgaard, "Ein Foto mit Hut — Bemerkungen zu Christa Wolf: *Kindheitsmuster,*" *Orbis Litterarum* 42 (1987) 376.

[24]M. Mitscherlich, "Die Frage der Selbstdarstellung" 294.

[25]Böll 11.

[26]Ryan, *The Uncompleted Past* 141.

[27]Caruth, Introduction 6.

[28]Øhrgaard 376.

[29]It is interesting to note that Nelly's reaction to Hitler, whom she glimpses firsthand at the age of five, is likewise described in physical terms. The narrator states that Nelly not only knew, but *felt* what the Führer was: "a sweet pressure in the stomach and a sweet lump in the throat" (67).

[30]Wolf, "Erfahrungsmuster" 815.

[31]Ryan, *The Uncompleted Past* 143.

[32]Some critics have added to this tripartite structure the first-person plural "we," arguing that the reader is implicitly included in Wolf's self-address, and therefore made a participant in her self-interrogation. See Marilyn Fries, "Problems in Narrating the Heimat: Christa Wolf and Johannes Bobrowski," *Cross Currents* 9 (1990); and Ursula Mahlendorf, "Confronting the Fascist Past and Coming to Terms with It," *World Literature Today* 55 (Autumn 1981).

[33]Wolf, "Erfahrungsmuster" 815.

[34]Robert Jay Lifton, *The Nazi Doctors: Medical Killing and the Psychology of Genocide* (New York: Basic Books, 1986) 64.

[35]In chapter six, for example, the narrator describes how Nelly is "split in two" during her mandatory appearance at Lori Tietz's birthday party. Aware of the insincerity and pretension being paraded around this upper-middle class household, the obedient Nelly nonetheless feels obliged to participate in a game of "The Jew has slaughtered a pig." The "other Nelly," however, watches from a corner and "sees through everything": "The other Nelly sees:

they all want something from her here. They're calculating. They've invited her in order to steal something from her, something that they can't get any other way." (181–82)

[36]Marianne Hirsch, *The Mother/Daughter Plot: Narrative, Psychoanalysis, Feminism* (Indianapolis: Indiana UP, 1989) 157.

[37]Lifton 64.

[38]Ursula Mahlendorf, "Confronting the Fascist Past and Coming to Terms with It," *World Literature Today* 55 (Autumn 1981) 556.

[39]Hirsch 155.

[40]Evelyn Juers, "Who's Afraid of Christa Wolf?," *The Cambridge Quarterly* 21 (1992) 216.

[41]Pickerodt underscores this lack of sentimentality in Christa Wolf's narrative, stating that "the ensemble of travellers resembles more a commission of critical experts than a group of persons who share an emotionally-charged fascination with the past." 300.

[42]Juers 217.

[43]Juers 217.

[44]Per Øhrgaard explains how in *Moskauer Novelle, Der geteilte Himmel,* and *Nachdenken über Christa T.* socialism substitutes for traditional familial structures. Not only do mothers and fathers not instruct their children, they offer them no real support. Authority figures in these early novels are much more likely to be teachers or friends than the protagonists' biological parents. 378–79.

[45]Hirsch 156.

[46]Critic Gerhardt Pickerodt contends that the narrator's family "fails in that it offers no alternative to the values and norms practiced in society at large. Rather, the family proves itself to be an agent of social adaptation, through which the child's character is shaped and formed." 301.

[47]Michael Schneider, "Fathers and Sons, Retrospectively: The Damaged Relationship between Two Generations," *New German Critique* 31 (1983) 18.

[48]The narrator recalls only one instance in which her father voiced a criticism of Nazi practices. While on leave Bruno Jordan learns from a friend that German soldiers have shot their Polish prisoners and responds by saying "That's not for me" (252). As his daughter will later discover, Bruno's reaction to this political and moral offense is not only conspicuously brief, but pathetic in its understatement.

[49]David Dollenmayer, "Generational Patterns in Christa Wolf's *Kindheitsmuster*," *German Life and Letters* 39 (April 1986) 230.

[50]Elaine Martin, "Women Right/(Re)Write the Nazi Past: An Introduction," *Gender, Patriarchy and Fascism in the Third Reich* 24.

[51]"The child's restricted perspective has the advantage of portraying the petit-bourgeois family from within, probing it as a breeding ground of fascism even while observing the effects of events produced by fascism . . . Moreover, because the adults . . . do not take the child seriously, they unguardedly reveal themselves as they are . . . their insecurity, lack of feeling, rationalizations, denial of reality, their lovelessness and their sweltering anger against each other, their complete inability to express themselves." Mahlendorf 555.

[52]Mahlendorf 557.

[53]Ohrgaard 380.

[54]Elaine Martin shows how a number of German women writers who were children or adolescents during the Third Reich describe the *Bund deutscher Mädel* as an organization that offered "physically strenuous outdoor activities, comradeship, leadership roles, creative outlets, and feelings of being both useful and taken seriously." Such freedoms, Martin argues, created a special appeal for German girls, who had historically been both physically and emotionally trapped within restrictive, patriarchal families. "Women Right/(Re)Write the Nazi Past" 24.

[55]Per Øhrgaard views the narrator's painful acknowledgment of Nelly's volitional involvement in National Socialism as central to Wolf's confrontation with the past. While it heightens the author's estrangement from her former self, it also answers her need for an honest analysis of her childhood, one which, in resisting the desire for innocence, comes closer to the truth. "Ein Foto mit Hut" 380.

[56]Juers 220.

[57]In his influential work *Discipline and Punish*, Foucault states that disciplinary power is exercised through its invisibility. "In discipline, it is the subjects who have to be seen. Their visibility assures the hold of the power that is over them. It is the fact of being constantly seen, of being always to be seen, that maintains the disciplined individual in his subjection." Michel Foucault, *Discipline and Punish: The Birth of the Prison*. Trans. Alan Sheridan. (New York: Vintage Books, 1979) 187. I am indebted here to Marie-Luise Gättens' mention of Foucault in her essay "Language, Gender and Fascism" 45.

[58]Gättens 52.

[59]Gättens 60.

[60]Mahlendorf 558.

[61]Henry Krystal, "Integration and Self-Healing in Post Traumatic States: A Ten Year Retrospective," *American Imago* (Spring 1991) 114.

[62]Christa Wolf claims in a 1982 interview that contradiction is her "fundamental form of life." She states that while such discrepancies "can be uncomfortable . . . [and] can make you doubt yourself," they are never wholly negative, "especially when it's a question of contradictions that move each other toward solutions." Francke Meyer-Gosau, "Culture Is What You Experience: An Interview with Christa Wolf," *New German Critique* 27 (Fall 1982) 93.

[63]Ryan, *The Uncompleted Past* 145.

[64]In the words of Judith Ryan, "Nelly, in both her earlier and later versions, must disappear into the black hole to allow her narrator to emerge into newly aligned categories of thought." *The Uncompleted Past* 147.

[65]Maria Luise Gättens writes that the eruption of Germany's fascist past into contemporary consciousness causes intense anxiety "as it signals that National Socialism, a period one has tacitly agreed to conceal, still has a profound impact on the present . . . and reveals that the postwar period is based on evasion and avoidance." "Language, Gender and Fascism" 43.

[66]Wolf, "Interview mit Hans Kaufmann" 785.

[67]"Isn't it possible that we have gotten used to describing fascism as a 'phenomenon' that existed outside us and which ceased to exist as soon as its power centers and organizations had been destroyed? Haven't we devoted our energies toward constructing for ourselves, and for ourselves alone, a tradition of being the anti-fascists and resistance fighters?" "Interview with Hans Kaufmann" 785.

[68]Ryan, *The Uncompleted Past* 146.

[69]Love 41.

[70]Pickerodt 296.

[71]Roshnowski 434.

[72]Gättens 62.

[73]Ryan, *The Uncompleted Past* 142.

[74]Love 66.

[75]M. Mitscherlich, "Die Frage der Selbstdarstellung" 295.

[76]Meyer-Gosau 97.

[77]Pickerodt 305.

[78]Hirsch 155.

[79]Love 6.

[80]Hirsch 158.

[81]Jutta Birmele, "Christa Wolf: A Quest for Heimat," *Der Begriff 'Heimat' in der deutschsprachigen Literatur*, ed. H. W. Seliger (München: iudicium verlag, 1987) 72.

[82]Mitscherlichs, *Die Unfähigkeit zu trauern* 23.

[83]David Dollenmayer is right to note that in collapsing the distinction between understanding and forgiveness, Lenka establishes an attitude toward history incompatible with her mother's cross-examination. Although the narrator is rigorous in her investigation of her childhood, at no point does she exonerate Nelly for her involvement in National Socialism. Indeed, the closer Wolf's subject gets to Nelly (by moving further and further into the past) the more she dislikes her.

[84]In Dollenmayer's assessment, the narrator's daughter has been raised too well: "Lenka's greatest barrier to understanding is at the same time her greatest virtue: 'Gerechtigkeitssinn.' Her sense of justice is imbued with a rigorous moralism that the narrator . . . has eschewed at the beginning of the novel precisely because it would render her task impossible." "Generational Patterns in Christa Wolf's *Kindheitsmuster*" 232.

[85]Alexander and Margarete Mitscherlich observe in *The Inability to Mourn* that the generation of Germans who grew up after the Third Reich seem oddly unencumbered by the burden of Nazi crimes and quickly "repudiate any imputation of responsibility for the infamous behavior of their elders." It should be added, however, that the Mitscherlichs view the younger generation's disassociation from National Socialism as merely the exterior disguise covering their feelings of shared complicity. The Mitscherlichs argue that there exists in Germany two distinct psychic processes: "the retrospective warding off of real guilt by the older generation and the unwillingness of the younger to get caught up in the guilt problems of their parents." Alexander and Margarete Mitscherlich, "The Authors' Forward to the American Edition," *The Inability to Mourn*, trans. Beverly Placzek (New York: Grove Press) xx.

[86]Böll 8.

[87]Juers 220.

[88]Caruth, Introduction 5.

[89]Pickerodt 298.

[90]Ryan, *The Uncompleted Past* 147.

[91]Mitscherlichs, *Die Unfähigkeit zu trauern* 9.

[92]From *The Fourth Dimension: Interviews with Christa Wolf*. Quoted in Juers, "Who's Afraid of Christa Wolf?" 219.

[93]Mitscherlichs, *Die Unfähigkeit zu trauern* 24.

[94]Böll 8.

Heredity, Heimat, and Hatred:
Thomas Bernhard's *Auslöschung*

> Interviewer: You see Salzburg as a deadly city, death museum, and deceitful facade. In your opinion, its residents are "perishing slowly and miserably on this thoroughly lethal soil ... with its mindless blend of National Socialism and Catholicism."
>
> Bernhard: I am after all a Salzburger, am I not? My relationship to this city holds a special place in my heart.[1]

READERS OF THOMAS BERNHARD have long come to expect the worst. The most eccentric and tortured protagonists; the most claustrophobic and stultifying cities; the most violent and degenerate citizens; the most corrupt and destructive institutions. Before his death in 1989, Bernhard had earned a reputation as a "misanthrope's misanthrope," a writer whose literary output was, in the words of one critic, "subjective, unkind, without generosity, stilted, and furious."[2] Bernhard was an unabashed critic of Austria and the Austrians. He denounced the sensationalism of his country's media, the hypocrisy of its elite, the ruthlessness of its politicians, and the abuse of its natural resources. Bernhard reserved his most vitriolic rhetorical assault, however, for Austria's complicity in National Socialism. Bernhard relentlessly condemned Austria's Nazi past, as well as his country's refusal to own up to its guilt in the years that followed. According to critics, Bernhard's primary goal in much of his fiction was to unmask Austria's complacent self-perception as the unwitting, unwilling victim of National Socialism.[3] The author adamantly rejected the view that Austria had been invaded in 1938 and rescued in 1945, and reminded his fellow Austrians not only of the cheering crowds that greeted Hitler's cavalcade, but of those Austrians who enthusiastically took up positions in the SS and in concentration camps.[4] Bernhard never forgave his country for its involvement in the Third Reich. And although the Holocaust is rarely mentioned in his works, his fiction is permeated by its crippling moral consequences for the postwar Austrian state.[5] Bernhard offered no apologies for his denunciations of Austria and had little respect for his detractors. In the words of one critic, the author remained until the end "a Jeremiah, the last angry, honest Austrian" of his generation.[6]

What is equally striking about Bernhard is his ambivalence — the simultaneity of efforts to vilify his country and a persistent inability to extricate himself from it. Bernhard confesses in an interview that he is deeply connected to his native land; not because Austria warrants such attachment, but because it has made him, for good or ill, what he is. He tells his interviewer: "I am bound to it by a terrible, indissoluble bond. My whole being has its origin . . . in this landscape."[7] Several years later Bernhard summarizes his attitude toward Austria as a mixture of love and hate, and declares that his *Haßliebe* "is the key to everything I write."[8] Thus, despite his lifelong animosity toward Austria, and his eagerness to expose its many flaws, the author found it impossible to abandon his country either geographically or emotionally.

Critics agree that Bernhard's fiction is largely autobiographical and identify this same ambivalence in many of his protagonists.[9] Bernhard's central figures are eccentric and reclusive characters; they share an inclination toward misanthropy and paranoia. Similarly, they are writers who find it difficult to write and harbor "a special odium for Austrians."[10] At the same time, these protagonists do not view Austria in wholly negative terms. They denounce their country's lack of environmentalism but readily acknowledge the beauty of its landscape. They ridicule famous composers, artists, and writers yet are scholars of Austrian music, literature, and art. They despise social hierarchy yet are fascinated by Austria's aristocracy. In short, Bernhard offers us few uncomplicated heroes.[11]

This narrative trademark is perhaps nowhere more apparent than in Bernhard's last novel, *Auslöschung* (Extinction, 1986),[12] published three years before the author's death and widely considered the most autobiographical of all his fiction.[13] Franz-Josef Murau, the first-person narrator of the novel, leads a life steeped in contradiction. He lives abroad but is obsessed with his homeland. He is incensed by the urbanization of Austria's countryside yet is a city-dweller. He ridicules the German language yet provides lessons in German literature. He covets the authenticity of the "simple folk" yet is proud of his aristocratic heritage. But Franz-Josef Murau is not simply a man in conflict. He is a man for whom ambivalence will prove fatal. His lifelong division of affection toward his country of origin results in a division of identity, which only amplifies the destructive counterbalance between his love and his hate. The death of Murau's parents triggers a torrent of childhood memories: about growing up in an upper-class household, about his difficult family relationships, about the perversities of Austrian culture, and about the "intimate connection between National Socialism and Catholicism."[14] Murau's return to Austria for his parents' funeral brings him to face to face with the people, places, and attitudes that have both fascinated and repelled him, and facilitates an excavation not only of his own familial legacy, but of a national legacy still very much alive. As the novel progresses, it becomes evident that Murau's initial confessions involve much more than a parent-son conflict, or the private ruminations of a disgruntled expatriate. What unfolds in the course of Bernhard's narrative is the story of a family's complicity in National Socialism and the deep-seated fascist beliefs that continue to infect an entire nation. And what begins as a journey of discovery ends as a project in extinction.

In the opening pages of *Auslöschung*, the reader is faced with an enigma. Franz-Josef Murau, an Austrian national living in Rome, has just received word that his parents and brother are dead. Killed in a gruesome car accident while traveling home from the theater, they are to be buried at Wolfsegg, the family's estate in Upper Austria. The reader cannot help but notice a curious lack of affect in Murau's response to the news, a response which seems as cold and impersonal as the missive itself. "With the telegram in hand," Franz-Josef announces, "I kept a clear head, walked calmly to my study window, and looked down on . . . the Piazza Minerva" (7). The coolness of the narrator's behavior is further amplified by his assurance that he had "no fear of succumbing to sentimentality" (14).

Given the dispassion of Franz-Josef's attitude, it would seem that Bernhard's protagonist feels little or nothing for his family in Austria. But such behavior is deceiving. As the novel progresses, the reader discovers that Murau's response to the telegram conceals an intensity of emotions unchecked by his years in Rome. By his own admission, Wolfsegg has haunted him day and night. The prospect of returning for the funeral elicits agitation, anxiety, and self-doubt, and ultimately leads to Murau's realization that the trip will require "all my strength, all my willpower" (11). The arrival of the telegram is the initiating event of Bernhard's novel. It serves as the catalyst for Murau's journey to Wolfsegg, his re-examination of his family history, and his recapitulation of these experiences in the form of a memoir. But, as the first scene portends, Franz-Josef's return to Austria will be fraught with conflict. Despite the benefits of his self-imposed exile and his repeated attempts to sever all familial and cultural ties, Franz-Josef Murau remains pursued by a past he cannot escape. His obsessions regarding Wolfsegg have followed him throughout his childhood, adolescence, and adulthood. And they have proved lethal. According to Murau, his boyhood experiences are to blame for a mysterious heart ailment from which he will soon die. Did Franz-Josef love the parents and brother who ironically predeceased him? He really cannot say. It is a question, he claims, "that remained . . . fundamentally unanswered" (12).

Bernhard's division of the novel into two parts, "The Telegram" and "The Will," mirrors the tension between Murau's dual identities: the cynical Austrian enamored of Rome and the urban sophisticate turned lord of the manor.[15] Although it is difficult to reconstruct the timeline of Bernhard's narrative, moving as it does between things "remembered, imagined, or dreamed,"[16] Part One concerns itself primarily with the narrator's initial reaction to the accident; Part Two recounts his return to Wolfsegg. In "The Telegram" Franz-Josef makes clear that his earlier departure from Wolfsegg was not one of choice but of necessity. The decision to leave his family and his homeland was the last of many plans to escape, attempts which previously included London, Paris, Ankara, and Istanbul. Rome is for Murau the ultimate haven, a "beloved," "revered," and "wonderful" place (111) where he can carve out a new identity. A resident of Rome for the past twenty years, Franz-Josef has done much to separate himself from his former *Heimat*. He has developed a close circle of international friends, acquired a job which provides financial comfort, and keeps all visits to Austria both infrequent and brief. In addition to these more positive attempts at independence, Murau has worked to insure his country's hostility. According to his detractors, his newspaper articles "are always dragging Austria in the dirt" and make insupportable claims that the country is "vulgar and despicable" (20). Murau is largely immune to such censure. His critics' attempts to redeem Austria's reputation are ignored; their threatening letters are destroyed. Murau's time in Rome has, in fact, bolstered his self-esteem. His friendship with the poet Maria provides a safe, honest arena where he can express both his dreams and failures.[17] His conversations with his student Gambetti confirm his intellectual prowess. And his outings with Archbishop Spandolini create a sense of vicarious wealth, elegance, and refinement.[18]

Rome is also everything that Wolfsegg is not. It is a city steeped in tradition yet fully modern, a city which cultivates an appreciation of the arts even among the simplest of its citizens. In contrast to Wolfsegg, described by Murau as a "stronghold of mindlessness" (17) without "the slightest bit of taste" (112), Rome actively promotes the life of the mind

and creates the perfect setting for Murau's pursuit of his one true passion — literature.[19] This is not to say that Franz-Josef grew up without
books. He informs the reader that there are five libraries at Wolfsegg, an
impressive collection of literary works established by his great-great-
great-grandfather. It is with considerable derision, however, that Murau
then tells us that these books are merely decorative. He recalls that as a
child the closed windows and locked doors of the libraries were barriers
not only to the fresh air of the surrounding countryside, but to the
more figurative fresh air of new ideas. What was once the pride of his
"crazy intellectual" grandfather (56) is now a curiosity piece for inquisitive visitors. Murau considers Wolfsegg the antithesis of intellectualism,
a place where conversations about literature or painting are drowned
out by talk of shallow and mundane concerns — "money, hunting,
vegetables, grain, potatoes, wood, coal, nothing else" (109). This "hostility to the intellect" (112) is for Murau a disastrous impediment to his
own creativity. The fresh air he so desperately needs he finds in Rome.
The open-air piazzas and cafés provide the ideal physical and mental
setting for his conversations with his pupil Gambetti, his enjoyment of
literature, and his artistic aspirations. In his own words, he cannot exist
without fresh air, "let alone engage in any mental activity" (71).

Murau's family sees nothing admirable in his Roman identity. They
consider Franz-Josef's flight from Wolfsegg a betrayal of his familial
obligations, a misuse of the family's funds, and a thinly-veiled attack on
their entire way of life. They likewise have no respect for Italy, a country they consider "the epitome of chaos" (394). Murau asserts that his
decision to move to Rome effectively terminated all hopes of positive
familial relations. During his twenty-year stay in Rome, his brother has
resented his "megalomaniac self-sufficiency"; his sisters have re-
proached him for his "inconsiderate pursuit of freedom" (12). In short,
Murau's family responds to his rejection of Wolfsegg with hatred, a
feeling which the narrator reciprocates: "They despised me, *their Roman*, just as I despised them, *the Wolfseggers*" (13).

Franz-Josef would like us to believe that he has grown impervious
to his family's antipathy and that his own animosity has given way to
indifference. Early in the narrative, he declares that "for decades I suffered under their hatred . . . but I haven't suffered from it for years;
I've become used to their hatred and it no longer hurts me" (13). Yet
immediately after making this pronouncement, Murau provides strong
evidence that he remains vulnerable to his family's criticism and indeed
counters their attacks on his carefully constructed identity with a virulent assault of his own. Upon hearing that his parents and brother are

dead, Murau retrieves from his desk three photographs: one of his parents at Victoria Station; one of his brother in Sankt Wolfgang; and one of his sisters in Cannes. Murau insists that he detests photography, "a vulgar addiction that is gradually consuming the whole of humanity" (29) and assures the reader that he has never owned a camera. Nevertheless, Franz-Josef refuses to part with the photographs he has taken of his family. He brought them with him from Wolfsegg and admits to showing at least one of the photographs to Gambetti. In explaining his possession of the photographs, Murau asserts that his fascination with these images is inextricable from a deep sense of revulsion. Unlike most photographs, he maintains, these three do not falsify reality, they capture it. They portray his parents and siblings as they really are: "unhappy, ugly and stupid" (127). Franz-Josef's discussion of the photographs is less a description of events than a dissection of his parents' and siblings' identities. As one critic perceptively observes, the narrator relishes the photographs because they present his family in miniature. The photographic images reduce, in effect, both his parents and Johannes to "Lilliputian dimensions," thereby reducing their power over him.[20] Interestingly, Murau has no photograph of himself. The narrator's conspicuous absence from these "ridiculous pieces of paper" (46) reveals a dual desire: to minimize and satirize his family and to confirm his own sense of superiority and control. Franz-Josef objectifies and scrutinizes his parents and siblings, but is careful not to incriminate himself. Importantly, however, Murau's discussion of the photos is not simply an act of self-assertion; it is one of self-defense.[21] By his own admission, it is an opportunity to bolster his fragile self-esteem and provides a momentary opportunity to "fortify myself during sudden attacks of weakness" (249).

Murau begins his assessment of the photographs by ridiculing his parents' pretensions. Illustrative of a lifelong desire to be something they are not, Murau's parents attempt while in England to be "more British than the British." Franz-Josef draws attention to their Burberry umbrellas and raincoats, his father's artificial posture, his mother's outstretched neck. He then concludes that the photo fails to convey what his parents had intended. What it does do is show Murau's parents the way he sees them, as "grotesque rather than refined and elegant" (23). Murau attributes to his brother Johannes the same propensity for pretense. The figure he describes is "an embittered man, ruined by living alone with his parents." According to Murau, Johannes, like himself, has been corrupted through association with Wolfsegg; his forced smile and sporty attire do little to hide "the illnesses that have already taken possession of him" (24). The photographs of his sisters Amalia and Caecilia come under similar scrutiny and attack. Their mocking, disdainful expressions, Murau proposes, are their sole defense against their imprisonment at Wolfsegg. The narrator finds rich irony in the fact that these same looks "scared off all the men they wanted" (60), thereby ending all hope of rescue.

Murau attempts to convince himself that, in spite of his family's disapproval, his Italian identity remains firmly intact. A closer inspection of his life in Rome exposes both the paradox of this persona and the narrator's assumption of the very characteristics he disdains in his family at Wolfsegg. Murau's actions are inconsistent with his ideals and gradually reveal a man of extreme contradiction and ambivalence. An early example of this contradiction is Franz-Josef's criticism of his family's love of money. He condemns his mother's designer dresses, his father's obsession with turning a profit, his brother's expensive sporting habits, and his sister's loveless marriage to a wealthy wine cork manufacturer. Given such disapproval of his family's materialism, one might expect from Murau a simple, modest lifestyle. This is certainly not the case. By his own admission, Franz-Josef leads a life of wealth and ease. He rents a luxury apartment in the heart of Rome and spends his days sipping coffee in cafés. Ironically, Franz-Josef supports this lifestyle through the money he receives from Wolfsegg, and by deceiving the affluent Italians who have hired him as tutor. Unable to confront his family with the "hand he was dealt at birth" (16), Murau projects the hostility he feels towards Wolfsegg against the unsuspecting Gambettis. The narrator appropriates, in effect, the malevolent habits of his own reviled household to destroy the happiness of another. He sees himself much as the Gambetti's have come to see him, "not only as the seducer of their naturally beloved son, but as his destroyer, and consequently their own" (210).

A further paradox of Murau *der Römer* is his profession as Germanist. Despite his knowledge of Russian, French, and Spanish literature, Murau chooses to teach a literary canon he considers inferior in a language he finds unredeemable. According to Murau, the German language is incompatible with creativity. German words, he insists, "hang like lead weights on the German language." German thought and speech, he adds, "quickly become paralyzed under the insufferable weight of the language, which suppresses any thought before it can even be expressed" (8). Murau likewise has little good to say about German-speaking authors. For at least a century, he exclaims, German novelists have produced nothing but "binder literature," uninspired, bureaucratic scribbling designed to please the lower middle class. This vilification of his native language and its literature has not stopped Murau from teaching it. Not only does he introduce Gambetti to the works of Musil, who along with Thomas Mann was "dominated by three-ring binders" (608), but teaches the worst offender of all — Goethe. As the novel opens, Murau assigns Gambetti Goethe's *Wahlverwandtschaften* (Elective Affinities). We later learn that Bernhard's narrator lacks all respect for Goethe, Germany's "foremost intellectual trickster." What, on the one hand, is required reading is, on the other, the "height of German charlatanry" (576).

A final example of Murau's conflicted Roman identity is his ironic choice of domicile. The narrator presents Rome as a place of refuge, a city geographically and culturally disconnected from his painful years at Wolfsegg. But Rome is not the world apart it appears to be. It is the center of Catholicism, a religion Murau describes as "a falsification of nature" (142) and the "great instiller of terror" (141). The narrator actively courts Archbishop Spandolini, a powerful representative of Catholic hierarchy. Murau considers Spandolini the most sophisticated, charismatic, and irresistible of all his acquaintances; neither the archbishop's position as a "natural born prince of the Church" (248) nor his blatant disregard for his spiritual vows stand in the way of the narrator's admiration. Franz-Josef admits rather late in the novel that Spandolini is largely responsible for his move to Rome. Because of this, Murau will always be grateful to Spandolini, the much admired "man of the world" (498). There is considerable irony in the fact that Spandolini is simultaneously his mother's paramour. Murau is complicitous in this adulterous affair; he neither denounces the lovers' deceit nor defends his father's honor. Although Murau resents his position — "between a lying mother and a hypocritical ecclesiastic" (287) — he chooses to maintain a discreet silence. His unwillingness to condemn the two lovers perpetuates the myth propagated by his mother: that she is in Rome to visit her son. It should also be noted that the relationship between Spandolini and Murau's mother long predates the narrator's decision to move to Rome, existing, according to Murau, for thirty years. It is with full knowledge of Rome's ubiquitous Catholicism, the duplicity of Spandolini, and the continued influence of his mother that Murau makes the city his home.

Bernhard's narrator is convinced that his Roman-ness will follow him to Wolfsegg. Although anxious about returning to Austria, Murau is also confident in his twenty-year identity and believes it will sustain him through the trying days to come. Franz-Josef insists that his time

in Austria will be brief and perfunctory. His decisions regarding Wolfsegg will be matter-of-fact and final. He will then return to his beloved
Italy and resume his lessons with Gambetti. As Part II begins, Franz-
Josef seems to have the situation in hand. His taxi ride from the train
station conjures pleasant thoughts of Rome and takes Murau through
what he considers "one of the most beautiful places in the world"
(312). The narrator also prides himself on arriving at his parents' estate
unannounced and savors the thought of his sisters' shock and resentment. It is soon obvious that Murau's intentions do not prepare him
for Wolfsegg. The narrator's present responsibilities — to provide for
his sisters' welfare and to determine the future of his parents' estate —
are overshadowed by memories of his painful past and quickly confront
him with a history that can neither be ignored nor escaped. No sooner
does the narrator enter the gates of Wolfsegg than his Roman identity
begins to crumble. Old hurts are reborn, old insecurities resurface. In
the words of one critic, the self-esteem Franz-Josef enjoys in Italy is
merely borrowed. Safe only within the confines of Rome, Murau's
adult sense of self remains vulnerable to the truths of his childhood and
will eventually collapse.[22] Rome, the idealized haven, the second *Heimat*, proves no match for the first.

   Murau's reaction to Austria is, like his Roman persona, riddled with
contradiction. He acknowledges the splendor of the Austrian landscape
yet decries its disfigurement by architects and "mercenary politicians"
(115). He dismisses Austria's aristocrats as "disgusting creatures" (56)
yet relishes his own status and wealth. He despises the rural Austrian
dialect but is drawn to those with the least education. Murau's attitude
toward Wolfsegg is much the same. The narrator does not hesitate to
avow the charms of his family's estate. He describes for the reader
Wolfsegg's majestic, austere beauty, its unrivaled view of the Alps, the
colors and fragrances of the Orangerie, the camaraderie of the gardeners. He recounts for Gambetti how, as a child, he sat for hours amidst
the camellias, conversing with his Onkel Georg and learning his first
words of Latin.[23] Murau admits that this early introduction to beauty
and refinement was a "great luxury." It instilled in him a lifelong love
of nature, as well as a deep appreciation for those who tend the earth.
Franz-Josef cherishes this portion of his childhood and confesses to his
pupil Gambetti that "this was one of my greatest pleasures" (166).

   The narrator harbors this same love of nature and learning as an
adult and carries it with him on his return to Wolfsegg. Murau considers his newly acquired status as executor of the estate an opportunity to
revitalize Wolfsegg. He plans to imbue the estate with his triumphant

intellectualism and the vitality of his life in Rome, and hopes to liberate his home from his parents' mediocrity. Franz-Josef asserts, in fact, that his sole reason for journeying to Wolfsegg is not to attend his parents' and brother's funeral. It is to "open wide the windows and let in the fresh air" (150). Murau's optimism is short-lived. His return to Wolfsegg brings with it a renewed awareness of the darker aspects of his childhood and a renewed hostility toward those responsible. As the taxi approaches his parents' estate, Murau is reminded of how this "most pleasant and restful countryside" (312) has been corrupted by its association with Wolfsegg, and how his decision to leave was, in actuality, "an escape from the damage directed at me by my parents" (36). Murau's fondness toward Wolfsegg soon becomes hatred. His appreciation of the estate's physical beauty gives way to memories of repeated psychological abuse and wanton political and moral corruption. Murau's hatred of Wolfsegg is, the reader discovers, inextricable from his parents who are inextricable from Austria which is inextricable from its history. What follows is an indictment not only of Murau's immediate family, but of a larger cultural heritage predicated upon obedience, conformism, and hypocrisy.[24]

Franz-Josef Murau initially equates the death of his parents with his own liberation. Staring at the photograph of the "demonic couple" (25) from his study in Rome, Murau states with relief that his *Verfolgungswahn* (persecution complex) is finally over and that he is now free. It is not long before he realizes that this freedom is an illusion. The removal of Murau's parents from Wolfsegg eliminates the most obvious cause of the narrator's neurosis. It does not obliterate its consequences.[25] Similarly, Murau's account of his life is more than a record of his boyhood experiences. It is an attempt to overcome the emotional damage that continues to plague him. By divulging the harm inflicted upon him as a child, Murau endeavors to come to terms with the family history or *Herkunftskomplex* which has been his "lifelong theme" (201).[26] It is important to note, however, that the narrator does not simply make peace with the origins of his unhappiness. Murau's excavation of the past, a project that is wholly self-imposed,[27] is likewise meant to destroy. Its goal is to end, once and for all, the myth of the respectable family promulgated by his parents and the pain associated with his own knowledge of the truth. Murau's denouncement of his parents' appearance in the photograph is merely the beginning. His criticism will extend far beyond physical affectations and will assault almost every facet of his parents' existence. According to Murau, his mother and father were masters of deception. Their devotion to pretense masked their unhappy marriage, their lack of learning, their social inadequacies, and their deplorable parenting. More importantly, it allowed them to appropriate, and later disguise, a fanatical commitment to Nazism.

Murau holds his parents directly responsible for his psychic turmoil as well as his failing health.[28] And he considers his mother the worst offender. "My heart has little capacity for resistance, having been abused since childhood. My heart has never been given the rest it needed, I thought, and now it's finished" (622). In Part One of the novel, Franz-Josef introduces his mother in the most unflattering of terms. She is greedy, vulgar, unfaithful, and unattractive. She is a committed Catholic without an ounce of Christian virtue. She is a "malevolent puppet master" (124), who ruthlessly manipulates the lives of her husband, her daughters, and Johannes. In sum, his mother is the source of all that is evil and destructive about Wolfsegg. "A person like my mother," Murau asserts, "makes a family bad that was never bad before and is the undisputed source of all evil that takes over a home" (298). As the novel progresses, we are given numerous examples of the dismissive, humiliating treatment Murau suffered at his mother's hand. The narrator recalls how from an early age his mother considered him her albatross. He was the child she never wanted, "the source of her unhappiness," "the bringer of misfortune" (289), "the most superfluous child one can imagine" (290), "the son of Satan" (276).[29] The negative effect of this treatment is exacerbated by Murau's inability to flee his mother's watchful eye. His escapes to Wolfsegg's libraries bring punishment and ostracism; his forays into the village result in charges of disloyalty and deceit. Given the extremity of his mother's cruelty, it comes as no surprise that Murau is morbidly fascinated by her death. Murau reads in the local tabloids that his mother's head — the locus of her mental cunning and verbal assaults — had been severed from her body, while Johannes and his father suffered only minor bruises.[30] Testimony to the mother's continued power over Murau, he suspects that she is still alive and insists on seeing her decapitated corpse as proof of her demise. It is only through the vigilance of Wolfsegg's huntsmen, and his mother's tightly bolted coffin, that such confirmation is denied.

Franz-Josef describes his father as a fundamentally weak and ineffectual man, a pseudo-patriarch who tolerated his wife's indiscretions and did nothing to curb her financial and disciplinary excesses. According to Murau, his father was obsessed with the idea of being a farmer and devoted his entire life to the creation and preservation of this ideal. The narrator recounts how his father would spend hours atop his tractor without tilling an acre of soil, and how he meticulously recorded each profit and expenditure. Murau characterizes his father's activities as the "simulation of work," a role meant to hide his actual ineptness and indolence. Both Johannes and his father, Franz-Josef argues, were consummate actors, feigning the activity they both so admired until they "could no longer see it as pretense" (93). The narrator likewise criticizes his father for insisting both sons follow in his footsteps. He vividly remembers the "toughening methods . . . that only made us unusually sensitive" (180) and assures his reader that, even as an adult, his father "had no compunction in putting me down in front of everyone" (604). According to Murau, his decision to move to Rome only intensified his father's hostility. Once it became clear Franz-Josef would never return to Wolfsegg, all hopes of positive mutual relations effectively came to an end.

Murau's most venomous attack on his parents focuses on their passionate support of National Socialism. Murau charges that his parents were Nazis not out of convenience, but out of conviction. Although he admits that his father was at first reluctant about the movement, he goes on to say that his father's moral cowardice made him easy prey to his mother's propaganda and to the thinly-veiled threats of Wolfsegg's pro-fascist huntsmen. Murau describes Wolfsegg as a hotbed of National Socialist ideology. He cites the swastikas that flew from the windows, his mother's "hysterical" (193) desire to be the model *deutsche Frau*, his father's Nazi badge and spirited *Heil Hitler*, the storm troopers who paraded through their courtyard, and the Party meetings held on Wolfsegg's grounds. Murau claims that, despite his father's initial hesitation, he eventually became a full-fledged advocate of the National Socialist cause and even profited financially from this affiliation. After the war, Murau recalls, his parents remained committed to the cause. They offered the Children's Villa as a hideout to Nazi fugitives and refused to remove their Nazi flags until American troops arrived at their gates. Murau underscores how his parents perpetuated their Nazi lifestyle long after the Allies had departed: "in them it was inborn, and they continued to cultivate it. Like their Catholicism, it was the very stuff of their lives, an essential element in their existence; they could not live without it" (291).[31] His mother converts her Nazi flags into aprons. His father joins the League of Comrades, an organization composed of former veterans and Party members. And both correspond regularly with these friends until their deaths. In short, Murau's parents not only emerged unscathed from the Hitler era, they remained "inveterate and unrepentant Nazis."[32]

According to Murau, this same seamless tradition from wartime to peacetime, and the stubborn continuation of Nazi ideals, can be witnessed in the Austrian population at large. For Murau, both his parents and his country provided fertile ground for the dissemination of fascist ideas and proved unwilling to relinquish these ideas even when ideology gave way to injustice. The narrator is outraged at the postwar prosperity of former Nazi officials, by their "agreeable circumstances" and "enormous pensions" (447). And he is sickened by the respect accorded them by the Austrian people: "These are the people my so-called countrymen regard as role models . . . These National Socialists are the people they look up to and secretly consider their leaders" (443). Murau converts, in effect, Austria's image as Europe's *Kulturlandschaft* into that of a spiritual *Ruinenlandschaft*, an environment devoid of both conscience and remorse.[33] It is clear from the narrator's disclosures that he adamantly rejects a revisionist attitude towards the past, whether it serves to redeem his family's honor or hide those crimes kept silent for generations.

The narrator's account of his childhood juxtaposes images of parental cruelty with familial devotion to Hitler's regime. Franz-Josef insists that, regardless of their differences in personality and lifestyle, his parents' corrupt political and moral values had the same bleak results — the disruption of his childhood identity, the need to create an *Ersatz*-persona elsewhere, and a debilitating ambivalence toward those who caused him so much pain. Franz-Josef summarizes his upbringing at Wolfsegg as a process of being "brought down," an intensely cruel and tumultuous period that extinguished all hopes for a positive and secure self-concept. He was not only denied physical warmth (sleeping for years in a damp and unheated room), but emotional warmth as well. And although Murau's siblings suffered much the same neglect, their willingness to obey their parents' wishes spared them the surveillance and resentment Franz-Josef felt from infancy onward. Murau states early on that his parents treated him with constant suspicion, "even with a subliminal hatred that later came into the open" (76). The narrator emphasizes this aspect of his parents many times throughout the novel and ultimately concludes that he had no place in his parents' hearts. "In time," he writes, "I have given up trying to force myself into them" (255).

Along with these negative depictions of his mother and father, Murau includes in his account startling admissions of continued love and compassion. *Auslöschung* is full of passages in which the narrator questions, amends, or retracts his uncharitable assessment of his family, and still others in which he claims to document "my own baseness, my own shamelessness, my own lack of character" (249). Franz-Josef states in the opening pages of the novel that his professed hatred for his parents and siblings is evidence of his own guilt. "We only feel hatred," he declares, "when we are in the wrong," and considers his own way of thinking not only contemptible, but a blatant attempt to assuage his bad conscience. Murau then ends this unexpected pronouncement by saying that "on the whole, I consider myself lucky" (105). Murau also elects at certain moments in his memoir to take pity on Caecilia and Amalia, whom he claims to love and hate in equal measure. He recalls how his sisters were robbed of their individuality and freedom and remarks that "even at forty, these dolls, my sisters, are still subject to my mother's puppeteering" (122). Similarly, Murau laments his father's loss of individualism and vitality, a diminishment Franz-Josef attributes not only to his mother's domination but to the narrow confines of a tyrannical bureaucracy.[34] In Murau's assessment, his father's *Lebensraum* extended no further than the walls of his gloomy and suffocating study. "Such breathtaking natural beauty, I thought, and such a magnificent estate, yet my father led this pathetic desk-bound existence!" (605). Perhaps not surprisingly, it is Murau's mother, the target of his most vociferous attack, who receives his most charitable retraction. Despite all that he has suffered, Murau confesses that he loves her. To feel otherwise, he argues, would be unfair.

> It would be completely ridiculous to blame her for all the wrongs that have occurred. We do this only because we have no alternative, because it's too difficult to think differently, too complicated, or simply impossible. So we simplify the matter and say, *Our mother is a bad person.* From this one thought we construct an attitude that stays with us for a lifetime. (298)

Murau's position as sole remaining male heir confers on him a new feeling of power and provides him the opportunity not only to right his parents' wrongs, but to resolve the nagging ambivalence, the "mental chaos" (141), he has suffered since his youth. Bolstered by the positivism of his years in Rome, Murau arrives in Wolfsegg with a desire to make things better. He intends to talk freely with his parents' staff, to enjoy the "simple folk" of the village, to revive his grandfather's libraries, and to renovate the estate's dilapidated buildings. Just as in Rome, however, Murau's attitudes and behaviors are contradictory and provide increasing evidence that he is not free of the negative psychological repercussions of his childhood. Franz-Josef wants to believe he can radically extricate himself from his family legacy. What we discover from Murau's confessions is that he remains bound to Wolfsegg, both financially and psychically.[35] Murau's Roman independence cannot stave off his insecurities; nor does his condemnation of his parents prevent him from replicating their behaviors. As Murau is forced to admit, "I have to show myself as I am, as these parents of mine made me" (159).

In the opening pages of "The Will," Murau battles conflicting impulses. Initially upon his approach to Wolfsegg, he is overcome by curiosity. The silence of his parents' estate produces an irresistible urge to see their bodies, and Murau runs directly to the Orangerie in hopes of viewing them without delay. Within moments Murau's attitude changes. His inquisitive and aggressive desire to observe the three corpses is transformed into a fear of being seen. Franz-Josef positions himself behind a wall, where he watches the gardeners' calm and careful movements. Murau admits that his actions are driven by fear. "Perhaps I was afraid of a confrontation with my dead parents and my dead brother," he speculates, ". . . and chose to remain pressed up against the wall for a little while longer" (161). What is striking about this scene is that Franz-Josef seems equally afraid of the gardeners. Hiding among the trees, Murau glibly assures himself this is all a well-rehearsed drama, that "the lines I had to speak . . . would come automatically" (161). Shortly thereafter, he is struck speechless. The narrator is unable to approach his parents' gardeners, whom he has always regarded as friends, and feels too full of "shame and timidity" to divulge his presence. Murau's behavior is strongly reminiscent of his childhood. The reader is reminded of young Murau's clandestine hours in the library, the anxiety that accompanies his visits to the village, and the watchful parental eye that guarded his every move. Franz-Josef's fearful, infantile compulsions reveal that, regardless of his virulent hostility toward his parents, he has nevertheless internalized their prohibitions. Caught between a will to transcend the narrow world of Wolfsegg and a desire to reclaim a sense of belonging,[36] Murau lacks both the "natural self-confidence" (337) he had as a child and the sophisticated, urbane persona he acquired in Rome. As the novel continues, the narrator grows increasing disoriented and unsure, and repeatedly displays external signs of psychological distress: a mechanical repetition of gesture and speech, awkward, unmotivated laughter, and the fear of leaving his room to mingle with the arriving guests.[37]

Along with these feelings of inferiority comes feelings of superiority. The narrator's actions express, in effect, a battle between two extremes:

between fantasies of grandeur which alienate him from others and feelings of emptiness that make him crave attachment.[38] Murau's emotional tug-of-war is powerfully captured in another of the novel's key scenes. Played out in the kitchen at Wolfsegg, it is here that the narrator's fear of discovery gives way to aggression. The kitchen scene is preceded by Murau and Caecilia's visit to the Orangerie, where their parents and brother are lying in state. Murau professes to be sickened by the experience. The "unmistakable smell of bodies" leaves him feeling nauseated and disgusted. By the narrator's own admission, he is "far from moved" (199); he feels neither sadness nor regret. What he does find striking is the contrast between his own indifference and the grieving face of his sister.

This emotional detachment does not last. Virtually on the heels of Murau's visit to the Orangerie, the narrator discovers in the kitchen a stack of newspaper articles recounting his parents' fatal car crash. Safe, he believes, from prying eyes, Franz-Josef devours the gory details of the event. He is fascinated by the articles' headlines: "Family wiped out." "Three concert-goers mutilated beyond recognition." He stares captivated at a photograph of his mother's severed head and remarks how a "metal rod had penetrated right through the vehicle" (204). Franz-Josef attempts to offset his insatiable curiosity by criticizing the sensational tabloids, referring to them as "provincial garbage sheets" that represent the worst of the Austrian press. Their chief goal, he maintains, is to "outdo each other in vulgarity" (205). As in the previous scene of his arrival, Franz-Josef's curiosity gives way to fear. The footsteps of the approaching cook cause him to panic. He quickly tries to arrange the papers exactly as they were before. What sets this scene apart from the arrival scene, however, is the narrator's fear of being not only physically exposed, but morally exposed as well. Murau's fear and guilty conscience combine to make him feel trapped and threatened. And his discomfiture leads him to extremes. The narrator blames the unsuspecting cook for taking advantage of his distress. He accuses her of exploiting the situation in order to gain power over him, of treating him with disrespect, of failing to know her place. Revoking his praise for the "simple people" of Wolfsegg, Murau views the family's employee as a peasant "larded with stupidity." Murau goes on to describe the cook as "base and contemptible," shameless, sneaky, and repugnant. And, for a moment at least, he hates her.

Murau's behavior in the kitchen scene marks a turning point in Bernhard's story. It is here that the novel's subtitle, *Ein Zerfall* (a decline) shifts from the visible decline of the Wolfsegg estate to the mental and moral deterioration of its last remaining male heir. With his Roman identity in ruins, Franz-Josef Murau falls back on the only identity that remains: his defensive and vengeful Wolfsegg self which must protect itself at all costs. The scene in the kitchen reveals Franz-Josef at his worst. The narrator diverts attention from his own "shameless curiosity" by accusing the cook of presumptuousness. He seeks to redeem his personal integrity by making her, and others of her class, physically repellent. Finally, he tries to gain power over the situation by presenting himself as the cook's lord and master. Murau attempts, in short, to replace his faltering Roman *Über-Ich*[39] with the privileges his status affords him: an ability to evade the truth under the guise of aristocratic birth. Franz-Josef will ultimately take pleasure in the fact that time-honored divisions and prejudices remain firmly in place.[40] And he expresses considerable satisfaction that he, the prodigal son, now holds the reins of control. "The deserter who had been rejected, detested, and execrated had suddenly become the master, the provider, the deliverer. In this moment of reunion they staked everything on me" (385). Ironically, what begins with the donning of his father's dressing gown ends with the assumption of his father's feudalistic and punitive attitudes.[41]

It is not until the end of the novel, when Franz-Josef stands at his parents' grave, that he realizes he can never escape the inherited nightmare of his family. Nor can he reconcile the two opposing identities which followed in its wake. Surrounded by corrupt clergymen, former Nazis, and Gauleiters, the narrator observes that the sinister aspects of Wolfsegg — with it specter of complicity, persecution, and denial — did not die with his mother and father, but rather live on in the son who bears their name. Murau is forced to acknowledge that he is part of the family and the society he so despises, and now knows that his attacks will double back upon himself.[42] He has distanced himself geographically and emotionally from Wolfsegg. He has not, he realizes, escaped its corrupting influence. As Stephen Dowden rightly observes, the narrator remains a "lucid critic" of his family history. He is also, however, its captive. "He changed cultures and languages in an attempt to free himself of his own tainted blood, but there is no escape from genetic inheritance."[43] Murau will himself conclude that his "inborn spirits" can be exorcised only for a time, "at tremendous cost, and never permanently." He summarizes his existence as a struggle against the "disease" of his Austrian nationality, a disease "which constantly reinfects me" (293). In addition to this burden of inherited guilt, the death of Murau's parents eliminates his psychic justification for a second distinct persona, one created solely in opposition to Wolfsegg and applicable only as long as both worlds remain intact. Having rejected his Wolfsegg self, and having lost his motivation for a Roman one, Murau is left with no definable identity at all. The incriminating, destructive nature of this insight is expressed both in Murau's reference to his impending death and to the content of his forthcoming memoir.

> When I set out to take Wolfsegg and my family apart, when I annihilate and extinguish them, what I am actually doing is taking myself apart, dissecting, annihilating, and extinguishing myself. (296)

The narrator's final project is, as Thomas Bernhard's title implies, one of destruction, of erasure, of annihilation. Franz-Josef had hoped through the process of writing *Auslöschung*, his "anti-autobiography," to bid farewell to his parents a second and final time, to wipe them from his awareness, to destroy their power over him.[44] What he discovers, however, is that he cannot separate this emotional obliteration of Wolfsegg from his own physical demise. Murau's decision on the last page of the novel to sell his family's estate, "along with everything it entails" (650), and donate all proceeds to a Jewish organization in Vienna, underscores his awareness that a new and positive beginning for Wolfsegg — indeed for Austria as a whole — can only be achieved through a radical change in ownership, through the empowerment of those "who never speak about what they suffered"; that is, the targeted victims of Nazism.[45] Seen in this light, Murau's action regarding Wolfsegg represents more than an act of penance for his parents' complicity in Nazism or a final demonstration of filial revenge. The narrator's gift to the Jewish community represents a last attempt to discard his parents' model and break free of their attitudes and behaviors. Just as importantly, it marks the end of Murau's obsession with his own conflicted identity and his championing of those whose persecution exceeds his own. Ironically, it is this third dimension of Franz-Josef Murau, an identity born of self-abnegation, that endows the sale of Wolfsegg and his eventual memoir (dedicated to the camp survivor Schermaier) a deliberate moral authority. After a lifelong search for a new and better identity, it is Murau's subordination of self that brings closure and, one might even argue, liberation.

Notes

[1]Arnim Eichholz, "Morgen Salzburg," *Von einer Katastrophe in die andere: 13 Gespräche mit Thomas Bernhard*, ed. Sepp Dreissinger (Weitra: Bibliothek der Provinz, 1992) 38. The translation is my own.

[2]Michael Stephens, "Homage to Thomas Bernhard," *Pequod: A Journal of Contemporary Literature and Literary Criticism* 33 (1992) 87.

[3]Judith Miller draws attention to the fact that Austria had a higher proportion of Nazis than the Germans and argues that, even today, "most Austrians see themselves as victims of the war rather than as major perpetrators of it." Cited in Gabriel Motola, "Thomas Bernhard's Austria," *Pequod: A Journal of Contemporary Literature and Literary Criticism* 33 (1992) 54.

[4]Bernhard includes in much of his fictional and non-fiction writing characters who passionately embrace the National Socialist cause. Examples include the prefect Grünkranz in Bernhard's autobiographical work *Die Ursache* (An Indication of the Cause) 1975; the former concentration camp commandant Rudolph in *Vor dem Ruhestand* (Eve of Retirement) 1979; the estimated 100,000 Viennese who welcomed Hitler in *Heldenplatz* (Heroes' Square) 1988; and Murau's committed Nazi parents in *Auslöschung* (Extinction) 1986.

[5]Motola 55.

[6]Phillip Lopate, "On Not Reading Thomas Bernhard," *Pequod: A Journal of Contemporary Literature and Literary Criticism* (1992) 33, 78.

[7]Quoted in Motola 57.

[8]Jean-Louis de Rambures, "Alle Menschen sind Monster, sobald sie ihren Panzer lüften," *Von einer Katastrophe in die andere* 112.

[9]Bernhard's propensity for blurring the lines between his personal life and his fictional characters is virtually undisputed. Michael Stephens interprets Bernhard's frequent inclusion of personal details as a creative blending of narrative genres and concludes that "these singular qualities in Bernhard's writing raise questions on every page about what fiction is, what autobiography, or even what is *aide memoire* jotted down in the course of life." Stephens, "Homage to Thomas Bernhard" 90.

[10]Robert Craft, "Comedian of Horror," *The New York Review of Books* (27 Sept. 1990) 44.

[11]Gerard Fetz proposes that it is precisely the complexity of Bernhard's narrators, their "paradoxical and contradictory formulations," their "exaggeration and giant leaps in logic," that provides not only their appeal but their greatest didactic power. Bernhard's irascible and imperfect protagonists, Fetz

contends, are meant to provoke and challenge us "to look beyond and beneath the clichés and artifices with which we all usually shield ourselves, our eyes, and our thoughts." "Thomas Bernhard and the Modern Novel," *The Modern German Novel* (New York: Berg Publishers Ltd, 1987) 96.

[12]Thomas Bernhard, *Auslöschung* (Frankfurt am Main: Suhrkamp Verlag, 1986). All future quotes refer to this edition and are indicated parenthetically. All translations are my own.

[13]*Auslöschung* contains extensive material taken from the author's own life: his Catholic and National Socialist upbringing, his unconventional teacher and mentor (changed in the novel from Bernhard's maternal grandfather to a fictionalized paternal uncle), his intensely ambivalent relationship with his mother, and his eclectic circle of friends and acquaintances. In the words of critic Hermann Helms-Derfert, nowhere else in Bernhard's fictional writings does one find a more extensive analysis of the "psychic and social constellations of his childhood and youth." *Die Last der Geschichte. Interpretationen zur Prosa von Thomas Bernhard* (Weimar/Vienna: Böhlau Verlag, 1997) 151. Bernhard's narrator, Franz-Josef Murau, is loosely based on the biography of Count Franz-Ferdinand Julien-Wallsee, whom the author met in 1971 during the filming of Bernhard's drama *Der Italiener*. For further biographical details see Ulrich Weinzierl, "Bernhard als Erzieher. Thomas Bernhard's *Auslöschung*," *German Quarterly* 63 (1990) 455–61; and Hans Höller, "Menschen, Geschichte(n), Orte und Landschaften," *Antiautobiographie. Thomas Bernhard's Auslöschung*, ed. Hans Höller and Irene Heidelberger-Leonard (Frankfurt am Main: Suhrkamp, 1995). Citing Weinzierl's study, Manfred Mittermayer speculates that *Auslöschung* was largely completed by 1981 and that its wealth of autobiographical details establishes a fictional companion piece to Bernhard's autobiography, released several years earlier. In Mittermayer's view, *Auslöschung* is, in actuality, a "Parallelaktion" to Bernhard's autobiography, and serves as a fictional commentary to Bernhard's attempt at self-definition. Manfred Mittermayer, *Thomas Bernhard* (Stuttgart/Vienna: J. B. Metzler Verlag, 1995) 110.

[14]Gitta Honegger, "Bernhard's Last Novel," *Partisan Review* 63 (1996) 528.

[15]Hermann Helms-Derfert observes this same technique in Bernhard's autobiographical work *Die Ursache. Eine Andeutung* (*An Indication of the Cause*), where the dual structure of the narrative ("Grünkranz" and "Onkel Franz") facilitates a comparative analysis of Catholic and National Socialist education and discipline. *Die Last der Geschichte* 150.

[16]Honegger 528. Gerald Fetz identifies Bernhard's elliptical narratives as an extension of the modernist tradition in German literature. According to Fetz, modernist writers (who include such authors as Kafka, Musil, Broch, and Aichinger) express "a strong scepticism about the possibility of narrating in a logical, chronological, or linear fashion a forward-moving story." Fetz like-

wise notes that Bernhard referred to himself in the 1970s as a "Geschichten-zerstörer" (a story-destroyer). Fetz, "Thomas Bernhard and the Modern Novel" 92.

[17]The fictional character Maria is widely believed to be modelled on the author's real-life friend, Ingeborg Bachmann. Bachmann, who died in Rome in 1973, was greatly admired by Thomas Bernhard, who describes her as "the most intelligent and most signficant poet of our country." *Der Stimmenimitator* (Frankfurt am Main: Suhrkamp, 1978) 167f.

[18]Christian Klug, "Interaktion und Identität. Zum Motiv der Willens-schwäche in Thomas Bernhard's *Auslöschung*," *Modern Austrian Literature* 23:3–4 (1990) 25.

[19]Charles Martin maintains that Franz-Josef Murau's devotion to the intellect is characteristic of many of Bernhard's heroes. Bernhard's protagonists are frequently men who escape the trivial and mundane concerns of society by immersing themselves in a *Geistesleben* of their own creation. All persons who reject this intellectual lifestyle are considered philistines and are treated with contempt. *The Nihilism of Thomas Bernhard* (Amsterdam: Rodopi, 1995) 191.

[20]Kathleen Thorpe, "Reading the Photograph in Thomas Bernhard's Novel *Auslöschung*," *Modern Austrian Literature* 21:3–4 (1988) 36.

[21]Mittermayer 117.

[22]Klug 26.

[23]Onkel Georg, modelled on Bernhard's grandfather Johannes Freumbichler, is credited not only with introducing Franz-Josef to the "secrets of music and literature" (45), but is, according to Murau, the only family member who successfully escaped Wolfsegg and "went his own way" (47). The presence of Onkel Georg during Murau's formative years is said to have presented him with two options: self-sacrifice or autonomy. Because of him, the narrator sees that he has "the choice between two worlds, the world of my parents . . . and that of Onkel Georg" (46).

[24]Matthias Konzett, "*Publikumsbeschimpfung*: Thomas Bernhard's Provocations of the Austrian Public Sphere," *The German Quarterly* 68.3 (1995) 267.

[25]Thorpe 46.

[26]For a discussion of the psychological dilemmas typically faced by Bernhard's narrators, see Thomas Fraund, *Bewegung, Korrektur, Utopie: Studien zum Verhältnis von Melancholie und Aesthetik im Erzählwerk Thomas Bernhards* (Frankfurt am Main: Peter Lang, 1986).

[27]Thorpe 46.

[28]As in many of his previous works, Bernhard is not explicit about the narrator's illness. Murau suffers, and eventually dies, from ailments that remain

mysterious and unnamed. Critic Stephen Dowden sees in the author's fixation on sickness, degeneration, and death strong historical and moral dimensions. According to Dowden, physical suffering and death are for Bernhard external reminders of the "inner truth of National Socialism and its debilitating consequences," and are an expression of the author's "historically rooted moral pessimism." Stephen Dowden, *Understanding Thomas Bernhard* (Columbia, SC: U of South Carolina P, 1991) 65. In an interview with editor Kurt Hofmann, Thomas Bernhard speaks of his own fragile condition and of the incurable heart ailment which has informed his attitude toward death: "A fear of death is not something I understand, because for me death is as normal as eating lunch." Kurt Hofmann, "Eine katholische Existenz," *Aus Gesprächen mit Thomas Bernhard* (Vienna: Löcker Verlag, 1988) 53.

[29]The depiction of the narrator's mother, in particular her abusive treatment of her younger son, replicates in many respects Bernhard's depiction of his mother in his autobiography, and therefore confirms critics' claims that Bernhard makes frequent use of material from his own life. To quote Stephen Dowden, Bernhard offers us "no elaborate ruse about masquing his own autobiographical compulsions." "Homage to Thomas Bernhard," *Pequod: A Journal of Contemporary Literature and Literary Criticism* 33 (1992) 87.

[30]Robert Craft contends that Bernhard's insertion of this grisly detail represents another example of the author's figurative "revenge on motherhood." Craft agrees with most critics that Bernhard's work is "transparently autobiograpical" and considers the author's negative portrayal of his fictional mothers a way of evening the score with his own. Robert Craft, "Comedian of Horror," *The New York Review of Books* (27 Sept. 1990) 40.

[31]Murau's condemnation of Catholicism as the co-conspirator of Nazism closely resembles Bernhard's own. Bernhard recounts in his memoir *Die Ursache*, for example, how in postwar Salzburg the National Socialist School for Boys quickly substituted images of Hitler with pictures of Jesus and how the Nazi uniforms of school administrators were replaced by the frocks of incoming priests.

[32]Martin 192.

[33]A. P. Dierick, "Thomas Bernhard's Austria: Neurosis, Symbol or Expedient?," *Modern Austrian Literature* 12:1 (1979) 83.

[34]Mittermayer 115.

[35]Klug 24.

[36]Martin suggests that Murau's ultimate incompatibility with the "simple folk" of Wolfsegg reveals that any "identification with the rural proletariat, so often seized upon in Bernhard's fiction as a possible means of transcendence, is finally discredited." *The Nihilism of Thomas Bernhard* 197.

[37]Dierick 84.

[38]I am indebted here to Christian Klug's use of Kohut and his theory of narcissisim to explain the narrator's erratic and self-destructive behavior. For Kohut's original study see *Narzißmus. Eine Theorie der psychoanalytischen Behandlung narzißtischer Persönlichkeitsstörungen* (Frankfurt am Main: Suhrkamp, 1976) 228f.

[39]Klug 26.

[40]Martin 198.

[41]In a preceding scene Murau likewise appropriates his father's Nazi vocabulary, spontaneously declaring that all the pigeons at Wolfsegg must be "decimated" (*dezimiert* 402), an utterance that shocks even Murau himself.

[42]Martin 189.

[43]Dowden 66.

[44]Werner Jung, "Die Anstrengung des Erinnerns," *Neue Deutsche Hefte* 35.1 (1988) 99.

[45]There are commentators who take a more critical view. Gitta Honegger, for example, considers Murau's gift to the Israeli *Kultusgemeinde* as a final act of retaliation ("Bernhard's Last Novel" 530), while Kathleen Thorpe interprets the narrator's donation and death a means of escaping "his self-imposed responsibility of exposing the truth about Austria's past" ("Reading the Photograph" 49).

The Sins of the Fathers:
Peter Schneider's *Vati*

> The guilt still haunts me, you know. And whoever is
> guilty will be punished. If not here and now, then at
> another time and in another place. The guilt will catch
> up with me sooner or later . . . My parents are already
> burning in hell. They've been dead a long time; they've
> put this life behind them. I'm the one they left behind.
> Born guilty. Still guilty.[1]

> I was always told that my father had been missing in
> Russia. My father had always been Dr. Mengele who
> spoke Greek and Latin and who had been so brave. . . .
> Now that I was told the truth, I would have preferred
> another father.[2]

IN JUNE OF 1985 A TEAM OF SCIENTISTS from West Germany, the
United States, and Brazil declared bones exhumed from a South
American grave to be those of Josef Mengele, *Todesengel* (Death Angel)
of Auschwitz. The former SS physician, believed to have sent some
400,000 people to the gas chambers, was now confirmed dead. His
remains had been positively identified, the bounty offered for his capture rescinded. News of Dr. Mengele's demise spread quickly through
the international press, unleashing a torrent of reports on the infamous
Nazi doctor, who had never been brought to justice. Yet only one
magazine, the popular West German weekly *Bunte Illustrierte*, could
boast the ultimate exclusive: interviews with Dr. Mengele's son. Rolf
Mengele, a forty-one year old lawyer, had entered *Bunte*'s headquarters
in Munich and declared that "he wanted to get rid of everything."[3]
Rolf volunteered to be interviewed and submitted to reporter Inge Byhan his father's personal effects: the doctor's photographs, research
notes, and diaries. In presenting these documents for public scrutiny,
Rolf Mengele sought to inform the world about his father's activities at
Auschwitz, his 1949 escape from Germany, and the years he had spent
in hiding. More importantly, however, the son wished to conclude his
long-standing complicity. Rolf had remained silent about his father for

thirty years. He had promised to conceal the doctor's whereabouts and had likewise vowed to protect the privacy of family members still living in Germany. Within days of the coroner's report, Rolf Mengele came forward, eager to ease the burden of silence that, by his own admission, "had simply become too great."[4] According to *Bunte*, Rolf reacted to his father's death with relief, hoping that, once and for all, the past could be laid to rest.

Rolf Mengele's disclosures to *Bunte* caused an international sensation. Josef Mengele had become the most wanted man in the world, and alleged sightings of the doctor in South America were featured in papers worldwide. What the public now learned was that the famed Dr. Mengele had a son, a successful Freiburg attorney, who for years had corresponded secretly with his fugitive father. Peter Schneider was among the readers fascinated by these revelations and in 1987 published *Vati* (Papa), a fictional re-telling of the Rolf Mengele story. Asked several years later what had prompted him to write the book, Schneider candidly acknowledged that *Bunte*, "typically considered a gossip magazine," had captured his attention in the summer of 1985.[5] He had read its six-part series on Josef Mengele and was struck by the similarities between his own biography and that of the Auschwitz doctor's son. Rolf Mengele was born in 1944; Peter Schneider in 1940. Both were natives of Freiburg. It is likely they had attended the same schools. Yet, despite these obvious parallels, there was one crucial difference, one fateful "coincidence," that fascinated the author most. As Schneider comments in a 1990 interview,

> I could tell myself that my father was a music director; my father never had a gun in his hand. And there was this other guy who had to say: my father, by sheer coincidence, is Josef Mengele. I could not get this contrast out of my mind. I thought if such a thing could happen to this man Rolf, then the rest of us were just plain lucky. And it became clear to me that this revelation affects all of us, not just one individual. It was for that reason that I tried to shape the events into a story, so that the reader would be forced to imagine how it would be if, as a son or a daughter, they suddenly learned that their father is the mass murderer Mengele. This is — in Germany at any rate — the story for an entire generation.[6]

While *Vati* follows closely upon the 1977 encounter between Rolf and Josef Mengele, the protagonist's conflict mirrors that of numerous children of Nazis forced to choose between loyalty and legality. Schneider's subject must decide between two options: to keep silent about his father out of filial loyalty, or to betray his father for the sake of justice. This dilemma forms the crux of Schneider's narrative and is intensified by the author's choice of title. The affectionate term "Vati" (Papa) articulates the son's intense desire for a father, a desire diametrically opposed to his moral obligation to denounce him.[7] At its most basic level, the author writes, *Vati* depicts a son trapped between two equally strong emotions: the bond forged by birth and the abhorrence caused by his father's crimes.[8] Schneider's story proceeds from the premise that for Rolf Mengele, indeed for all those saddled with a dark family history, resolving the parent-child relationship is a balancing act between attraction, sympathy, anger, and disgust. As the daughter of a Wehrmacht official puts it,

> The actual tragedy is that my father's life triggers such varied reactions
> . . . As long as we live, his fate will never leave us in peace — even
> when he has been dead a long time and will stay that way even
> longer.[9]

For Schneider, Rolf Mengele's decision to come forward in 1985 marked a turning point in Germany's response to its Nazi past. By publishing his father's papers and in openly discussing their relationship as father and son, Rolf Mengele provoked others among his generation to speak out. Rolf's testimony soon was joined by statements from Niklas Frank, the son of Hitler's governor in Poland, and by the publication of Peter Sichrovsky's groundbreaking work *Schuldig geboren: Kinder aus Nazifamilien.* Yet what Schneider finds most compelling in Rolf Mengele's account, as well as in those that followed, is not that a silence had been broken, or that the German public, once disinterested in the families of prominent Nazis, now clamored for details. In telling the story of Rolf Mengele, Schneider chronicles the preservation of a secret. His novel *Vati* focuses not on Rolf Mengele the celebrity,[10] but on the troubled son who, even as an adult, was unwilling to publicly divulge his father's whereabouts or communicate his own ongoing struggle with the doctor's heinous legacy. As Schneider himself has noted, the generation born too late to have participated in Nazism was by no means free from the "biographical complications" tying them to history.[11] And in keeping silent for forty years, these sons and daughters became co-conspirators in a half century of repression and denial.

In his fictional revision of the Rolf Mengele story, Schneider conflates the personal and historical by examining the burden placed upon a son by his Nazi father's crimes. Rather than restricting himself to the narrator's exposure of his parent's infamy, or restating the factual information already available on the Mengele family, Schneider's text un-

derscores how history is borne out in the conflictual relationship between father and son. Like other novels of this period, *Vati* represents
the intersection of history and the self; it stresses the personal element
within the political events of the postwar years. Unlike the *Vaterbücher*
(father books) of the previous decade, however, Schneider's work focuses not on his generation's posthumous confrontation with their
largely apolitical parents, but on the direct encounter between a mid-
dle-aged son and a member of Hitler's elite.[12] *Vati* reinforces the notion that German novels of the 1980s continue an interest in subjective
or everyday experiences and, at the same time, remain committed to
the controversial issues of history. Schneider's novel also serves to illustrate an essential project of this new type of literature: it reveals not
only the guilt of the parents, but illuminates the next generation's
moral and psychological legacy as "Hitler's children."[13]

The narrator's journey to his father's home in South America is the
culmination of his twenty-year battle with a painful family history. Like
Rolf Mengele, Schneider's protagonist is separated from his father first
by war, and then by the doctor's flight abroad. The narrator does not
learn his father's true identity until puberty, and with the exception of
one ski vacation in Switzerland (when the doctor is introduced to his
young son as an uncle), the narrator's image of his father is based solely
on letters, photographs, and hearsay. The son's trip to Brazil is motivated by a desire to confront his father face to face and to hear from his
father's mouth the truth of the doctor's wartime activities. At the same
time, however, the narrator's visit signals an examination of his own
identity. In forcing his father, the world's most famous Nazi fugitive, to
speak, Schneider's subject hopes to finally understand what it means to
be his son.

Alexander and Margarete Mitscherlich propose in *The Inability to
Mourn* that the maturation process during adolescence requires that the
child assume a more accurate, less idealized assessment of his parents.
They contend that this process is liberating but also very painful, and
assert that the child's realization that the father does not fit an idealized
image is accompanied by a feeling of personal devaluation. The
Mitscherlichs argue further that the struggle for such identity forma-
tion, while always difficult, was greatly intensified during the German
postwar era. They cite not only a decline in paternal authority, but the
disappointment felt by German children whose fathers, in the aftermath
of Nazism and defeat, could no longer fulfill their vision of a strong
and confident guardian. Although these children still looked to their

parents as models for their own identity, any sign of parental weakness was considered evidence of their own diminished self-worth.[14]

Vati goes one step further. The narrator's statements reveal that the conflict with his infamous father extends beyond the loss of an idealized parental image or the abdication of his childhood narcissism. In presenting the strategy behind his visit to São Paulo, Schneider's protagonist professes a sense of entanglement in his father's Nazi crimes. Although an infant during the final years of the war, the narrator of *Vati* has lived a life "laden with guilt" (31).[15] He cannot say, like many others, that his father was a passive bystander during the Third Reich, or even an obedient bureaucrat. His father was a member of Hitler's elite, a scientist dedicated to racial purity, head physician at Auschwitz. The son is aware not only of his parent's guilt, but of the awesome burden that is his inheritance. His search for clues leads him to the realization that the man who gave him life is simultaneously the man who sent thousands to their death. In learning the details of the doctor's activities, the son is faced with the potential implications of his paternal parentage, and increasingly fears he has somehow been contaminated. To what extent does he share his father's genetic makeup? Is he tainted, through biology alone, by his father's culpability?

> What did I have in common with him other than my name? What does one inherit from a father one doesn't know? His eyebrows, his bald head, his hands, what else? (21)

The subject of Schneider's narrative actively questions the nature of his biological inheritance and is haunted by the possibility that he shares not only his father's name and external features, but his moral depravity as well. In forcing his father to confess his sins, and by making him atone for the horrors of Nazism, the narrator seeks to cleanse his own conscience and sever all ties to a murderous past. As one critic has suggested, the son's visit to Brazil is not simply an expression of conflicting loyalties, but ultimately comes to represent a "quasi-religious quest for redemption."[16]

The issue of inherited guilt emerges in *Vati* through the content of the son's revelations, but also in the way he tells his story. The narrative structure of Schneider's story is straightforward and can be divided into three separate parts: the narrator's arrival in Brazil, his recapitulation of the father-son relationship, and the description of his stay in São Paulo (ending with a brief account of his father's death). The uncomplicated nature of this presentation reveals both the genesis of the son's guilt as well as its eventual effects. There is, however, an added element to the author's method: the mysterious "you" (*du*) to whom the story is told. It is this figure who, although never allowed to speak, will expose the pervasiveness of the son's troubled legacy.[17]

This implied recipient of the son's account, whom we later discover is a former classmate, is an integral part of Schneider's story. The narrator organizes his revelations around questions allegedly posed by this second-person subject: why he decided to visit his father in South America, what he had expected to find there, and the reasons for his continued loyalty. The narrator never records these questions verbatim, but his response to the friend's supposed curiosity reveals a distinct uneasiness. He claims, for example, to have no illusions about the motives behind his estranged companion's recent telephone call, attributing it more to the publicity surrounding his father's death than to a renewal of old ties. The narrator refers to his caller's inquiries as "accusatory questions" and to his own replies as "stumbling explanations" (18–19). It is clear that the son feels not only interrogated by his listener's queries but blamed. And although Schneider's subject is sometimes willing to entertain his friend's opinions, he more often considers them simplistic and disingenuous. The narrator's story is an attempt to explain the nature of his familial conflict; it is also an opportunity to vent his frustration at his friend's implicit lack of sympathy and support.

The presence of a questioning "you" in Schneider's story serves to problematize the identity of the subject-narrator. The son is forced to defend his attitudes and actions, and the insecurity, aggression, and defensiveness that result are evidence of his disrupted self-perception. *Vati* focuses, in effect, not only on the son's confrontation with his criminal father, but on the narrator's confrontation with himself and with those who have made him the target of his father's shame. His story is, in the truest sense of the word, his self-defense. The former classmate, who remains for the most part invisible throughout the son's narrative, contributes to this process by piquing the narrator's uneasy conscience and confronting him with a kind of moral authority.[18] And yet despite the unmistakably defensive tone that often colors the narrator's disclosures, his account is also highly confessional. The son is drawn into his father's guilt by virtue of keeping the doctor's secret and responds to this complicity by experiencing an acute moral crisis. The narrator feels he must explain why pleasing his father was more important than exposing him, and devotes much of his account to exploring why he feels guilty, when it is his father who was the war criminal.[19]

The narrative structure of *Vati*, established ostensibly through the narrator's responses to his companion's inquiries, also invites a second, imaginary audience into the novel. The son's answers imply questions which could have been put by Schneider's own readers, a technique that brings the reader into the fictional narration and makes him an active participant in the protagonist's dilemma. The author extends, in effect, the role of interrogator beyond a fictional persona to all those reading his story and challenges his audience to become involved in the problem of inherited guilt.[20] In doing so, the reader is asked to consider both the son's personal familial legacy and how he himself might have reacted in similar circumstances. Schneider suggests that although one clearly cannot condone Rolf Mengele's behavior, it is much more productive to analyze his quandary than to simply condemn his choices. "It is easy," the author writes, "to be indignant about Rolf Mengele's behavior. It is more difficult to answer the question of how one would have acted in the same situation."[21] Reminiscent of the biblical Cain, who is marked for life by the murder of his brother, Schneider's subject is haunted by a name made synonymous with unparalleled crimes against humanity. Just as geographical names such as Auschwitz "function as shorthand"[22] for the widespread brutality committed and suffered during Hitler's Reich, the narrator's father personifies the many individual acts of barbarism sanctioned, indeed encouraged, by the National Socialist regime. The name Mengele never appears in *Vati*. The impact of such a name, however, is unmistakable.

> At first I was irritated by the tone my teachers used whenever they called on me — the hesitation, the way they lowered their voices before pronouncing those three syllables — as if the good Swabian name were totally unutterable. My name seemed to suggest something terrible, or maybe something impressive; at any rate it was something that could not be said. But what I never found out. (13)

This passage, coupled with the large number of biographical details included in *Vati*, leaves little doubt as to the historical subjects behind Schneider's narrative. Nevertheless, critics have taken issue with this omission. The narrator's irritation at hearing his name pronounced seems matched only by that of literary scholars who cannot find the name at all. One writer states, for example, that in place of any direct reference to the Mengele family, Schneider simply substitutes "a coquettish allusion to the effect its three syllables have on those who speak or hear it."[23] For Wolfgang Nagel of *Die Zeit*, the omission signals a frustrating inconsistency. If Schneider sought to make his story universally applicable, the journalist contends, he should never have included biographical details pointing to a single, well-known Nazi. If, on the other hand, the author intended to concentrate on a specific personality, he should have been more illustrative and precise in his characterization of the famous doctor.[24]

Critics are correct in asserting that the name Mengele is hinted at only through its phonetic composition. It is also true that the reader is left to ponder the author's reasons for excluding it. What these critics fail to consider is the essential relevance of what is not said. Schneider's extensive discussion of the narrator's mysterious appellation suggests that it is precisely the absence of this "good Swabian name" that provides a key to the son's central conflict and dramatically exposes the extremity of his suffering. Having been physically separated from his father since birth, the narrator's last name is his only link to the man he has never known. It serves, in other words, as the son's most tangible inheritance from his absentee father. The poignant irony of the narrator's story, however, is that this same surname epitomizes the son's psychic wound. The burden imposed upon him by his father's culpability extends to the most basic component of his identity, his name. And it is in the articulation of these vaguely identified three syllables that the son's loss is resurrected and relived. The enunciation of the protagonist's last name recalls not only the narrator's abandonment by his father and his family's fifteen-year deceit, but unleashes images of his father's crimes, crimes which have come to epitomize the unspeakable horrors of Auschwitz.

The narrator compares the mystery attached to his name to a hieroglyphic text that only he cannot decode. The cautious attitude of others both confuses and alarms him. He feels he is "stricken by an illness" but is not told the nature of his malady. Yet, despite the hardships caused by his unfortunate family connection, it is evident that the narrator is also sheltered by his name, a name that absolves him of responsibility and allows him to escape the reprimands he frequently deserves. As one critic perceptively observes, Schneider's protagonist shares a kinship with the Old Testament Cain not only in his isolation from others, but in his protection by those in authority.[25] While the son is ridiculed by his classmates for being the child of an infamous SS officer, he is pampered by his teachers due to the "father trauma" he has endured. And although the narrator is repeatedly the instigator of schoolyard brawls, his delinquency is dismissed by school officials as a sad, self-fulfilling prophecy.

> If I got a bad grade in biology the teacher apologized by saying this
> was no reflection on any of my relatives! If I lost my homework, no

one called me lazy, but rather spoke in terms of my "difficult family situation." There was hardly a scuffle that didn't end with a teacher offering me a helping hand. How can he help it, they'd always say, if his name isn't Müller. (14)

The discomfiture caused by the son's invisible flaw is thus doubly manifested; once in the narrator's sense of alienation, again in the secrecy and circumlocutions employed by his elders. The narrator's schoolmates eagerly vocalize their disapproval of his criminal father. His teachers, on the other hand, seem to avoid the uncomfortable topic at all costs. Ironically, it is not the aggressiveness of his peers that oppresses Schneider's subject; it is the favored status granted him by his instructors. This secrecy on the part of the older generation illustrates the more general tendency of postwar Germans to ignore the reality of recent political events. Schneider states, for example, that for West German schoolchildren in the 1950s, their "so-called re-education amounted to only two hours on the history of Nazi fascism."[26] The reluctance of the German educational system to engage in discussions of National Socialism can be attributed in large part to the personal involvement of teachers and parents in Hitler's regime. The author recalls how in his own Gymnasium an instructor once admitted such complicity and stubbornly refused to teach a subject in which he had been personally implicated.[27] This avoidance of the subject of Nazism in postwar German classrooms, a tendency extensively documented by other authors of Schneider's generation, is echoed in *Vati* in the narrator's description of his history instruction. He recalls that when it came to the Third Reich, all discussion ceased. The period was, in essence, passed over without a word. "Our history teacher had spared us — whether for my sake or his own is not clear — all the pertinent information regarding those years" (13).[28]

Prior to his visit to South America, the narrator of *Vati* attempts at various points in his development to discover the truth of his father's wartime service. He lives in a community unresponsive to the subject of Nazism, describing Freiburg as city in which weekly pictures of the war seemed "produced in a studio" (20). Nevertheless, he endeavors to confront his difficult legacy and to examine the familial influences that shape his current sense of self. As the story progresses, it becomes increasingly evident that, despite what the narrator learns about his father, he is unable to sever his emotional ties to the former Auschwitz physician. What begins as a mere fact-finding mission ends as his quest for a father. The son is progressively bound to a man whose history he despises. It is ultimately the desire for paternal guidance that triumphs over the pursuit of justice, and the narrator's longing for filial attachment that allows his father to remain free.[29]

The trauma associated with the narrator's infamous heritage, an inheritance that attaches itself to him like a disease, is revealed in his compulsion to simultaneously expose and avoid the reality of his father's crimes. The narrator's conflicted reaction to his father, and his subsequent confused assessment of his own physical and spiritual legacy, first surfaces when his mother and aunt enlighten him about the truth of his father's identity. The family's conviction that he is old enough to comprehend such a revelation is countered by the narrator's own assertion that "no son will ever be able to grasp that he is the son of such a father" (20). Upon hearing that his father was an SS physician at Auschwitz, the narrator seeks to reconstruct his genealogy by consulting pictures of the uncle he now knows to be his parent. Although he is shocked by the reality of the officer's activities, he has also been granted a father. The narrator eagerly endeavors to offset his bewilderment by verifying that, despite his father's absence, the doctor has always loved him. The narrator consults numerous photographs of the uncle turned father and sees a man surrounded by idyllic images of children, dogs, and flowers. What the son does not find, however, is proof of his father's affection. In each photograph it is his cousin Werner who is the object of his father's gaze. The narrator is quick to comment that this comes as no surprise, that his cousin "always won my father's love while I got nothing but coldness" (25). Yet the father's obvious attachment to Werner greatly intensifies the narrator's emotional pain. The son feels, in essence, doubly betrayed: once by his father's physical absence; twice by the biological ties that fail to ensure his father's devotion.

It is not until many years later that the narrator is able to confront the photographs of "die anderen" — his father's victims. Although the son does not seek to avoid these images, he reportedly experiences a blinding dizziness whenever he encounters them. By his own admission, the crimes at Auschwitz, recorded in black and white before him, prompt a "defense mechanism or escape reflex" (22) that prevents him from fully comprehending what he sees. Tellingly, the narrator places quotation marks around the word *Opfer* (victim) in this passage, implying that the horrors perpetrated by his father are merely alleged. The son openly acknowledges the problematic nature of his ambivalence and hesitates before qualifying the status of his father's victims at Auschwitz. Nevertheless, he chooses to do just that, and justifies his decision based on his duty as lawyer and son of the accused.

The narrator's conflation of these two distinct roles reveals a persistent effort to deny his difficult moral choice. He tenaciously desires to be both advocate and son: to act according to what is legally and morally responsive to his father's victims and, at the same time, to be the loyal son. The narrator's response to the photographs proves, however, that the two are incompatible. It likewise serves to foreshadow his eventual decision. The son separates the photos of his family and those of his father's victims into two separate piles and claims he must decide between those of his relatives and the prisoners at Auschwitz. As his later visit to Brazil bears out, the narrator continues to partition his family history from the history containing the death camp and ultimately will abdicate his role as attorney in favor of his filial attachment.

It is clear that the narrator's continued alliance with his father is a bond he not only perpetuates but at times encourages. This complicitous aspect of Schneider's narrator elucidates the son's emotional dependency upon a father whose deeds he abhors. The narrator's inability to break free of his parent's influence is apparent long before his visit to Brazil and has its origins in the written correspondences between the doctor and his son.[30] This interpretation challenges the notion that Schneider's subject is merely the victim of a cruel fate. And it is corroborated by the narrator himself. The narrator reports, for example, that despite the shock and disgust he initially felt for his father, the disclosure of his family secret later led to defiance. The son asserts that, in becoming his father's pen-pal, he had entered the hallowed "circle of initiates" and claims to have offered himself up to his father as both friend and confidante. The narrator had hoped such candor would be reciprocated. He had expected, through mutual correspondence, to better understand his father and, whenever possible, to protect him. Upon his arrival in São Paulo, the son's attention is quickly drawn to his father's writing desk. He surveys the voluminous notes and essays his father has compiled. What he hopes to find is a "message that was meant for me and me alone" (11).

As the son reaches adulthood, his personal inquiry into his father's past coincides with the newfound interest in National Socialism that emerged in the late 1960s. The narrator's discussion of his fellow students underscores Schneider's conviction that Germany's *Studentenbewegung*, characterized by an uncompromising commitment to the future, fell far short of a total reckoning with the past. Himself a participant in the political activism of the late 1960s, the author nevertheless uses the term *Unschuldsvermutung* (presumption of innocence) to describe his generation's belief that, because its members were born either during or after the war, they were in no way implicated in the crimes committed under Hitler.[31] He notes that what first appeared as an awareness of the crimes perpetrated under Nazism and a concerted effort to expose the vestiges of fascist thought in modern-day Germany was soon transformed into an attack on all "superfluous forms of authority."[32]

The narrator of *Vati* initially views the rebellions of 1968 as his salvation. He becomes increasingly disenchanted with his father's role in the war and joins others his age in seeking ideological solutions to familial conflicts. Like his contemporaries, the son chants "a few hastily acquired quotes from Mao and Che Guevara" (29) and hopes that by rebelling against the older generation he can sever all associations with his father's hateful past. The narrator's statements likewise suggest, however, that although his peers effectively shattered the silence regarding Germany's support of Nazism, their attempts to disassociate themselves from these fascist and patriarchal roots amounted to yet another form of evasion. Echoing Schneider's own recollections of 1968, the majority of the narrator's contemporaries feel untainted by their parents' problematic past. They are ready to condemn their purportedly Nazi fathers based on the scantiest of evidence, yet are unwilling to investigate the potential implications of such parentage for their own lives. Not surprisingly, the narrator's classmate carries with him written proof of his father's alleged complicity and simultaneously announces that every connection with him has been effectively terminated.[33]

The narrator observes that other students can simply denounce their fathers, flamboyantly rejecting everything but the monthly allowances that finance their revolution. He also realizes that, for him, such tactics are unavailable. In contrast to others his age, the narrator holds the key to his father's very existence: he will either remain silent and preserve his father's safety, or publicly condemn his father and deliver him up to be executed. The narrator's conviction that his own generation cannot assist him in his painful dilemma, that he must carry the burden of his father's identity alone, contributes in large measure to his decision to meet his father one-on-one.[34]

By the time the narrator confronts his father in Brazil, he not only acknowledges the inadequacy of his generation's militant and often hypocritical lifestyle, but has tired of the antagonistic content of his father's correspondences. For years, the son has yielded to his father's wishes: giving up the collarless shirt that his father derides as an emblem of American culture and accepting the doctor's recommendations for appropriate reading materials. Yet, despite the narrator's compliance with his father's demands, the letters he receives from abroad appear directed at a state attorney rather than a son. And although he claims to avoid any and all complaints that might provoke or offend his fugitive father, the narrator feels he must constantly defend himself against the onslaught of his parent's rebuke. According to the doctor, his son's letters reveal an intolerable superficiality, softness, and bookishness, all of which stem from the "pseudocosmopolitan" atmosphere in which he lives. After years of such criticism, the narrator is convinced that his every move is observed "by the watchful eye of my distant father" (24).

Schneider's protagonist now feels it is time to turn the tables, to divert the scrutiny and critique away from himself and focus exclusively on his father's Nazi past. A lawyer by trade, the narrator plans to use these skills to his advantage. He will be the aging physician's son, but also aspires to be his prosecutor — relentlessly questioning him on every accusation levied by the doctor's victims and making it impossible for him to escape. As Schneider's revision of the Mengele story reveals, such parental accountability is never forthcoming. What the narrator thinks will be a simple game of question and answer becomes a frustrating game of cat and mouse. The father is not only unrepentant of his crimes at Auschwitz, he is also adept in the art of psychological maneuver. The son soon realizes he is not the only one who has planned for this encounter and who hopes to exploit the father-son relationship in order to get what he wants. The former SS physician, too, has prepared himself well in advance.

> His tactic was to trace my reproaches back to their 'philosophical roots' and to entangle me in a debate over the fundamental tenets of my own worldview. He answered my cautious inquiries about his membership in the SS, the time he spent on the eastern front, and his activities in the camp with such a jumble of philosophical and 'scientific' explanations, that I feared I would be intellectually overrun. And all the while, as he babbled on with frightening certainty about it all, he stared at me with a sly look on his face. He knew that my attempts to close in on his thoughts and motives were aimed at his actual deeds, and he waited for my attack. (33)

In his essay "German Postwar Strategies," Schneider refers to the role reversal that emerges during Rolf Mengele's visit to South America, a feature of the son's confrontation that likewise appears in his own fictional re-telling of the event. In spite of the letters he has received over the years, the young lawyer remains ill-informed about his father's specific activities at Auschwitz: what the doctor had done, and by what motives he had been guided.[35] Rolf Mengele goes to interrogate his father, but it is he who becomes the accused. He is by this time aware of his father's criminal reputation. Nonetheless, he feels compelled to justify his choices and defend his character. As Schneider himself observes, Rolf's strategy for forcing a confession out of his Nazi father fails. It is he who ultimately stands trial.

Despite the years that separate him from his service to the Reich, and the miles that distance him from his native German soil, the father remains an ardent supporter of National Socialist ideals. The aging doctor perpetuates the image of Josef Mengele as a physician and researcher passionately committed "to bringing science into the service of the Nazi vision."[36] In spite of his declining health and meager resources, the father continues to immerse himself in philosophical and scientific explanations, devoting hours to long discredited biological inquiries and patently refusing any awareness of, or atonement for, the crimes committed in the name of this so-called science. This continued adherence to racist ideology is expressed vividly in the doctor's reaction to his son's blond, blue-eyed fiancé. He is overjoyed at his son's decision to graft a "shoot of our family tree with a woman from the other side of the northern border." The Auschwitz physician is convinced that from this new combination of genes "one can expect only the best results" (41).

Although the father is proud of his membership in Hitler's SS, he emphatically denies any part in the crimes perpetrated by members of this elite corps. He swears that he never hurt another human being and, as in his letters, presents his son with a worldview whose legitimacy he considers self-evident. The doctor expresses no bitterness over his moral corruption and no disillusionment towards a regime that, through its failure, destroyed his professional ambitions. On the contrary, the narrator's father has composed a memoir about his years with the SS and reserves his most stringent criticism for German postwar democracy. It is a system, he feels, that has betrayed its National Socialist heritage. According to the doctor, all one must do to accept his views is to observe Europe's obvious and ongoing deterioration since the Führer was defeated.

The narrator's inability to sever the ties to his Nazi father reflects the ambivalence observed among many of Germany's youth by Alexander and Margarete Mitscherlich. In *The Inability to Mourn* the Mitscherlichs note that, while the younger generation appeared anxious to break free of paternalistic and authoritarian tradition, they seemed to be simultaneously in a desperate search for it. Similarly, the narrator of *Vati* confesses that, despite his repeated efforts to defy his father, the years and continents that have divided them, and his occasional feelings of hate, he can never fully abandon the desire to win his father's favor. His attachment to his father seems, in fact, to be in direct response to his early loss of paternal authority. Schneider's subject appears reluctant to surrender his vision of the erudite, charming uncle who once composed for him fairy tales about "gauchos, river rides, horses, and campfires in primeval forests" (11). He shares with his listener his impressions of the doctor's continued charisma: his searing intellect, his steadfast commitment to his ideals, his distinguished and well-groomed appearance. And although the son cannot explain why, he continues to accord his father — "the most hated and despised man on earth" (30) — the respect and obedience demanded of him. Even after the doctor's blatantly inaccurate assertion that he never hurt another living soul, the narrator's first reaction is to believe that his father is telling the truth. It should be noted, however, that the narrator's reaction to his father in Brazil is expressive not only of an idealized sense of admiration, but also of fear. His repeated references to the hospital-like cleanliness of the tiny house in São Paulo and his father's fastidious appearance underscore the SS physician's reputation as a callous, emotionally bankrupt man obsessed with order and personal hygiene. His statements call to mind images of the doctor wearing crisp, white overcoats and cologne while his victims shivered malnourished and half-naked, an officer who whistled his favorite arias while performing selections for the gas chambers. When angered by the doctor's praise for his fiancé, the narrator feels compelled to challenge his father's authority and to refute his crude and obvious racism. Yet before he can do so, the son is faced with a terrifying vision of Auschwitz and immediately cowers before his father's renowned potential for sadism and violence.

> He stood before me unbelievably large and powerful. I saw his muscular, hairy arms in his short-sleeved shirt. I recognized the awful strength in his body, something incalculable, violent. And suddenly a picture sprang up before my eyes, sharp and clear, as if I myself could testify to these events. I saw a well-groomed, placid man in an SS uniform, a man who could become insanely angry by a single forbidden movement, who could smash in the head of a prisoner completely without warning, or stomp on the belly of a pregnant woman with his boots. Any minute now, I thought, he'll drop the shoes he has in his hand and throw himself at me. (43–44)

Schneider derives his descriptions of the narrator's father from biographical information on Josef Mengele,[37] including testimonies from former inmates of Auschwitz. His characterization draws upon eyewit-

ness accounts of the young Dr. Mengele, reports that portray the physician as a handsome, well-dressed, and charismatic doctor who, with
god-like impartiality and no visible emotion, wielded power over life
and death. Documents show that even for those persecuted by Josef
Mengele, the SS officer often held sway over his subjects, appearing to
them as Clark Gable or Rudolph Valentino, a man who seemed to enjoy contrasting his own elegance with the prisoners' barely human state
and who could capriciously commit the most barbarous of acts. As one
Auschwitz survivor recalls, "he was brutal, but in a gentlemanly, de-
praved way."[38]

Biographers have likewise noted that, for many, Josef Mengele has
come to symbolize a demonic personality, an image of pure evil caused
not only by the horrific nature of his crimes, but by his uncanny ability
to elude capture until his death in 1979. Posner and Ware write, for example, that

> as a fugitive, Mengele was variously rumored to be involved in ex-
> periments on Indian tribes in South America, to have the ear of dic-
> tators, and to have had numerous brushes with death. He was
> portrayed as a ruthless power broker, who could call upon the services
> of armed guards and killer dogs and who moved among a score of im-
> penetrable fortresses deep in the jungle. According to this legend, the
> only clue to his whereabouts was a trail of dead Israeli agents and in-
> dependent Nazi hunters, whose corpses washed up on the banks of
> the Parana River.[39]

Robert Jay Lifton makes a similar observation in his 1986 work *The
Nazi Doctors,* noting that "no Nazi criminal has evoked so much fantasy and fiction,"[40] but he goes on to argue that such accounts merely
serve to mythologize the infamous Auschwitz physician. Lifton asserts
that such depictions may well have set out to dehumanize Josef Mengele, to denounce him not only as inhumane but inhuman. They
ended, however, by transforming the doctor into something *other than*
human, someone perversely sacred. Lifton maintains that although individual accounts and attitudes may vary, Josef Mengele — whether re-
called by former friends and colleagues as a committed Nazi and
dedicated scientist, or by his victims as a murderous madman — has
taken on a disturbingly exalted status.

In spite of Schneider's recourse to available biographical data on
Josef Mengele, critics have reacted negatively to his fictional characterization of the infamous doctor. Some contend that by employing such
images in his story the author perpetuates what has come to be known

as the "Mengele myth." Several take the writer to task for diminishing the doctor's barbaric cruelty. Others chastise Schneider for his failure to portray the father as an ordinary, mundane bureaucrat. Gordon Burgess considers it unfortunate, for example, that unlike *Bunte*, Schneider neglected to "arrest the eye and assault the senses" with graphic depictions of Dr. Mengele's activities at Auschwitz. What had made for good journalism in the case of *Bunte*, Burgess writes, qualifies as bad literature in the case of *Vati*. In his estimation, Schneider had transformed an "extraordinary real-life person into a fairly colourless, almost innocuous person."[41] A similar attitude is echoed in *Die Zeit*, where Schneider's craft as a writer is said to be no match for the "monstrousness of the theme,"[42] and by *Spiegel*'s contention that the author's fictional perspective was incapable of doing justice to a "phantom of horror."[43]

A possible factor in much of the criticism levied against *Vati* is the popularization of Hannah Arendt's theory of the banality of evil. In accordance with this view, Nazi war criminals had come to be seen not as inhuman monsters, but as "ordinary people who had committed extraordinary crimes."[44] An article appearing in the *Frankfurter Allgemeine Zeitung* at the time of *Vati*'s release seems to bear this out. In a 1987 review, titled "Vati's Tod" (Vati's Death), journalist Uwe Wittstock takes exception to what he considers the mythic proportions attributed to the narrator's father. He argues that by having the doctor appear larger than life, the author implies that the Holocaust was perpetrated by a select group of superhumans. In his opinion, Schneider denies the obvious and unpalatable fact that the majority of those responsible were, in fact, ordinary citizens. Wittstock writes that

> in one scene Schneider describes the gray-haired SS murderer as 'large and powerful,' possessed by 'animal-like speed' and 'awful strength.' In doing so, he stylizes [the father] into a demonic apparition with almost superhuman abilities and ultimately shuts his eyes in the face of the most shocking insight one can glean from Germany's past: namely, that most of the war criminals, camp guards included, were average, run-of-the-mill citizens.[45]

When one looks closely at Schneider's text, however, it is evident that *Vati* does not simply appropriate these popular images of Josef Mengele, but rather sets out to desacralize the legend by undermining this concept of the vigorous, omnipotent *Todesengel*. The narrator's impression of his father's life in São Paulo is that of a fearful and aging

hermit; his home is a "doghouse" where he hides like a hunted animal.
Schneider's subject states, for example, that

> I saw for the first time how frail my father was. His skin looked gray
> and crumpled like dried out clay. His hands shook whenever he put
> the cups in place; it also seemed to me that his right arm was lame.
> (52)

And again,

> Sometimes he woke up from a nightmare and would hear the
> swooshing sound of an executioner's blade over his covered head. Re-
> cently the misfiring of an engine nearly scared him to death, because
> he thought the explosion came from the gun of an assassin. He says he
> feels empty, burned out, abandoned. He is plagued by the wish to free
> himself from his pain and from a thankless world by committing sui-
> cide. (56)

The narrator's portrayal of his father's considerable intellectual and
physical presence is carefully contrasted with repeated references to the
father's age, loneliness, and poverty-stricken surroundings. These impressions present the former SS physician without his Auschwitz stage;
they expose his gradual metamorphosis into a paranoid old man, his
deterioration mentally and physically, and ultimately, his passage into a
corpse. By employing this technique, Schneider simultaneously calls to
mind the doctor's indisputable cruelty and his mortality, a depiction of
the Nazi doctor that makes his crimes appear all the more unsettling.

Although critics desire a more polarized and straightforward depiction of the doctor in *Vati*, the fact that the narrator's father is capable
of tears in one scene and, in the next, celebrates his "historical task"
and his work in the field of eugenics is much more true to fact. Schneider addresses, in effect, on a fictional level the deep-seated contradictions that epitomized Dr. Mengele's behavior. As Lifton has noted,
neither the assessment that Josef Mengele was a kind man driven to his
crimes by a passion for science, nor a monster who merely feigned
kindness towards his subjects at Auschwitz proves satisfactory. According to Lifton, all Nazi doctors underwent a process of "doubling" in
the camp; that is, took on a second, autonomous self in order to adapt
to evil. But Dr. Mengele, he contends, "was special in the seemingly
extreme compatibility of the two components of his double self."[46] In
Lifton's view, such psychological compartmentalization allowed the SS
doctor to select victims for the gas chambers without seeing himself as
a killer, a psychological maneuver which Dr. Mengele apparently mas-

tered and one that is vividly portrayed in Schneider's fictionalized rendition.

The narrator is well aware of the rumors spread about his father and is surprised to discover how starkly they conflict with the actual circumstances of his father's life. His visit to São Paulo leads him to challenge the constant stream of photographs prevalent in newspapers and magazines, images that allegedly depict the elusive Nazi fugitive in various luxurious South American venues. And yet Schneider's protagonist does not limit his objections to the press alone. He likewise suspects that his friend will not believe his story, that the former schoolmate will see his account as yet one more attempt to divert attention away from his father's whereabouts. In responding to this anticipated accusation, the narrator states that his companion's reluctance to accept the truth is symptomatic of a more general societal tendency to see his father as a myth, and thus to avoid the more disturbing possibility that this SS criminal was, like them, a human being: "The world does not want to let my father die because they cannot bear the thought that my father also belongs to the human race" (82). While it might be charged that the narrator's defensiveness in this passage exposes his own guilty conscience, one can also interpret his words as a challenge to those who continue to evade their own guilt by focusing on the moral failure of a single son and the horrific crimes committed by his infamous father. The narrator states in the opening pages of his account that his father was protected less by his family's deceit than by the fantasy of those who pursued him, and claims that the "monster image" they constructed of him made the doctor virtually invisible (10).[47]

This does not mean that the narrator seeks to erase his own culpability. Rather, he combines an investigation of personal guilt with society's reluctance to view the real-life, mortal side of his father, a reluctance that not only perpetuates the doctor's extra-ordinary status, but absolves other individuals of their moral responsibility for the Holocaust. The narrator concedes he may never know the full extent of his father's crimes, but he does profess to know this: that "no single individual, only a country, has it in its power to extinguish an entire race" (22). Therefore, in spite of the mixed expectations of Schneider's critics — to create a character that is either monster or man — *Vati* succeeds in combining both. In so doing, the author proposes that the doctor's behavior, indeed Auschwitz itself, was a "product of specifically *human* ingenuity and cruelty."[48]

It is doubtful that the narrator of *Vati* inherits his father's name and nothing of his personality. Schneider challenges *Bunte*'s assertion that the son of a brutal SS officer "really didn't inherit anything from his father other than his name, the mere mention of which made people flinch."[49] While the narrator's mother breaks away from his father, ending the marriage because of alleged personality conflicts, his own separation from his father has neither the same clarity nor finality. Schneider raises this troubling question in the early pages of his story. The narrator, who has recently learned of the doctor's role at Auschwitz, decides to burn the family photos in his possession. But as the flames begin to destroy the images of father and son, it is impossible to decipher which face is which.

> I watched how the flame took hold of the cut up photographs, how it faded out the rocky landscape and the face on the corner, and saw how the heat caused the picture to roll itself up. When I looked at it again I could no longer distinguish if it was his face or mine that was being consumed. (21)

The son appears, in fact, to have inherited portions of his father's character and, at various points in the novel, makes note of their seemingly compatible tastes. He, like his father, is inspired and comforted by Brahm's String Quartet in G-major. When, as a schoolboy, the narrator is unjustly accused of stealing his teacher's pen, he finds solace in the composer's melodious work. Years later in Brazil, the son is horrified to learn that his father, the Death Angel of Auschwitz, cherishes the same piece. It is this similarity which kindles in the narrator the suspicion that he shares other aspects of his father's personality. The son speculates that if musical preferences can be passed from one generation to the next, then he quite possibly has inherited the doctor's more sinister qualities. As one scholar rightly suggests, "part of the reason for the narrator's visit to his father is to confront his fears that he may be like him."[50]

What is equally significant and disturbing about the narrator's connection to his father are those aspects of his identity that seem to elude his awareness and thereby perpetuate a legacy he consciously attempts to resist. The son states, for example, that he suffers from a "pathological jealousy" (17), the same trait that led his mother to divorce his father after the war. The narrator's jealousy is perhaps nowhere more evident than in his reaction to his schoolmate's alleged betrayal. In this scene, the son discovers his friend playing chess with another boy their age (whom we discover is his cousin Werner). At the sight of the two boys together, the narrator flies into a rage, responding violently to what he considers a blatant act of deceit. The narrator's indignation is combined with a desire to humiliate and subordinate his friend. And, like his father, his need for revenge is excessive. The son wants to see his friend crawl on his hands and knees and plead for mercy. The similarity between the narrator's behavior as an adolescent and his later description of the father's "outburst of rage" in São Paulo is unmistakable.

> Oversized, spewing sparks I stood there in the room, I was so full of indignation that I couldn't speak. I thought to myself: now you'll throw yourself down on your knees and beg for forgiveness; you'll crawl over to my side and swear that you'll never betray me again. (17)

The narrator's commonalities with his father are likewise exhibited during his later visit to South America. When frustrated by his father's insensitivity and lack of remorse, the son is overcome by a violent desire to "throttle" him, an act reminiscent of the doctor's outbursts at Auschwitz. The son later stalks an unknown woman through the streets of São Paulo and feels an obsessive urge first to tear the clothes from her body and then to throw himself at her feet. His ultimate choice is aptly termed by one critic the "classic *volte-face* of oppressors": he convinces himself that he is the one being exploited and accuses the woman of seducing him. The narrator excuses his behavior, in other words, by blaming the victim and, characteristic of his father's Nazi mentality, implies that the target of his fixation brought such treatment upon herself. Schneider's subject fends off a sense of personal culpability regarding the woman by employing the same rationalizations that enabled his father to perform his activities as a concentration camp doctor virtually without regret.[51]

The culmination of the son's unconscious alliance with his father, a connection intensified by his failure to denounce the criminal doctor, is played out during his altercation with a local São Paulo hotel. The scene is prompted by the alleged theft of five hundred dollars from the narrator's suite. In taking legal action against his Brazilian innkeepers, whom he accuses of the crime, the son seeks to assuage his own conscience concerning his father's escape from justice. He attempts, in effect, to substitute a trial involving petty theft for his father's trial as a mass murderer, hoping to absolve himself of the guilt caused by his misguided loyalty. As in the earlier scene involving the female stranger, the narrator embraces his father's disposition, concerned less with recouping his financial loss than with the harsh punishment of the suspected thieves. The son's earlier comments about the "half-naked, dark-skinned" inhabitants of his father's village are transformed here into an urge to prosecute such persons without a shred of evidence and take on the racially motivated quality of a Nazi witch-hunt. At one point, the narrator screams at the hotel receptionist that "nothing is sacred to you people, not even your own children!" (72). This declaration represents not only a crass stereotype, but assumes a chilling irony given his father's participation in the massacre of countless children at Auschwitz.

By assuming the role of the aggressor, and thereby imitating his father's behavior, the son finds it ever more difficult to denounce his father's past activities and report him to the authorities. Because he reacts to situations as his father might have done, any temptation on the narrator's part to rebuke his parent becomes not only hypocritical, but tantamount to exposing his own guilt. The psychological paradox of this identification is that in avoiding his father's criminality, and in perpetrating his own misdeeds, the son's suffering is intensified. In addition to committing spiteful, injurious acts, the narrator berates himself for assuming the very traits he seeks to reject. The son's actions seem to bear out in concrete form what he formerly presented as a mere abstraction: "we are, no matter how we react to it, the sons and daughters of the perpetrators; we are not the children of the victims." (42).

Following his outburst concerning the missing money, the narrator wishes to retract his accusations. He also fantasizes about the possibility of terminating his inquiry. Yet he is unable to do so. The narrator makes his way slowly towards the police station, walking as if in a daze and repeating the precise sentiments he previously had used in reference to his father: "He is lying. He is guilty. He must stand trial" (73). The narrator becomes complicitous in his father's guilt, both by failing to seek restitution for the doctor's victims and in committing his own acts of injustice. He is likewise a passive bystander in real acts of cruelty and violence. The narrator does not intervene, nor even protest, when he sees a petty thief severely beaten by local Brazilian police. In spite of the "blows and whimpers" that emanate from an adjoining room, the narrator can think of nothing but his own safety and attempts to escape the premises by claiming that he has a plane to catch. The son's moral cowardice in this scene is striking, as is the graphic depiction of the detainee's disfigured appearance.[52] The violence represented here, as well as the author's use of the term "victim" to describe the man brutalized by police, is again reminiscent of the father's activities at Auschwitz. The narrator's response not only replicates his father's capacity for extreme emotional detachment, but dramatizes the son's persistent moral paralysis when faced with the truth of his father's past.

Interviews conducted with children of Nazis reveal a tendency among these children to seek a reconciliation with their parents. In spite of the sometimes brutal crimes their mothers or fathers condoned (or in some cases actually committed), many of the children interviewed claim they would come to terms with this burden, if only their parents would acknowledge their guilt and express some semblance of remorse. In the words of one daughter,

> If my mother had only said a single time, "You know, I've been thinking it over, and what I did was the worst thing a human being can do. I shut my eyes. And I'll probably take the guilt of that silence with me to my grave." I could have made peace with a mother like that. Even if she had been a guard in a concentration camp.[53]

The narrator of *Vati* ultimately fails to reconcile the doctor's dual role as father and murderer. The narrator's exploration of his paternal legacy simultaneously exposes his desire for a strong and confident guardian, his shock at the truth of his father's identity, his fear that he may be like his father, and his incapacity, in spite of what he learns, to sever these painful and confusing ties. Bearing out what the Mitscherlichs observe in 1967, the son appears to be in desperate search for a father. At the same time, he remains ambivalent about his father's position as role model and hesitates to view him as either hero or ideal.[54] The narrator's investigation of the past is not only the quest for a father, but an excavation of his own role as son, a pursuit that ultimately ends in confusion and frustration.

After his visit to São Paulo, the son attempts to withdraw both physically and emotionally. He never returns to his father's home; he sheds no tears at his father's grave. Nevertheless, the narrator's inability to mourn the doctor's death leaves him haunted by a murderous history he can neither fully confront nor successfully wish away. The doctor's lack of remorse concerning his crimes, as well as his postwar escape from capture, robs the son of a means of coming to terms with his father's life. He faces at his father's grave the consequences of his loyalty. And he finds no resolution to his feelings of attraction, pity, anger, and disgust. The narrator's desire to tell his story, and the tone of "guilty defiance"[55] often characterizing his account, powerfully express the son's inescapable and unresolved dilemma: that the bonds of familial duty and the father-son relationship remain forever at odds with the demands of natural justice.

Schneider candidly acknowledges the open-endedness of his story, anticipating an uneasiness among readers who expect the son to break all ties with his murderous father and dutifully fulfill his civic and moral obligation. The author concedes that, in many respects, *Vati* is the story of an attempt that fails. While his narrator does reach an eventual decision concerning his father, he never manages to reconcile the more painful issue of his conflicting emotions. Central to Schneider's discussion of *Vati* is his rejection of the belief that this absence of a solution implies a lack of progress and insight. He argues that, in spite of the narrator's life-long ambivalence, there is much to be learned from his struggle.

To illustrate his point, Schneider compares Rolf Mengele's disclosures in *Bunte* to Niklas Frank's 1987 interviews in *Stern*. The author shows how, in the case of Frank, all emotional attachment to the father is graphically (indeed grotesquely) obliterated during the son's confrontation with the past. He recounts, for example, how the son achieves orgasm in a public restroom while imagining his father's death by hanging, and summarizes Frank's approach as a "pitiless attempt to even the score."[56] Schneider maintains further that although Frank's autobiography may have the merit of having no literary predecessors, inducing as it does considerable shock and disgust, this autobiographical report is problematic precisely in its desperate repression of any family feelings.

> My uneasiness with Frank's account is that it proceeds too smoothly. His intention — an unsparing tallying up of the balance sheet — overruns the story and blends together all of the ruptures and conflicts in order to achieve this goal. At no point does Niklas Frank seem troubled by the question of what he might have inherited from his father. The question as to why it took him forty years to write what by all appearances is a spontaneous expression of hate never gets answered.[57]

Schneider argues that, in spite of Rolf Mengele's pronounced ambivalence, or perhaps even because of it, one finds in his dilemma a crisis of conscience, a struggle between the bonds of family and the demands of justice. Although both stories reveal a shared inability to come to terms with a painful inheritance, Niklas Frank vehemently suppresses the psychic dilemma caused by his father's infamy. Rolf Mengele's account, on the other hand, exposes an arduous, painstaking inquiry not only into his father's Nazism, but also into what it means to be the infamous doctor's son. The question of inherited guilt is central to Rolf Mengele's quest. In defending his criminal father, Rolf ultimately chooses to live with his guilt. His sustained exploration of this moral, psychological, and emotional predicament stands in stark contrast to Niklas Frank's pretensions that no such crisis ever existed.

In fashioning his story upon the real-life experiences of Rolf and Josef Mengele, Schneider unleashed a debate which, as one critic notes, was remarkable for the sheer "vehemence of the attack."[58] In March of 1987, just three days prior to *Vati*'s scheduled release, an article appeared in *Spiegel* that suggested the author had borrowed too closely from the 1985 *Bunte* series and had, in fact, taken large portions of his narrative directly from Byhan's interviews. Gerda-Marie Schönfeld, whose article incited legal charges against Schneider for plagiarism, describes the author's treatment of the *Bunte* material as "obscene," "irritating," and "blatantly copied."[59] Burda Verlag, *Bunte*'s publisher, responded to *Spiegel*'s disclosures by issuing an injunction against *Vati*, and temporarily halted its distribution. What followed was a proposal Schneider has described as the transformation of a dispute over authorship into a moral offense. Burda offered to withdraw its objections to *Vati* if the author donated all proceeds from his book to a Jewish charity dedicated to Holocaust victims. Schneider promptly rejected this proposal. He argued that to accept such terms constituted a confession of guilt concerning the charges of plagiarism and an acknowledgment that his book did badly by Josef Mengele's victims. More disturbingly, the author maintained, the proposal demanded a monetary settlement for what critics had concluded was a moral transgression. In his letter to Burda the author writes,

> I consider the compromise that you submitted to Luchterhand [Schneider's publisher] a public relations stunt. And I will have nothing to do with this shady trade deal that once again victimizes the Jews; this time in the form of a debate over who owns the comments of Rolf and Josef Mengele.[60]

After several weeks of deliberation, the legal system sided with Schneider. *Vati* was granted permission for release. Yet the vociferous nature of the *Vati* debate did not stop there. Literary critics quickly took up where the lawyers had left off. The *Frankfurter Allgemeine,* for instance, derided the author's use of the "cheapest clichés" and concluded that "the best that one can hope from Peter Schneider is that his clumsy little book will be forgotten as soon as humanly possible."[61] *Die Zeit* expressed dismay at the author's "senseless word-acrobatics," "failed formulations," and "misplaced metaphors."[62] Gordon Burgess inferred from Schneider's use of ordinary language that *Vati* "fails to be literature."[63] Equally disparaging is Gabriele Kreis's description of the novel as a "hopelessly bad book. Poorly researched, poorly conceived, poorly written."[64]

It has been suggested that the critics' aggressive attacks on Schneider were motivated neither by the author's failure to cite his sources, nor by a heartfelt conviction that the story was insensitive to Holocaust victims. After all, the authors of the popular *Vaterbücher* of the 1970s had already dealt with such subject matter — the relations between children of Nazis and their parents — but had never received the same harsh treatment. Why was it then that *Vati*, a fictional re-telling of actual events that avoided the fractious tone of earlier autobiographical works, ignited such outrage in the German press? For some reason, Schneider's slim volume had seemed "to touch a raw nerve."[65]

The charge of plagiarism is easily rebutted. The *Bunte* articles were so widely read and the case of Josef Mengele so well known, that the author could not have had the slightest hope of deceiving anybody. As Schneider himself has written,

> The *Bunte* exclusive was *the* newspaper sensation of 1985 and was sold worldwide. The assumption that I hadn't wanted people to notice any similarities was like saying that Charlie Chaplin wanted the film title *The Great Dictator* to hide the fact that the movie was about Hitler.[66]

Schneider's response to his critics focuses less on questions of plagiarism and literary style than on what he considers a more fundamental and sensitive issue in the *Vati* debate: the use of fiction to address the Holocaust. For many of the author's critics, *Vati* had ventured into territory inaccessible, indeed inappropriate, to fiction. The story of Josef Mengele, they argued, was incompatible with the art of aesthetic embellishment, which served merely to trivialize the concrete, unspeakable horrors of Nazism. In the words of one critic, Schneider's account "endeavors to deal imaginatively with the unimaginable, and fictionalizes dreadful fact." This same critic goes on to state that, in contrast to the more factual approach taken by *Bunte*, *Vati* "is not equal to the subject-matter."[67] An equivalent view is expressed in *Die Zeit*, which maintains that, when faced with the infamous *Todesengel* of Auschwitz, Schneider, adept in the area of creative fiction, was robbed of both "the imagination and the means."[68]

For Schneider, Adorno's famous phrase of 1949 — "To write poetry after Auschwitz is barbaric"[69] — has become for contemporary German-speaking writers a question of how literature can be produced *about* Auschwitz. The author challenges the notion that novelists should cede to journalists and filmmakers the responsibility for depicting the Holocaust. He argues that although the documentary approach may provide unrelenting proof about the historical facts, what it cannot do, and what fiction must take as its ultimate goal, is to transform the unimaginable into the imaginable. It is the task of the writer, in other words, to undermine the belief that the reality of Auschwitz surpasses our ability to conceive of the atrocities committed within its gates.[70]

Vati's critics are correct in asserting that Schneider's story presents the reader not with simple, irrefutable facts about National Socialism and the Holocaust, but rather with an account of Nazi crimes as seen through the highly subjective, even biased, lens of an Auschwitz physician's son. The narrator fails to resolve his dilemma concerning his father and, in the end, places the safety of a Nazi criminal over justice for his victims. At the same time, Schneider creates in *Vati* a fictional persona who, because of his infamous paternal legacy, confronts a history others have chosen to ignore. In spite of his friend's admonishments, for example, to stay away from Brazil and simply pretend his father never existed, the narrator considers such an attitude tantamount to suggesting that he was delivered to his mother by a stork. It is obvious that the son's investigation into his family history has painful consequences. It exposes his father's enthusiastic participation in Nazi evil and illuminates the doctor's continued refusal to mourn his victims. Even more disturbing, however, is the narrator's realization that he is not free of his father's taint. Schneider's protagonist concludes during his visit to São Paulo that he has inherited not only his father's traits, but much of his guilt. He acknowledges that although he himself has committed no atrocities, he nonetheless shares with other Germans, both young and old, the burden of passive tolerance, silent complicity, and ineffectual resistance. The narrator is unable to report his father to the authorities, but he is likewise incapable of escaping a painful historical and familial legacy. After twenty years, the son is ultimately convinced that he — indeed his entire generation — must find a way to accept it.

Perhaps what has most disturbed readers and critics of *Vati* is the fact that the narrator's inability to conclusively resolve his emotional and moral dilemma applies not only to the experiences of this fictional persona, but represents a larger failure on the part of the Federal Republic.[71] Schneider's story reveals that while postwar Germany's older generation gave little attention to such men as the narrator's father, and remained silent about their experiences during the Third Reich, so too did the younger generation avoid a reckoning with their tainted familial and cultural inheritance. The tendency of critics to chastise Schneider for the weakness and indecisiveness of his narrator, and to suggest that the author is morally suspect for portraying a character that does not conform to acceptable ethical standards, seems to convey more than a naive equation of author and fictional subject. *Vati*'s critics appeared to be "indulging in wishful thinking."[72] They not only distanced themselves from the son's undesirable behavior, but allied themselves with the victims of Nazism rather than with the perpetrators and their children. Any insinuation that postwar generations had failed to confront their parents about the Third Reich and were actually complicitous in their parents guilt was apparently intolerable.

Peter Schneider contends that, due to the benevolent hand of fate, his own personal history differs in many crucial respects from that of Rolf Mengele. He is quick to acknowledge, however, that they do have something in common: a confrontation with the period of National Socialism that is painful and ongoing. Schneider feels compelled to understand Germany's fascist past and its continuing impact on the present; but his intellectual curiosity is mixed with apprehension. By the author's admission, his interest in history is "ambiguous, afflicted with the emotions of suspicion, shame and unwanted complicity."[73] The son's ambivalence in *Vati* mirrors, then, Schneider's suspicion regarding any attempt to resolve or "overcome" the traumatic legacy of the Third Reich and replaces the project of *Vergangenheitsbewältigung* (coming to terms with the past) with the task of facing — and facing up to — the past. Like other novels of its decade, *Vati* does not seek to ensure certain answers but rather to give rise to new questions. Perhaps, as Judith Ryan suggests, the former aim of mastering the past has ultimately given way to analysis.[74]

Notes

[1] Peter Sichrovsky, *Schuldig geboren: Kinder aus Nazifamilien* (Köln: Kiepenheuer & Witsch, 1987) 50.

[2] Gerald Posner and John Ware, *Mengele: The Complete Story* (New York: McGraw Hill, 1986) 160.

[3] Inge Byhan, "Von Reue keine Spur," *Bunte Illustrierte* 30 (July 1985) 117.

[4] Byhan, "So entkam mein Vater," *Bunte Illustrierte* 26 (June 1985) 30.

[5] Colin Riordan, editor's introduction, *Vati: German Texts Edition*, ed. Colin Riordan (Manchester, UK: Manchester UP, 1993) 8. Future citations from this edition referred to by editor.

[6] Peter Schneider, interview with Colin Riordan 8.

[7] In his essay "German Postwar Strategies," Peter Schneider explains how Rolf Mengele used the word "Vati" to describe a man "whom he had never met and whose crimes he detested." Schneider observes that as late as 1986 Rolf Mengele was unable to call his father a murderer, or even a criminal. During a TV interview Rolf declared that "nobody can ask a son to denounce his own father." Peter Schneider, "Postwar German Strategies in Coming to Terms with the Past," *Legacies and Ambiguities: Postwar Fiction and Culture in West Germany and Japan*, eds. Ernestine Schlant and J. Thomas Rimer (Baltimore: The Johns Hopkins UP, 1991) 200.

[8] Peter Schneider, *Deutsche Ängste: Sieben Essays* (Darmstadt: Luchterhand Verlag, 1988) 86.

[9] Sichrovsky 81.

[10] By the time *Vati* appeared in 1987, Rolf Mengele had become a well-known personality. He had been interviewed for numerous publications and had also appeared on a talk-show in the United States.

[11] Riordan 4–5.

[12] In his discussion of the "father literature" of the late 1970s, Peter Schneider locates the "common point of departure" for these autobiographical stories in the sickness or demise of a parent, writing that "only the death of a parent . . . made it possible for people of my generation to admit their emotional wounds." "Postwar German Strategies" 284. Michael Schneider (younger brother to Peter) draws similar attention to these belated attempts to fill in the gaps of parental histories, and considers it significant that the parents themselves were never questioned. In his opinion, this popular genre exposes his generation's complicity in Germany's postwar silence and can best be characterized as a series of "obituaries." Michael Schneider, *Den Kopf verkehrt aufgesetzt oder die melancholische Linke: Aspekte des Kulturzerfalls in den siebziger Jahren* (Darmstadt: Luchterhand Verlag, 1981) 9.

[13] Margarete Mitscherlich, *Erinnerungsarbeit: Zur Psychoanalyse der Unfähigkeit zu trauern* (Frankfurt: S. Fischer Verlag, 1987) 37–46.

[14] Alexander und Margarete Mitscherlich, *Die Unfähigkeit zu trauern: Grundlagen kollektiven Verhaltens* (Munich: R. Piper & Co 1967) 230–32.

[15] Peter Schneider, *Vati* (Darmstadt: Luchterhand Verlag, 1987). Page numbers in parentheses throughout this chapter refer to this edition. All translations are my own.

[16] Riordan 20.

[17]Riordan 16.

[18]Wolfgang Nagel, "Zu Besuch bei einem Ungeheuer,"*Die Zeit* (17 April 1987).

[19]Riordan 18.

[20]Riordan 16–18.

[21]Schneider, *Deutsche Ängste* 88.

[22]Ernestine Schlant, Introduction, *Legacies and Ambiguities* 2.

[23]Gordon Burgess, "'Was da ist, das ist [nicht] mein': The Case of Peter Schneider," *Literature on the Threshold: The German Novel in the 1980s,* eds. Arthur Williams, Stuart Parkes and Roland Smith (New York: Berg Publishers, 1990) 114.

[24]Nagel, "Zu Besuch bei einem Ungeheuer."

[25]Riordan 81.

[26]Schneider, "German Postwar Strategies" 281.

[27]"Our history teacher . . . who was also our German teacher told us in no uncertain terms 'I am personally implicated in this' . . . And he made it perfectly clear: 'Please do not ask me to on about this wound in my life.'" The upshot of all this for a school guided by traditional humanist ideals is that we spent exactly two hours on fascism during my entire history class. I think that many others my age could tell a similar story." Interview with Colin Riordan 3.

[28]In interviews conducted by Israeli psychologist Dan Bar-On for his book *Legacy of Silence,* one finds repeated references to Germany's postwar reluctance to discuss the Third Reich. One interviewee states, for example, that the subject was "pushed out of the sphere of awareness" and that his generation was forced to inform itself about the country's fascist past: "Today I think it's a disgrace that in school, after the war, we didn't learn anything at all. Nothing! The word *Hitler* didn't exist. We just had to scrape it together for ourselves, my generation . . . We didn't learn anything except that the war started. That was all." Daniel Bar-On, *Legacy of Silence: Encounters with Children of the Third Reich* (Cambridge: Harvard UP, 1989) 33.

[29]Peter Schneider models his subject's ambivalence on that of Rolf Mengele, who, according to Inge Byhan of *Bunte,* would only speak of his father in the most tentative of terms. "So viele halfen ihm" 26.

> On the one hand, it's the father who swore to his son that he never killed anyone, that he had never done anything to hurt anyone. The son doesn't want his father to be associated with the word murderer or criminal. On the other hand, he knows that his father is objectively guilty. That is the source of his suffering. He inherited the name Mengele like a disease.

[30]Nagel, "Zu Besuch bei einem Ungeheuer."

[31]Schneider, *Deutsche Ängste* 72.

[32]Peter Schneider writes that during the 1960s the term 'fascism' was divested of its political specificity and that "anyone who opposed the 'revolutionary' order of the day was sent to the corner as a fascist." The author maintains that while this popular and "deadly" word became the trendy way to condemn and insult one's enemies, it was never used to refer to "the infamous twelve years in which it entered the vocabulary of international language." Ironically, the very generation who had declared war on the crimes of the past ended by diluting these crimes almost beyond recognition. "Postwar German Strategies" 284.

[33]This sentiment underscores Peter Schneider's assessment of the "antifascist impetus" characterizing the 1968 rebellions, an ideological platform that led his generation to believe, quite mistakenly, "that they had broken not only with the political but also the cultural inheritance of Nazi-fascism, especially with the culture of obedience." *Deutsche Ängste* 72.

[34]"It is comparatively easy to renounce a father who swindled his way through the postwar years by pretending to be merely a small-time sympathizer, all the while looking forward to his honorable pension. When I learned of my father's existence there was a five-digit bounty on his head. The father assigned to me never became a judge, high-school teacher, state secretary, chancellor, or general secretary of the UNO; he became the most wanted man in the world. There was nothing for the son of such a man to discover, nothing to sniff out, nothing to expose. For me there was only one choice: to protect my father or to betray him" (28–29).

[35]Rolf Mengele declared in 1985: "We had never met as father and son. I wanted to see him one time face to face and ask him: 'What did you do? What happened? How could it happen?'" Byhan, "Von Reue keine Spur" 110.

[36]Robert Jay Lifton, *The Nazi Doctors: Medical Killing and the Psychology of Genocide* (New York: Basic Books, 1986) 340.

[37]In his essay "Vom richtigen Umgang mit dem Bösen," Schneider enumerates the various documentary sources he consulted while researching *Vati*. These included not only the 1985 *Bunte* series, but a 1986 issue of *Stern*, Miklos Nyiszli's *Auschwitz* and *Mengele: The Complete Story* by Gerald Posner and John Ware. *Deutsche Ängste* 82–121.

[38]Lifton 343.

[39]Posner and Ware xvii.

[40]Lifton 338. To illustrate his point, Lifton chooses one American and one German source: Ira Lewin's popular 1976 novel, *The Boys from Brazil*, in which the infamous Dr. Mengele is portrayed as a "brilliant, fiendish scientist

engaged in the cloning of Adolf Hitler," and Rolf Hochhuth's 1963 play *Der Stellvertreter*, where the behavior of "The Doctor" (closely modelled on Josef Mengele) seems so inhuman as to resemble "an uncanny visitant from another world."

[41]Burgess 119.

[42]Nagel, "Zu Besuch bei einem Ungeheuer."

[43]Gerda-Marie Schönfeld, "So eine Nachbarschaft," *Der Spiegel* 11 (9 March 1987) 218.

[44]Riordan 28. In describing Hitler's director of transport, Arendt writes: "[Adolf] Eichmann was not Iago and not Macbeth, and nothing would have been farther from his mind than to determine with Richard III 'to prove a villain.' Except for an extraordinary diligence in looking out for his personal advancement, he had no motives at all." Hannah Arendt, *Eichmann in Jerusalem: A Report on the Banality of Evil* (New York: Penguin Books, 1963) 287.

[45]Uwe Wittstock, "Vatis Tod," *Frankfurter Allgemeine Zeitung* (11 April 1987).

[46]Lifton 151.

[47]The son's pronouncements in this passage are corroborated, in fact, by Mengele's biographers, who maintain that the "elusive aura" attributed to the SS doctor was not only the "wishful thinking engendered by Nazi hunters," but actually contributed to the fugitive's ability to avoid capture. Posner and Ware 129.

[48]Lifton 4.

[49]Byhan, "Keiner fragte nach seinen Taten,"*Bunte Illustrierte* 28 (July 1985) 29.

[50]Riordan 21.

[51]Riordan 22–23. It is interesting to note that the narrator's father states elsewhere in the text that concepts of right and wrong are meaningless, "just as in nature there's no 'good' or 'evil.'" The former SS physician concludes, in opposition to ethical or religious standards of virtue and integrity, that the "only decisive factor was the 'existential necessity' that determined a country's actions" (39).

[52]"The face and arms of the suspect were bloody and swollen. Whole handfuls of hair had been ripped from his head, and I could see how even now he fought back the tears. A long quivering wooden stick left no doubt where the wounds came from" (75–76).

[53]Sichrovsky 112. This view is echoed in Bar-On's *Legacy of Silence*, in which the child of an *Einsatzgruppe* commander is willing to admit her father's suffering, to offer sympathy for his three-year imprisonment, and to recognize his difficulty in avoiding "the situation he'd gotten into." The only prerequi-

site for such sympathy is that her father "acknowledg[e] at least once the fate of his victims." 251.

[54]Mitscherlichs 231.

[55]Riordan 19.

[56]Schneider, *Deutsche Ängste* 89.

[57]Schneider, *Deutsche Ängste* 89–90.

[58]Riordan 24.

[59]Schönfeld 218–19.

[60]Schneider, *Deutsche Ängste* 105.

[61]Wittstock, "Vatis Tod."

[62]Nagel, "Zu Besuch bei einem Ungeheuer."

[63]Burgess 119.

[64]Gabriele Kreis, "Ach Vati, deine Substantive," *Konkret* 6 (1987) 66 ff.

[65]Riordan 1, 25–27.

[66]Schneider, *Deutsche Ängste* 99–100.

[67]Burgess 120.

[68]Nagel, "Zu Besuch bei einem Ungeheuer."

[69]Theodor Adorno, *Prismen: Kulturkritik und Gesellschaft* (Frankfurt am Main: Suhrkamp Verlag, 1955) 31. Adorno would later amend this dictum, writing in 1965 of the legitimate tension between aesthetic stylization and the necessity of remembering Nazism's victims. For further elaboration of Adorno's views, see "Engagement," *Noten zur Literatur III* (Frankfurt am Main: Suhrkamp, 1965) 125ff.

[70]Schneider, *Deutsche Ängste* 90–91.

[71]Riordan 19.

[72]Riordan 27–28.

[73]Schneider, "Postwar German Strategies" 286.

[74]Judith Ryan, "Postoccupation Literary Movements and Developments in West Germany," *Legacies and Ambiguities* 205.

At Home with Fascism:
Elfriede Jelinek's *Die Ausgesperrten*

> It is not the political phenomenon of fascism that needs to be analyzed, but rather the connection between fascism and capitalism, the petty bourgeois as the facilitators of fascism. Fascism, as Bachmann has said, begins in the family, in the relationship between men and women. She announced this in the 1950s, when no one else dared, and it remains just as true today. Fascism is a general state of mind and can be seen in our horribly authoritarian child-rearing, in the beating down of opposing opinions, and in our completely intolerant and authoritarian ways.[1]

> Then I thought, well, this is no mere coincidence. I chose to fall in love with one of my father's victims, who is a victimizer of others at the same time.[2]

JAQUELINE VANSANT HAS NOTED THAT, for many Austrians, the arrival of Hitler's army in 1938 was experienced neither as a major disruption nor as a definitive break with the past. In spite of attempts by government officials to portray Austria and Austrians as victims of Nazi oppression, that is, "as the objects of historical events rather than as historical subjects," stories recounted by the population at large "demonstrate that 1938 was not the rupture it was purported to be." According to Vansant, many who experienced the *Anschluß* firsthand exchange fond memories concerning the early years of Nazi rule and claim to have suffered no personal upheaval in their lives until the Allied air raids of 1943.[3]

Elfriede Jelinek's 1980 novel *Die Ausgesperrten* (The Outsiders)[4] draws similar attention to the largely unobstructed political transitions of recent Austrian history. But, in contrast to the narratives cited by Vansant, Jelinek presents such historical continuity as an unbroken endorsement of oppression. Situated in Vienna in the late 1950s, *Die Ausgesperrten* depicts a country whose former territorial inclusion into Hitler's Reich served merely to valorize a politics of violence and subjugation already at work in daily social affairs. The novel unmasks the ways in which Austria's eager accommodation of a totalitarian regime emerged from existing social interactions "destructive of life, hierarchical in nature, and intolerant of the other,"[5] and seeks to expose how these same attitudes and behaviors remained firmly anchored in postwar Austrian life.

In characterizing fascism as a "general state of mind," Jelinek extends her definition beyond the realm of politics and class and locates both past and present structures of oppression within the lives of individual citizens. She considers the social and economic foundations of bourgeois capitalism, "with [their] unbelievable brutality,"[6] one step removed from the rigid monopolies of a dictatorship. Her concept of fascism collapses the barriers between public and private forms of tyranny and proposes that political despotism has its origins in covert, everyday abuses. The most threatening aspect of fascism is not that it may happen again, but that it already exists in the day-to-day relations between men and women and their children.

Die Ausgesperrten is set in the years of the Great Coalition, an alliance between the Socialist and People's Parties that was "thoroughly geared toward stability and conciliation."[7] In Jelinek's novel, the conservative mindset of the period does not allow for a recognition of the crimes committed under Nazism; nor does it advocate a return to the progressive politics of Austria's short-lived liberalism.[8] Substituting domestic stability for ethical engagement, Austria is presented in *Die Ausgesperrten* as a society which, trumpeting 1945 as a chance to start anew, eradicated any guilt that might stand in its way.[9] It is a time when the Russians have gone and the Nazis are free to resume their places. In the words of the narrator, "Nazis old and new could once again have their day in the sun, just like the flowers in their gray planter boxes. Welcome one and all" (109).

Jelinek inverts in *Die Ausgesperrten* the popular myth of postwar Austria, a myth predicated upon positive visions of economic renewal, political neutrality, and the imitation of American culture. Just as Austria's complicity in fascism is shown to be the logical extension of a repressive, authoritarian culture, so too are the country's reactionary political and social attitudes after 1945 shown to be closely intertwined. The narrator's sardonic reference to the economic miracle — "a German expression manifested in numerous films with kidney-top tables and wet bars" (28)[10] — is followed by repeated examples of self-centered individualism and repressed moral conflict. Whether it is Hans Sepp's glib dismissal of his mother's concentration camp stories ("To hell with the working class, long live Rock n' Roll" [26]), Rainer's conviction à la Sartre "that the past does not exist" (106), or Herr Witkowski's decision to put his war crimes behind him and "look forward into the future" (101), the society depicted in *Die Ausgesperrten* is one in which personal gain takes priority over collective guilt.

In Jelinek's view, the Austrian postwar era can best be defined as a facade of respectability, a carefully applied veneer behind which lurked the most horrific of offenses. Although the 1950s saw the glorification of traditional values and institutions — economic security, the strict division of gender roles, the sanctity of the Austrian home[11] — *Die Ausgesperrten* suggests that such ideologies served to hide, and thereby perpetuate, old patterns of repression and injustice. As Allyson Fiddler has noted, *Die Ausgesperrten* depicts a society where denazification has failed. The novel's middle-class protagonists profit financially from the postwar *Wirtschaftswunder*, but simultaneously preserve their country's latent or protofascist structures. *Die Ausgesperrten*, Fiddler writes, exposes the unpleasant reality of 1950s Austria. The author not only rewrites her country's history, she demystifies it.[12]

Interspersing images of political mass murder, domestic violence, and criminal assault, the "uglier facts brought to light"[13] in Jelinek's text trace the ubiquity of trauma in Austrian society; the presence of multiplicitous forms of cruelty that continued unabated from the period of National Socialism into the years following its demise. The Austrian environment detailed in *Die Ausgesperrten* is one which bridges the gap between political brutality and domestic perversions. And what have been heralded as the country's most cherished values and institutions — from friendship and marriage to love and intimacy — are shown to be the breeding grounds for violence and subjugation.[14] The author underscores Bachmann's fusion of public and private crimes. Fascism in Jelinek's novel goes beyond the power of governmental regimes, manifesting itself in the most brutal of terms in everyday human exchanges.[15]

Michel Foucault's analysis of power provides a useful point of entry into Jelinek's text. Foucault suggests that systems of oppression are deployed not only by the tyrannical rule of a single individual or group, but by innumerable variants of power circulating among each member of the social order. In an interview in 1977, for example, Foucault says that

> between every point of a social body, between a man and a woman,
> between the members of a family, between a master and his pupil,

between everyone who knows and everyone who does not, there exist relations of power.[16]

For Foucault, power is everywhere and forms a part of each social exchange: from the intimate affairs of men and women, to the interactions of the family unit, to the traditional structures of education. Foucault's conception of power rejects the notion that authority is limited to a hierarchical system of regulation or control, a sovereign force dominating a subordinate entity. This conventional construct, he argues, implies a linear framework, whereby power operates from a position of ultimate superiority downward. His theory, by contrast, suggests that while such vertical expressions of authority do exist, they are but single facets embodied within a larger network of power relations.

Foucault's discussion of power, therefore, is not limited to the isolated forces that channel their influence along narrowly circumscribed paths. Rather, he sees a circular dimension of power in which lines of domination cross the boundaries of sovereign and subordinate. There is seldom one supreme force immune to the power-plays of another force, even a seemingly subservient one. Foucault's theory of power relations calls into play the multiplicity of mechanisms continually invested, utilized, transformed, and displaced within society as a whole.[17] An analysis of power should not, in Foucault's estimation, be limited to the means by which one individual or group single-handedly exerts its supremacy over passive and ineffectual victims. In actuality, it is each individual who himself possesses the ability to produce and effect power. Each constituent of the social body is power's executor as well as its recipient.[18]

Die Ausgesperrten reveals how one generation's extreme destructiveness on a world-historical level finds expression in the violence and destructiveness of its children. Equally important are the ways in which punishing and coercive forms of power circulate — between different social classes, among family members, and within each individual. Just as Jelinek's narrative begins and ends with violence (a vicious attack on a Viennese pedestrian; the slaughter of the Witkowski family), the structures of oppression embedded within the novel emerge as continuous cycles of abuse. Illustrative of this cyclical configuration of power, *Die Ausgesperrten* offers a complex arrangement of cause and effect, innocence and guilt. The author problematizes the easy division of her characters into victims and perpetrators. She suggests that due to repressive ideologies engrained within the social fabric, the oppressed can easily become the oppressors, and those who suffer domination are often complicitous in their own abuse. Jelinek also shows how violence inflicted upon others can coexist with aggression turned inward against the self. *Die Ausgesperrten* illuminates a system of oppression that violates boundaries of age, sex, and class, as well as those of self and other. Although much of the violence depicted in the novel stems from "fascist tendencies that have become a way of life,"[19] one can discern within this dynamic of oppression the interaction of both sadistic and masochistic behaviors, domination and docility. As Susan Sontag points out in her discussion of Nazi aesthetics, fascist ideology encompasses more than the deification of extreme control; it embraces both "submissive behavior and extravagant effort." In her words, fascism exalts "two seemingly opposite states: egomania and servitude."[20]

A primary target of Jelinek's analysis of history, trauma, and power is the family. Traditionally considered the repository of experiences untouched by the outside world, it is here that the author erases the borders separating the personal and political, demonstrating that within the framework of the conventional Austrian household such distinctions cease to exist. Alice Miller characterizes the authoritarian home as the prototype of a totalitarian regime. The father is the "sole, undisputed, often brutal ruler"; his wife and children are "subservient to his will, his moods, and his whims." According to Miller, all members of the authoritarian household must accept humiliation and injustice unquestioningly. They must also be grateful for the privilege.[21] This assessment seems particularly applicable to *Die Ausgesperrten*. In Jelinek's novel, Herr Witkowski recuperates within the context of his family the power he possessed as a member of Hitler's elite. Robbed of his former "field of honor," Witkowski seeks compensation in the "field of family honor" (17), a territory he guards with a watchful and uncompromising eye. The narrator informs the reader that the domestic violence in the Witkowski home commenced on the very day the war was lost. "Before, the father could beat up strangers of various shades and stripes; now the only thing left was his wife and children (32)." And while the former SS officer once crossed the border into Poland, sending his enemies away "through the chimneys and crematoria of Auschwitz and Treblinka," the borders he now transgresses are those of the philistine — "those narrow borders of clothing and moral values" (15).

Witkowski's obsessive preoccupation with violent pornography epitomizes Austria's "smooth transition from warfare to hobby: pornophotographic shots replace human target shooting as a means of sexual arousal and the assertion of power."[22] Just as during the war Hitler's SS glorified the production of death as a way of life, Herr Witkowski seeks to arouse or enliven his male audience through the stylized destruction and debasement of his female subject.[23] Frau Witkowski is made vulnerable to the invasive gaze of her husband's camera. She is also exposed to the prying eyes of her husband's acquaintances, who will later be shown the photographs. Frau Witkowski is not merely objectified, but twice objectified — "once as the object of the action in the scenario, and once as the object of the representation, the object of viewing."[24]

Herr Witkowski's *Pornfotographie* is meant to re-institute the supreme power he once enjoyed in the SS. The Party "made him so great," we read, "that he grew beyond his wildest dreams; today he enlarges his pretty pictures" (101). Accordingly, the majority of the veteran's photographs revolve around images of failed female resistance. Witkowski carefully arranges each scene so that his wife (here a housewife spied on by a stranger; there a maid being punished by her employer) is seen attempting to fend off her male aggressor. And although her vagina is meant to confirm her sexual availability, it is simultaneously staged as the cite of her protest. As one scholar has observed, the female subject of the pornographic photograph should not only invite sex, she should also postpone it. Like Frau Witkowski, she most often appears with her hand "hovering" over her genitals.[25]

The pornographic images captured by Witkowski on film are designed to inspire fantasies of domination and abuse. They employ representations of rape, torture, and the threat of death. The positions he demands of his wife alternate with stories of mass executions. In the same way the SS officer "smashed down" the resistance of his wartime enemies and "liquidated numerous persons" with his own hands (16), Witkowski threatens to bash his wife's skull if she does not cooperate with his "flights into the realm of photography" (18). Where it was once his gun that penetrated his enemies, transforming them into "dark skeletons" frozen in the Polish snow (33), it is now his camera that freezes his cowering wife, and his children's watercolors that provide the grisly effects.[26] According to Jelinek's narrator, Witkowski is as dedicated to this new hobby as he formerly was to his military assignment, both of which "know no limits" (15).[27]

Witkowski's use of photography to both document and glorify abuse reappears in sinister fashion in Rainer's decision to be photographed by Anna holding his father's bayonet. The narrator's comment that Rainer's "murderous expression well suited his violent thoughts" (206) can be seen to foreshadow the bloodbath at the end of the novel, the horrific continuation of a legacy of murder initiated by his father under fascism.[28] If we conclude, as does one critic, that Herr Witkowski is the primary target of his son's violent aggression,[29] then one should likewise note that, in killing him, Rainer reproduces his father's brutality, not only through committing similar crimes but by using identical weapons. Rainer commits these murders after seeing the pornographic photos of his mother, thus reinforcing his father's use of the violated female body as the conduit for transmitting political violence into the private sphere.[30]

The physical and psychological terror practiced by Herr Witkowski in Poland carries over into the postwar abuse of his wife and children. But his authority does not go unchallenged. One of the many war invalids populating Vienna's streets, Witkowski shares with his former comrades a radical demotion in social status. These men, the narrator claims, "reminisce about their time abroad when they were really something, which is no longer the case" (27). Jelinek undermines the popular image of the stylishly-clad, jackbooted SS man by transforming Herr Witkowski into a one-legged porter dependent on his patrons' tips for income and on his camera for a sense of virility.[31] Although the "magic quality of his uniform" may have made him irresistible to women during the war, having relinquished his uniform, and a leg, his current attempts at masculine bravado are absurd. The strict military discipline to which Witkowski once adhered gives way to a dependency on crutches for his every move. In one scene, for example, the former SS officer attempts to molest his wife but is thwarted by his handicap. The narrator describes in detail Witkowski's efforts to regain control over his body, presenting at the same time a grotesque inversion of his former supremacy.[32]

> Papa is paddling around and around helplessly in a circle, paddling mistakenly from one side only, never from the other. In recent days he has been plagued by sciatica and rheumatism of all things; he has enough to worry about with his leg. He is rotating now on his axis and tries to get up on his feet, which he accomplishes only with the expert help of Margarethe's hand-up. Upsy daisy. (103)

Equally disturbing about this scene is Frau Witkowski's reaction. While, moments earlier, she had pleaded with her husband not to rape her, Margarethe now seeks both to comfort her despondent husband and to bolster his beleaguered self-esteem. In the narrator's opinion, this scene is yet one more example of how Witkowski's "former radiant authority always pulls his wife along behind him" (103). It is important to note, however, that Frau Witkowski's treatment of her husband in this and other passages is indicative not only of combined admiration and fear, but of a process of infantilization in which Herr Witkowski himself participates. Coupled with endearments like *Mausi* (honey), *Schatzi* (sweetheart), *Spatzilein* (darling) and *armes Manndi* (poor little man), Frau Witkowski cradles her "Otti's" head in her lap and promises to make things better. The use of such phrases as "there there" recalls conventional images of mother and child, as does the statement which brings the chapter to a close: "Today he'll get an extra dinner portion, to make up for his tears" (104).

Alice Miller's characterization of the traditional European family as a microcosm of the totalitarian regime is not limited to the father's role alone.[33] In Miller's words, the mother has her own "sphere of authority" in the household. She not only rules over the children when the father is not at home, "she can to some extent take out on those weaker than herself the humiliation she has suffered."[34] Elfriede Jelinek presents a similar view of maternal influence in *Die Ausgesperrten* and suggests that although the family patriarch may hold the most visible reins of control, the mother is not without her own resources of power.

Virtually nowhere in Jelinek's work is motherhood portrayed positively.[35] In spite of prevalent images of female suffering — at the hands of abusive husbands, callous lovers, domineering bosses, and ungrateful children — mothers in Jelinek's texts tend to operate simultaneously as victims and oppressors.[36] Illustrative of this view, Jelinek's portrayal of Frau Witkowski in *Die Ausgesperrten* reveals that the twins' mother is subjected to horrific abuse (which the narrator neither trivializes nor condones) and repeatedly endeavors to reclaim a sense of personal agency by manipulating her children's development. While offering slavish devotion to her cruel and domineering husband, Frau Witkowski insists that Rainer and Anna rise above their father's vulgarity and reject the tastes of the "average" Austrian citizen. Frau Witkowski sends her children to the local Gymnasium in order to cultivate in them the sense of beauty "in thought, word, and deed" (41) absent in their father. Rainer and Anna's education also compensates for her own girlhood dreams of art and culture, dreams that ended on the day of her marriage. Frau Witkowski puts enormous pressure on her children to succeed in their intellectual and artistic pursuits. She produces a daughter "blinded by her music studies" (19) and a son who, outside of his knowledge of literature, cannot seem to master much of anything.[37] The irony of Frau Witkowski's plans, however, is that the familial soil provided to nourish this receptiveness to nature and the arts negates all aesthetic inspiration. The Witkowski home is one in which genius must contend not only with brutality and madness, but with filth.

The head, where the ugly worm of Rainer's literary talents nested, is in any case already in the clouds, and looks down on a sea of musty old underclothes, worn out furniture, tattered newspapers, torn up books, piled up detergent cartons . . . bread crumbs, pencil stubs, eraser dust, completed crosswords and sweaty socks, all of which penetrated, against his will, the one refuge still left open to him, if he's lucky: the refuge of art. (14)

Referring to motherhood as "the only societally sanctioned form of female power,"[38] and to her own mother as "highly authoritarian and insanely opposed to desire,"[39] Jelinek includes in *Die Ausgesperrten* vivid images of maternal dominance over her young protagonists' sexual maturation. In the case of Rainer, Frau Witkowski violates her son's physical integrity by continuing to bathe him even after he has reached adolescence. The narrator describes Rainer sitting naked in the family's bathtub — an "improvised" tub on the kitchen floor — while his mother "makes sure he's clean all over." Rainer's humiliation during these episodes is ignored. His mother dismisses his embarrassment by saying she brought him into the world and that shame is a "healthy emotion" (181). Furthermore, she adds, his father "has exactly the same things and in the same places" (180). For Anna, this same ritual transgression of her physical privacy ("when your mother does it, it's as if you did it yourself" [181]) is intensified by her position as "Lieblingskind."[40] Anna is expected to accept such encroachments not only as evidence of her mother's love, but of her steadfast attentiveness and concern.

Rainer and Anna's early traumatization manifests itself in a state of mental and bodily surrender through which they escape the physical violations common to their abuse. Exhibiting indifference, emotional detachment, and profound passivity, the twins frequently relinquish their struggle against the father's violent attacks and the mother's demeaning intrusions. The narrator recounts how each child, while being beaten by Herr Witkowski, "rises out of its body and takes a position higher up, where it has a better view of the cruel scene below" (34).[41] The narrator goes on to warn, however, that although the Witkowski twins physically survive their traumatic ordeals and make their "troublesome and hesitant" way through adolescence, internally the seeds have been sown for a new generation of violence: "Something gets balled up inside their heads, and will later be released as an explosion of orange-colored light" (34).

Just as Rainer and Anna are faced with shifting and contradictory visions of power, where maternal and paternal domination alternates with patterns of extreme childishness and submission, the twins' behavior incorporates both domination and helplessness, suffering and revenge. Expressing on the one hand the power of Herr and Frau Witkowski to manipulate and punish their children, *Die Ausgesperrten* simultaneously satirizes Austria's deification of parental authority by showing how parental control is undermined. In the Witkowksi household, the twins' fear and humiliation frequently give way to anger and retribution. Rainer insists that his hate sets him apart from society's complacent middle class. He is joined in his negative campaign by his sister Anna, who, according to the narrator, "could earn a doctorate in hate" (12). The twins are frightened by their father, but they are also cruel: aping his movements, snatching his crutches, knocking him over, spitting into his food. The teens are equally vindictive towards their mother. They respond to Frau Witkowski's request for sympathy by ordering her to "Clear out!" and to her offer of a freshly-baked cake by leaving her "not a single piece" (37).

For Foucault, the body is the site of power, the place where docility and subjectivity converge.[42] Similarly, Foucault's conception of modern society views the body politic as something expressed through the "politicization of the body."[43] Foucault conceives of power not only as a force produced in every social interaction, but as one induced within the body itself.[44] Foucault speaks of power as an integral facet of existence, as an all-pervasive entity. Power is something which permeates the very bodies of individuals and ultimately determines their perceptions and behaviors.

> In thinking of the mechanisms of power, I am thinking rather of its capillary form of existence, the point where power reaches into the very grain of individuals, touches their bodies, and inserts itself into their actions and attitudes, their discourses, learning processes, and everyday lives.[45]

This corporeal assessment of power is central to *Die Ausgesperrten*, for it is upon the body of each character that Jelinek stages her drama of fascism's shifting power. Herr Witkowski's service in the SS is characterized by his physical strength and sexual potency, and the fate of his victims by their passage into corpses. The officer's postwar occupations are associated with the loss of bodily integrity and the carnal abuse (both representational and real) of his wife and children. Frau Witkowski's deployment and forfeiture of power likewise centers around the material self. She poses nude for her husband's camera, is physically battered and bruised, bathes her teenagers even during puberty, and seeks to instill in her abusive spouse a renewed sense of virility. In like fashion, it is through the bodies of the Witkowski children that this movement between aggression and submission, docility and violence will continue.

In his desire to escape the perversities of his homelife, Rainer seeks to deny material reality by cultivating a sense of something higher. Described by the narrator as the only alternative for those "who can't afford a better method of growing out of their environment" (20), Rainer's knowledge of literature and philosophy is his shield against his parents' depravity and provides him with a sense of superiority over those less learned, leverage that he hopes will mask his distinct social and economic disadvantage. Yet, at the same time Rainer attempts to rise above his brutal, middle-class origins, his narrow focus on his middle-school education and his need to dominate others mimics both his father's fascism and his mother's misplaced obsession with art. Rainer substitutes the infamous Nazi phrase "Arbeit macht frei" (freedom through work) with his own motto "Wissen macht frei" (freedom through knowledge [35]), and equates his carefully constructed ideologies with a right to subvert the opinions of others; to make them, in effect, subservient to his will. Rainer's passion for control, as well as his belief that through one's intellect "one can also acquire people" (20), finds vivid expression in his position as self-appointed *Anführer* of the gang and in his insistence that Hans, an uneducated member of the working class, remain solely a "recipient of messages, admonitions, [and] orders" (53).[46]

Rainer's refuge in intellectualism also serves as a substitute for the physical intimacy of which he is incapable. As the novel progresses, Rainer's trauma is seen to reside not only in his physical victimization. His subjection to violent and distorted displays of adult sexuality has virtually destroyed his relations with the opposite sex. Having witnessed the physical and sexual abuse of his mother (who "cries out for help from the bedroom" [38]) and the crass exhibitionism of his father (who masturbates in his son's presence),[47] Rainer has come to reject sexual relations altogether. For Rainer, the "immortality of the poet" (52) takes on almost mythical proportions. The body that houses such genius, however, is considered not only impermanent but grotesque.[48]

In response to his conviction that sexual intimacy is a contemptible and degrading experience, Rainer constructs an identity that is devoid of all erotic potential. He enacts, in effect, his own castration. Rainer asserts that his penis "does not exist because his father's does" and adds that whatever doesn't exist "cannot be disgraced at home by one's mother" (180). Herr Witkowski establishes his marital sovereignty through the sexual violation of his wife. Rainer conceives of male-female relationships essentially as a union of the mind. Frau Witkowski refuses her son the right to privacy and counsels him regarding the benefits of shame. Rainer refuses to look at his own naked body or to let it be seen by others. For Rainer, "what one does not see does not in fact exist" (185).

Rainer seeks repeatedly throughout the novel to shield himself from representations of female sexuality, images which remind him not only of his upbringing but of his own sexual inadequacies. When in the presence of girls his own age, the young Witkowski is content to "pass judgment on them from a distance" (41) and confines his infrequent sexual gratification to masturbating in the dark. Rainer's denial of sexuality — his own as well as that of others — is expressed by the photographs of pretty girls pasted in his wardrobe. In each one, Rainer has cut away the models' bodies, leaving only their faces for review. Thus, while Herr Witkowski graphically exposes his wife's breasts and genitals, Rainer can tolerate pictures of women only if proof of their sexuality is removed.

The narrator reminds us, however, that Rainer's needs are not eliminated by the trauma he sustains within the Witkowksi household. They are only "locked away" (167). With Sophie, Rainer's attempt to relegate the relationship to the exchange of philosophical ideas constantly wages war with carnal attraction. In one scene, Rainer takes Sophie "tenderly in his arms" (8) before she pushes him away. In another, he makes "clumsy advances" (46) as she glides past. Yet, despite the power of his tenacious adolescent lust, and his occasional ability to give way to erotic temptation, Rainer can never overcome the damage caused by his family. When he finally is alone with Sophie in her garden and has the opportunity to act on his attraction, what begins as sexual arousal ends in a debilitating attack of nausea.

Although both Rainer and Anna are subjected — visually as witnesses, physically as victims — to horrific scenes of domestic violence, it is Anna whose body is most powerfully inscribed with her traumatic childhood and adolescence. Underscoring Jelinek's contention that for every man who is exploited and downtrodden, there is a woman "who has it even worse,"[49] Anna's suffering is intensified by her sex. The garbage in the Witkowski apartment is, for Rainer, an inhibition to his creative genius. For Anna, this filth clings to her "like a magnet"; it not only intrudes upon her mental processes, but invades her body. Cleanliness has become something foreign to Anna. As Jelinek's narrator comments, Anna has the feeling that "she consists only of dirt" (23) and, in response to this feeling of physical contamination, repeatedly "purges" herself by emptying her stomach of its contents.

Anna likewise re-enacts in her sexual life the brutality and ugliness she experiences at home. Haunted by images of her mother's blood-stained panties, her father's pronouncement that all feminine products be removed "upon pain of death" (206), and the screams that emanate from her parents' bedroom, Anna, like Rainer, comes to associate human sexuality with repulsiveness and violence. Unlike her brother, however, who struggles to protect himself from all sexual contact, Anna actively seeks out demeaning and abusive situations. Rainer castrates himself metaphorically, merely pretending that his penis doesn't exist. Anna attempts at the age of fourteen to de-flower herself with a razor.

Anna's promiscuity, which appears at first glance to subvert society's dictates concerning "proper" female behavior, is upon closer examination intensely self-destructive.[50] Her decision, for example, to have sex in the men's room of her Gymnasium is by all appearances a provocative and rebellious act.[51] In the end, however, it is Anna who suffers. Waiting impatiently for Gerhard to reach orgasm, Anna is sickened by her pimple-covered classmate and by the stench of her surroundings. She finds herself, once again, on the verge of vomiting. It can therefore be argued that Anna's initial dare — the student must stab himself under the fingernail without crying out — and her subsequent participation in such sordid sexual intercourse reflect a negative, self-lacerating vision of sexuality based on violence and abuse.

Jelinek describes her writing as an act of survival. Begun in her early teens, it has given voice not only to her pessimism about modern Austrian society, but has provided access out of a catastrophic, and potentially debilitating, family history. In an interview with Donna Hoffmeister, the author recounts that

> Speaking out has saved my life. I have always written in order to survive. What would I do without language! I came out of such spiritually chaotic and catastrophic (albeit economically secure) circumstances, that language was my only means of survival. My sole escape. Without it I have nothing.[52]

In *Die Ausgesperrten* Jelinek draws upon her personal experience by combining Anna's descent into speechlessness with the intensification of her trauma. Anna's speech impediment is, like her eating disorder, the result of aggression turned inward upon the self, a protest against emotional pain that becomes written on the body. Anna initially seeks an outlet for her troubled sexuality in the form of lewd jokes. Once this is taken away (to prevent her from "poisoning" her fellow pupils), Anna finds herself increasingly unable to speak at all. "Her tongue became more and more inclined to say 'No. I refuse to work today'" (24).

The lack of effective communication in *Die Ausgesperrten* goes beyond Anna's silence to the overall language barrier between men and women. Men in Jelinek's novel assume a position of linguistic dominance. They consider themselves superior to the women around them and, despite their imprisonment within culturally-induced gender roles, enjoy the privilege of speaking their minds. Herr Witkowski is said to talk "like a waterfall" (98). Rainer reportedly indulges in "manic chattiness" (187). Anna, on the other hand, is robbed of speech altogether and "makes her way into silence." In contrast to her male counterparts, who are able to articulate their thoughts (even if these thoughts are socially conditioned), Anna is rendered incapable of making a sound. "She opens her mouth but nothing comes out. Not a single word. . . . Silence" (158).[53]

Anna is described by one critic as "the child of a wife abuser and a codependent mother."[54] She is an eyewitness to her father's glorification of violence as well as to her mother's submission to it. Anna's behavior in the gang reveals that her identity is shaped both by a will to conquer and by a compulsion to succumb. It is Anna's job in the foursome to be the "eternal temptress" (208), to lure the next unsuspecting victim into the waiting hands of his assailants. To do so, Anna uses her body. In each case, Anna's seeming innocence and vulnerability play a decisive role. Her male targets are drawn to her underdeveloped hips and tiny breasts, and entertain vivid fantasies of violating a virgin. While one man relishes the contrast between his more voluptuous wife and the "fresh young girl" pressed against him in the streetcar, another revels in the fact that, unlike his hometown of Linz (where young girls like Anna are protected by the police), "here in this decaying, foulsmelling city one can simply take advantage of them and then send them packing" (211).

Yet Anna's seductiveness only goes so far. First feigning a desire to be molested by male strangers, Anna rapidly becomes the aggressor: robbing, beating, and humiliating her victims. The paradox of Anna's attacks, however, is that they merely re-invent within the public sphere the violent events of her homelife — events which involve her as witness and recipient. Anna's blows are aimed at the head and genitals of her male targets and ironically mimic her own subjugation and loss.[55] Anna appears to achieve the upper hand in these assaults. She emerges successful in her attempt to brutalize and degrade her victims. At the same time, Anna's behavior recreates, and thus causes her to re-experience, her own familial trauma. And by assuming the role of the perpetrator, she identifies with the very persons who have abused her.[56]

Anna hopes that by having sex with Hans she will experience affirmation of her unique identity and will be infused with his physical power. Their love-making, she believes, will free her from her anger. Her body and her heart will articulate what her mouth can no longer convey. What Anna actually experiences with Hans is further loss, not only of her body but of her intellect. Like Rainer, Anna's education is ultimately of no use to her in her relations with the opposite sex. Unlike Rainer, she is expected to relinquish her intelligence altogether, to join the "millions of others" (89) who fulfill an identical sexual function. For Anna, it is not Hans's use of her body that strikes her as sad. It is that he has no use for anything else. Upon being rejected by Hans, Anna deteriorates both mentally and linguistically. We are told that Anna "loses her reason" (244) and is released from school after uttering an "inarticulate scream" (243). Anna later sees Hans at the Gymnasium's tea party. She tries desperately to speak to her former lover, yet can only signal with her hand that she has something to say. Having failed to get Hans's attention, Anna then "hops about" in an effort to be seen. The contrast in this scene between Hans, who is still in possession of "considerable power" (252) and Anna, who is physically emaciated and wordless (255), is striking.

Alice Miller has stated that it is part of the tragic nature of the repetition compulsion that "someone who hopes eventually to find a better world than the one he or she experienced as a child in fact keeps creating instead the same undesired state of affairs."[57] This assessment of the repetition compulsion can be applied to *Die Ausgesperrten*. In Jelinek's novel, Rainer and Anna, desperate visionaries of a more promising future, perpetually re-enact the traumas from which they hope to escape. As the novel progresses, it becomes increasingly evident that the arrogant, sadistic behavior of the Witkowski twins is not only a reaction against, but an imitation of, the governing principles of their parents' lives. The teenagers' attempts to dissociate themselves from middle-class society, as well as their efforts to evade their parents' control through intellectual achievement, are in actuality "engraved . . . by the lifestyles and relationships they see at home and are doomed to fail."[58]

It is the contradictory nature of the young Witkowskis' aggression that dissolves its therapeutic effect. Although Rainer and Anna hope to purge themselves of their suffering by committing their own injustices, such acts of violence merely serve to mark them ever more indelibly with the stamp of their familial heritage. Seen in this light, Rainer's proud declaration of rebellion, uttered as a manifesto against the bourgeois world of his parents, becomes in effect an ironic approximation of his own family dynamic. "We are monsters," Rainer asserts, "even though we've disguised ourselves as average citizens. On the inside we're consumed by evil deeds. On the outside we look like school kids" (54).

Jelinek focuses her novel on the repercussions of fascist attitudes and behaviors within the Witkowski household. But she in no way limits her depiction of postwar Austria to Nazi perpetrators and their children. In accordance with the author's contention that fascism extends beyond the political sphere and touches the lives of individual citizens, *Die Ausgesperrten* traces the effects of brutalizing power on Austrian society as a whole, including those victimized during Hitler's Reich. As one critic has noted, it is not just Herr Witkowski, a former SS officer, who establishes a connection to Austria's National Socialist past. Frau Sepp, the widow of a Communist Party member, does so as well.[59] In both the Sepp and Witkowski households, Austria's complicity in Nazism continues to have a profound impact. The physical and psychological terror perpetrated by Witkowski in occupied Poland is reinvented during his assaults on his wife and children, during Rainer and Anna's attacks on Viennese pedestrians, and in the bloodbath that brings the novel to a close. In like manner, the murder of Herr Sepp at Mauthausen dooms his widow to a life of poverty and is the catalyst for her adherence to socialism. For Hans, his father's failure to survive Austria's fascist regime is interpreted as a sign of weakness. Images of his father's emaciated, brutalized body fuel a disdain for the political Left, which he considers both ineffectual and obsolete. Such images also shape the young Sepp's deep-seated suspicion of physical and emotional vulnerability.

Frau Sepp is arguably the most positive of Jelinek's characters in *Die Ausgesperrten*. She is certainly the most politically aware.[60] Having sustained a series of losses under National Socialism — the death of her husband and friends, the decimation of the Communist Party — Frau Sepp is faced with additional trials in the years that follow. In spite of her country's blossoming economic miracle, Frau Sepp's sole means of survival is the money she earns addressing envelopes. The narrator maintains that she is not alone. Frau Sepp, we read, belongs to a class of citizens "for whom nothing good ever comes along and certainly no miracles. They open up their doors each day but nothing enters in. Except, of course, the cold" (28). It has been suggested that the garbage in the Witkowski home is a metaphor for the corrupting residue of Nazi crimes. In similar fashion, the piles of envelopes surrounding Hans and his mother offer visual reminders of the ongoing repercussions of such atrocities.

Frau Sepp remains ardently committed to the political ideals of the Communist Party and devotes all of her spare time to improving the lot of the working class. Yet she is not above exploiting her husband's death in order to gain control over her rebellious son. Frau Sepp becomes increasingly frustrated with Hans's philosophy of social advancement and considers her son's association with the Witkowski twins and Sophie Pachhofen not only egoistic, but a betrayal of his class.[61] Eventually Frau Sepp's disappointment over her son's rejection of socialism gives way to rage. If she cannot persuade him to join the Party by appealing to his sense of political and ethical duty, then she will do so by rehearsing a litany of Nazi horrors.

> The mother now makes the decisive mistake, just as she always does when she gets angry and can no longer control her son, and starts to tell stories about the concentration camp. About the child eating apples who was thrown against a wall until he died. . . . About the tortured children thrown out of a second-story window. About the mother who, along with her two-day-old infant, was sent to the gas chamber because she had begged the doctor to let her give birth. The doctor granted her request. (172)

Frau Sepp's stories have little or no effect on Hans. Following such outbursts by his mother, Hans typically responds with yawns or sarcasms. On one occasion, he can think of nothing better to do than put some styling gel in his hair. Hans is described by the narrator as a "fully modern person" (94), a young man focused on the latest fashion and the newest Elvis release. Hans concerns himself with the present and the future, not with the past. He seeks to put the Hitler years, and with it his father's death, behind him. Hans views his deceased father as a "sickly altruist" whose death accomplished nothing. By contrast, Hans endeavors to experience through athletics that he is very much alive. "Who'd want to lie frozen under the ground?" he asks his mother. "You can get all the warmth you need with sports and bebop" (228).

Hans Sepp's aloof dismissal of his father's death and his callous treatment of his mother serve as a defense against his loss. It is easier for Hans to condemn his parents' politicism than to admit the pain caused by his mother's poverty and his father's absence. It is not, however, simply the lack of material comforts and paternal guidance that leaves its mark on Hans. He is haunted by the fact that his father was unable to protect himself against his Nazi aggressors. Herr Sepp did not die in a bold confrontation between communists and fascists before the war, or as a resistance fighter after the *Anschluß*. He was instead the inmate of a concentration camp and spent the years before his death as a frail and powerless skeleton. Hans reacts to his father's fate by becoming obsessed with his physical strength. For Hans, power is located neither in the cooperative political efforts of the Communist Party nor in the spiritual solidarity of the working class. It is located in the strength of his own physique. Hans's muscular form is a protest against the weakness of his father. Because Herr Sepp was forced to suffer bodily abuse, his son is determined he will not. Ironically, Hans is not satisfied merely to be strong; he must prove his strength through violence. Transforming emotional pain into aggression, Hans re-enacts in his assaults on innocent pedestrians the sadism of his father's killers.

> Dripping with sweat, Hans pummels . . . his victim like a soul-less machine. His fists fall like a hammer and only rise to take another swing. Ouch, the victim groans softly. He hardly has the strength left to protest. . . . The man's terror has made him speechless, until he just lies there in a heap. (9)

Jelinek has stated that, although she considers herself a feminist, she has been criticized by her female readers for not depicting women as the "superior beings promoted by the feminist movement."[62] This is especially true of the character Sophie Pachhofen, described by the narrator of *Die Ausgesperrten* as an "evil carnivorous plant" (255). Sophie is the daughter of wealthy industrialists. Her father made his fortune during the war, profiting from the slave labor provided by the Nazis. The narrator emphasizes that Sophie is driven to crime neither out of financial need nor out of hate. What entices Sophie is the joy she experiences in random acts of destruction. Sophie's decision to detonate a bomb in the Gymnasium changing room, for example, is motivated by an overwhelming desire for "sheer bliss." She announces to her companions that she wants to experience ecstasy. And she considers it regrettable that "most people lead inhibited lives" (240).

Critics have noted that while Sophie exerts considerable power over Rainer and Hans, who continually vie for her favor, her power is based on attributes that articulate her imprisonment within the cultural values of the 1950s. In the words of one scholar, Sophie Pachhofen is the "ideal image of carefully crafted beauty [and] carelessly managed abundance."[63] She symbolizes her country's desire for wealth and public recognition. Dagmar Lorenz offers a similar assessment of Jelinek's young protagonist, stating that Sophie is "little more than her family's pawn" in the power plays of postwar capitalism. Lorenz goes to say that Sophie's "impeccable cleanliness and her sexual frigidity are her selling points for a later marriage."[64] In contrast to Anna, who refuses the "improvements" expected of her sex, Sophie focuses almost exclusively on the cultivation of her exterior persona. Like her mother (a social butterfly addicted to pain killers), Sophie is destined to pursue a life devoid of depth and meaning.

Die Ausgesperrten suggests that the patterns of oppression perpetrated by the teenage gang express not only the repetition of parental injustices and an effort to punish society, but are an attempt to break free of their environment by assuming command over it.[65] Jelinek's four young protagonists repeatedly engage in activities that reopen their psychic wounds. They hope that by re-experiencing their ordeals, they will recover a sense of control. The group takes on the role of sadist, exalting in the power they exert over their victims. But, at the same time, their acts of cruelty expose a desperate need to master their own lives. The various attempts by Jelinek's protagonists to achieve a sense of freedom and autonomy ultimately fail. The members of the Viennese gang neither resolve their problematic family histories, nor secure for themselves a role in Austria's postwar world. In the words of the narrator, they are thrown into a "whirlpool of feelings" (117). And there they stay.

Alice Miller suggests in her discussion of juvenile delinquency that the sadistic crimes of the young bear witness to the desperation of children "searching a way out of a hopeless situation."[66] Jelinek offers a similar appraisal of adolescent violence. The cruelty and arrogance displayed by her central protagonists have their basis in past and present suffering, but also in a sense of foreboding about the future. Rainer, mimicking the existentialists, proposes that "nothing is important," that the only thing certain in life is death (116). He prefaces the murder of his family by saying that "when hope has been taken away, all that exists is the present" (256). Elsewhere in the novel, the narrator describes Anna's hollow eyes and thin face as the portrait of a hopeless generation (202). Jelinek focuses her portrayal of postwar Austrian life on those she considers the most helpless, and hurting, sector of society: Austria's youth.[67] The intergenerational transmission of violence in the novel stems not only from sustained physical and psychological abuse, but from the absence of positive avenues for self-improvement, empowerment, and happiness.[68]

In declaring that "individualism is no longer possible,"[69] Jelinek proposes that in the postwar age attitudes and actions are programmed by one's culture. It is this preoccupation with the "social location of identity"[70] that distinguishes the author's novels from those of more mainstream postmodernists. Unlike many writers of contemporary fiction, Jelinek presents her readers with characters whose personhood is determined by the historical and cultural influences that fatefully bind them together. Illustrative of this view, the author's concept of fascism exceeds the isolated behaviors of individual figures and works to illuminate the effects of seemingly isolated forms of cruelty upon the wider social context. Thus, while Jelinek insists that the individual's personal identity is barred from full development, the intensely negative quality of her protagonists — whom she describes as "mere stereotypes"[71] — is forged by their imprisonment within an essentially abusive environment.

Rainer, the most outspoken proponent of individualism in *Die Ausgesperrten*, provides the most convincing evidence that such self-actualization is unattainable. Rainer's appropriation of existentialist philosophy, with its emphasis on man's unlimited freedom, is radically overturned by his inability to break free of his stifling surroundings and by the "sheer negativity of the novel's ending."[72] In the final moments of *Die Ausgesperrten*, Rainer is no longer all talk; he shifts from being a philosopher to a "man of action" (201). Rainer salvages, in effect, a sense of power by murdering his entire family. It is during this gruesome murder scene that Rainer's earlier words become clear, words which in retrospect expose how far Rainer will go to prove his strength: "I am capable of unimaginably horrible deeds and only control myself so that I don't commit them" (23).

Jelinek's ability to remain attentive to the inner life of her protagonists and, at the same time, demonstrate how their conflicts and actions are "behavioristically social,"[73] is accomplished largely through her narrator. Described by one critic as the "mouthpiece of the collective subconscious," the supervisory voice of Jelinek's narrator clarifies the reasons behind the characters' behavior and reveals the impact of their actions on others and the self.[74] The narrator of *Die Ausgesperrten* is presented as an omniscient persona. She is cognizant of the events taking place within the novel, the mental state of individual protagonists, and the correlation of these personal psychologies to Austrian political and cultural history. On the opening page of the novel, the narrator begins by informing the reader of the different "guiding principles" behind the teenagers' attack on a local attorney. For Anna it is rage, for Rainer pleasure, for Hans money, for Sophie diversion. Immediately thereafter, she relates such brutalization of innocent persons to the failed denazification of postwar Austria. In the narrator's opinion, the fact that the victim's moral character is far superior to that of his assailants is of little consequence — as history has tragically borne out.

Jelinek considers it one of the most "unbelievable experiences" of her career that, while in the process of writing *Die Ausgesperrten* she discovered its basis in fact. She learned that in 1965 a seventeen-year-old student named Wunderer had killed his entire family (father, mother, and brother) with a handgun, ax, and bayonet and had inflicted upon their bodies 180 wounds.[75] Despite the fact that she discovered this information belatedly, Jelinek claims to have known that such a figure must exist. The author maintains that her invention of the fictional character Rainer emerged from her conviction that the tradition of oppression in her country inevitably leads to extreme acts of violence.[76] Thus, it is not a documentary of an actual crime that Jelinek develops in *Die Ausgesperrten,* but a fictional portrait of the types of destructive behavior promoted daily by Austrian society.

Expressive of her view that violence and brutality are deeply engrained in contemporary Austrian life, Jelinek credits the crime novel for providing inspiration for her work. As one critic has noted, the author's love of the genre can be explained "not in terms of the compelling drama of a criminal act and the individual's relation to it, but in terms of the exemplary factors which she extrapolates from them."[77] In response to the question "What fascinates you about crime novels?" Jelinek claims that such stories represent "miniature models for society," situations in which operative forms of violence and brutality "make their way to the surface."[78] To the suggestion that the violence in her writing is gratuitous, Jelinek retorts:

> Who can deny that society is extremely violent, even when this violence is constantly being released through certain pressure release valves. It is for this reason that I am so interested in criminal cases; in the end, all my books are crime novels.[79]

In spite of her membership in the KPÖ and her outspoken criticism of capitalism, Marxist critics have charged that Jelinek presents an exaggerated picture of Austrian society and that, because her images are overly cynical and insufficiently realistic, the content of her work subverts any hope of raising the public's consciousness and effecting positive social change. Although Jelinek does not deny the abrasive quality of her work, she rejects the notion that her novels are unrealistic. In a 1991 interview, the author declares that she has always written "realistische Literatur" and goes on to say that her brand of realism can best be described as hyper-realism or super-realism.[80] *Die Ausgesperrten* is illustrative of this technique, in that the ugliness, cruelty, and violence in the novel are taken to extremes. Jelinek does this not to make Austria's everyday acts of fascism seem unbelievable, but rather to draw attention to those forms of oppression too often concealed from view and banished from discussion. As Sender Freies Berlin concludes in a discussion of the author's work, Jelinek's portraits are so distorted by her well-known evil eye that the "comfortable upholstery of the normal is torn. . . . She doesn't stop at the description of 'reality' but instead reduces it to its essential dynamic, namely exploitation and violence."[81]

Trauma, Judith Herman writes, challenges us to speak about horrible things, "things that no one really wants to hear about."[82] The reluctance of Jelinek's readers to contemplate such political and domestic abuses is evidenced by their largely negative reaction to this and other of her works.[83] Arguing that Jelinek's vision of Austrian life is too dark, too cynical, too pornographic, critics have perpetuated the notion that traumatic events are and should remain "unspeakable." Many readers have praised the author for taking on such controversial issues as female masochism, rape fantasies, and the maternal misuse of power.[84] Others have condemned her fiction for its "vulgarity, pessimism, and utter disrespect for some of the most popular people and institutions of modern European, and in particular Austrian, life."[85] Jelinek candidly describes her reputation in her native country as "more infamous than famous"[86] and has noted the frequent use of such adjectives as "merciless" and "brutal" to describe her work to date.[87] The author does not contest such assessments. She readily concedes that she is incapable of seeing her country in a positive light. Jelinek declares: "I cannot depict positive things. That is impossible, because I really see human relations as essentially negative." She then adds: "Of course I still hope this will change."[88]

Jelinek has also been taken to task for her seeming lack of empathy towards her protagonists. Hilda Gnüg of the *Neue Zürcher Zeitung*, for example, compares the author's aesthetic method to that of a surgeon incising a defenseless body. She writes that the author wields her "satirical scalpel in order to carve up her characters' feelings." Gnüg concludes her review of *Die Ausgesperrten* with the statement: "Unfortunately few survive."[89] According to some leftist critics, Jelinek's work is distinctly callous towards the working class and the underprivileged. Not only is her fiction unrealistic, they contend, it mocks the very groups whose victimization it sets out to expose. Jelinek defends herself against such accusations. She rejects the notion that her satire and irony are used to ridicule those who suffer oppression and insists that her "so-called medical rage"[90] works to subvert the corrupt ideologies to which helpless citizens fall prey.

> I do not ridicule people for the awful living situations they are forced to live under, but rather for the false ideology that, in the final analysis, they themselves innocently partake of and which destroys them completely.[91]

In deconstructing the "false ideology" propagated by postwar Austrian society, Jelinek seeks to broaden her readers' understanding of fascism and to highlight the myriad types of suffering often left out of monolithic equations of power. Although her cynicism is omnipresent, the author adamantly rejects the word *Haßgesang* (invective) to describe her work. For Jelinek, her negative aesthetic is employed solely in the service of disclosing how patterns of oppression are hidden behind a facade of traditional values and "natural" human relations. Her novels are marked by satire, but her attitude toward the tragic fate of her characters conveys anything but humor or hate.[92]

Elfriede Jelinek's assessment of Austrian society aims to provoke the reader to think seriously about the past and to avoid emotional or instinctive reactions that inhibit thorough analysis.[93] *Die Ausgesperrten* presents fascism as a personal as well as political phenomenon and challenges its readers to acknowledge the painful continuities between the crimes of domestic life, sexual relations, war, and dictatorship. The potential for cruelty exhibited by the novel's young protagonists is juxtaposed with Austria's history of political rivalries, foreign invasions, and genocide, yet also with the socially sanctioned values and institutions that mask the injustices of supposedly peaceful times. *Die Ausgesperrten* problematizes the notion that one can separate Austria's complicity in Nazism from the patterns of oppression evident in the immediate postwar and beyond. To use Judith Herman's phrase, the author's project in the novel is about "restoring connections" — between the present and the past, between the public and the private, between the individual and the community, between men, women, and children.[94] In exposing the traumas of everyday Austrian life, Jelinek sounds a warning about the ever-present power of fascism.

Notes

[1]Elfriede Jelinek, interview with Jaqueline Vansant, *Deutsche Bücher* 15.1 (1985) 5.

[2]Dan Bar-On, *Legacy of Silence: Encounters with Children of the Third Reich* (Cambridge: Harvard UP, 1989) 257.

[3]Jacqueline Vansant, "Challenging Austria's Victim Status: National Socialism and Austrian Personal Narratives," *The German Quarterly* 67. 1 (Winter 1994) 39–40. Vansant calls her reader's attention to Karin Berger's article "Aus Angst, uns ein Bild zu zerstören," in which the author relates stories she claims are typical for her generation. According to Berger, the uncles and cousins in her family proudly display photographs of themselves in National Socialist uniform; her female relatives reveal a similar pride in their pro-Nazi activities on the homefront.

[4]Elfriede Jelinek, *Die Ausgesperrten* (Reinbek bei Hamburg: Rowohlt Verlag, 1980). All further references correspond to this edition and will be indicated parenthetically. Translations from the German are my own.

[5]Jacqueline Vansant, *Against the Horizon: Feminism and Postwar Austrian Women Writers* (New York: Greenwood Press, 1988) 85.

[6]Donna Hoffmeister, "Access Routes into Postmodernism: Interviews with Innerhofer, Jelinek, Rosei and Wolfgruber," *Modern Austrian Literature* 20. 2 (1987) 115.

[7]Allyson Fiddler, *Rewriting Reality: An Introduction to Elfriede Jelinek* (Oxford: Berg Publishers Limited, 1994) 18.

[8]Jacqueline Vansant points, for example, to the passage of womens' suffrage in 1919 and to the Equal Rights Statute of 1920. The legal improvement in women's status was also central to the "Linzer Programm," the Social Democrats' 1926 party platform, which included the removal of all laws discriminating against women, equal pay for equal work, and the establishment of public daycare centers. This initial progressive phase in Austrian politics came to an abrupt halt, however, in June of 1920 with the coming to power of the conservative Christian Social Party. It is from this point on, Vansant writes, that Austria "moved slowly but surely in the direction of fascism." *Against the Horizon* 16–18.

[9]"History decided after 1945 to start over from the beginning, a decision which neatly paralleled a feeling of innocence" (98).

[10]Margarete Lamb-Faffelberger attributes much of West Germany's negative reaction to *Die Ausgesperrten* to Jelinek's critique of the *Wirtschaftswunder*, commonly associated with the German postwar era. In her opinion, "literary

criticism [mirrored] a certain displeasure about the newest socially critical contribution of the promising Austrian writer, because it dealt with social relations during the postwar reconstruction, years in which Germans strongly identified themselves with their country's economic miracle." *Valie Export und Elfriede Jelinek im Spiegel der Presse: Zur Rezeption der feministischen Avantgarde Österreichs* (New York: Peter Lang, 1992) 47.

[11]Vansant includes in her discussion of postwar Austrian politics the Socialist Party's efforts in the 1950s to improve relations with the Catholic church and thereby strengthen support among Catholic voters. She illustrates how in 1958 the Party instituted conservative policies on birth control, thus avoiding the controversial issues of family planning and abortion and highlighting the social significance of the family. Vansant adds that, "although the Socialists recognized the social and economic necessity of the work of women outside the home, housework was still considered the woman's responsibility." *Against the Horizon* 22–23.

[12]Fiddler, *Rewriting Reality* 90.

[13]Fiddler, *Rewriting Reality* 90. Fiddler proposes in her article "Demythologizing the Austrian Heimat: Elfriede Jelinek as 'Nestbeschmutzer,'" that this and other of Jelinek's novels also disrupt the commonly-held notion of the Austrian people as "peace-loving, simple, sociable and carefree," offering in its place images of stifling and oppressive political, social, and economic relations. *From High Priests to Desecrators: Contemporary Austrian Writers,* eds. Ricarda Schmidt and Moray McGowan (Sheffield: Sheffield Academic Press, 1993) 26.

[14]Dagmar Lorenz takes a similar view, describing the *Die Ausgesperrten* as an "iconoclastic assault on the collective's 'holy cows': disabled veterans, mother- and fatherhood, the home, love, and friendship." "Elfriede Jelinek's Political Feminism: *Die Ausgesperrten,*" *Modern Austrian Literature* 23. 3–4 (1990) 117.

[15]"[Fascism] does not begin with the first bombs that are thrown; it does not begin with the terror that one can write about in every newspaper. It begins in the relationships between people. Fascism is the first component in relations between men and women. And I have tried to say . . . that here in this society we are always at war." Ingeborg Bachmann, *Wir müssen wahre Sätze finden* (München: R. Piper & Co. Verlag, 1983) 144.

[16]Michel Foucault, *Power/Knowledge: Selected Interviews and Other Writings, 1972–77.* ed. Colin Gordon (New York: Pantheon Books, 1980) 187.

[17]Foucault, *Power/Knowledge* 99.

[18]"Power must be analyzed as something which circulates, or rather as something which only functions in the form of a chain. It is never localised here or there, never in anybody's hands, never appropriated as a commodity or piece of wealth. Power is employed and exercised through a net-like organisation.

And not only do individuals circulate between its threads; they are always in the position of simultaneously undergoing and exercising this power. They are not only its inert or consenting target; they are always also the elements of its articulation." Foucault, *Power/Knowledge* 98.

[19]Vansant, *Against the Horizon* 85.

[20]Susan Sontag, *A Susan Sontag Reader* (New York: Farrar, Straus and Giroux, 1982) 316.

[21]Alice Miller, *For Your Own Good: Hidden Cruelty in Child-rearing and the Roots of Violence*, trans. Hildegarde and Hunter Hannum (New York: The Noonday Press, 1990) 146.

[22]Sylvia Schmitz-Burgard, "Body Language as Expressions of Repression: Lethal Reverberations of War in *Die Ausgesperrten*," *Elfriede Jelinek: Framed by Language*, eds. Jorun B. Johns and Katherine Arens (Riverside, CA: Ariadne Press, 1994) 195–96.

[23]Witkowski can be seen to carry on the tradition of death-centered photography popularized by the Nazi army during the war. Stuart Hall underscores, for example, the connection between Hitler's SS and the "pornography of death" captured on film during the Third Reich. He notes that not only was German photographic equipment highly advanced (the first hand-held 16 mm cameras were used by Nazi troops on all fronts), but that German soldiers took endless snapshots of what became "the irrefutable evidence of genocide" — shootings, hangings, and gas chamber selections. Arguing that this pervasive use of photography by Hitler's military "partly explains why the crimes of the German army and the SS were so fully documented," Hall adds that "POWs were often found with examples of this pornography of death as souvenirs." *Introducing Fascism* (New York: Totem Books, 1994) 102.

[24]Susan Kappeler, *The Pornography of Representation* (Minneapolis: Minnesota UP, 1986) 52. Susan Suleiman, in her discussion of pornography, likewise frames these representational practices in terms of power relations. She argues that whether the images produced are violent or more subtly "erotic," the female nude is always subordinate to her viewer.

> The person whose body is displayed is generally somebody who has less power than the person who looks. . . . The person who looks and is fully clothed is definitely in a position of dominance over the person who is naked and being looked at, whether it's in a photograph or in real life or in a beautiful 16th century, priceless work of art.

Interview with Susan Suleiman, *Harvard Newsmakers*, UPI Radio Network. The above quote is taken from a tapescript of this interview which appeared in the *Harvard Gazette* October 5, 1990.

[25]Gary Day, "Looking at Women: Notes Toward a Theory of Porn," *Perspectives on Pornography: Sexuality in Film and Literature*, eds. Gary Day and Clive Bloom (New York: St. Martin's Press, 1988) 90.

[26]Elisabeth Bronfen offers fascinating insight into the conjunction of death, art, and femininity. Using artistic renderings of the female corpse as examples, Bronfen shows how "the feminine body appears as a perfect, immaculate aesthetic form because it is a dead body, solidified into an object of art." The female cadaver presents the viewer not only the "translation of an animate body into a deanimated one," but is captivating precisely because "it is about to be cut into." *Over Her Dead Body: Death, Femininity and the Aesthetic* (New York: Routledge, 1992) 5.

[27]It is interesting to note that Witkowski defines the acts of butchery that serve to foreground his "hobby" as a form of mastery. He claims that his experiences in the SS caused him to "overcome" his inhibitions about inflicting bodily harm, and that having achieved such self-control, he was then able to let violence happen "of its own accord." Witkowski translates, in effect, a code of military discipline into an ethics of self-discipline, which he then converts into the subjugation of his wife, "frozen" into position and artificially engraved with the marks of combat.

[28]The narrator alludes a second time in this scene to Rainer's future murders, stating that "under his leadership and guidance a crime will take place, hopefully even two; that is the beginning of a life of crime." (207).

[29]Lorenz 116.

[30]Rainer's mutilation of his mother and sister's bodies mirrors Herr Witkowski's earlier raids on Polish villages, during which the officer's company waded "up to the ankles of our riding boots in blood" (17). Klaus Theweleit has documented similar instances of brutality in his book *Männerphantasien*. In this study of the German Freikorps, Theweleit notes how assaults were carried out on women primarily through the use of boots, rifle butts and bullets. "Bare-handed attacks," he writes, "almost never happen." While both Rainer and his father wish to penetrate their female victims — initiating through violence a perverse sense of closeness — this savage contact is made, as practiced by their Freikorps counterparts, without any sort of bodily contamination (reflected on a representational level by Witkowski's camera). As Theweleit writes, the woman must be kept always "at arm's length." One can likewise read in the murderous acts of Rainer and his father a union of the sexually debased female form with the reduction of her body to, in Theweleit's words, "a shapeless, bloody mass." Just as Herr Witkowski found erotic satisfaction in the "mountains" of naked female bodies (102) strewn across the Polish landscape, Rainer converts the pornographic photographs of his mother, as well as his visualization of Anna's lovemaking, into the actual an-

nihilation of their bodies. *Male Fantasies,* vol.1: *Women, Floods, Bodies, History,* trans. Stephen Conway (Minneapolis: Minnesota UP 1987) 192–96.

[31]As Susan Sontag suggests, the power of Hitler's elite military community (which she describes as "the most perfect incarnation of fascism") resided in its combination of brutality and aesthetics. The SS, she writes, was to be "not only supremely violent but supremely beautiful." Susan Sontag, "Fascinating Fascism," *A Susan Sontag Reader* (New York: Farrar, Straus and Giroux, 1982) 371.

[32]Michel Foucault concludes in his analysis of disciplinary coercion that the military's primary function — whether sanctioned by Frederick II or Adolf Hitler — consistently has been to increase the body's utility by regulating its most minute movements and gestures. *Discipline and Punish: The Birth of the Prison* (New York: Vintage Press, 1979) 136–38.

[33]Miller applies the term "poisonous pedagogy" to child-rearing practices that impart false information and beliefs, as well as to those that seek to obtain mastery over the child through the use of threats, isolation, ridicule, and the withdrawal of love. For further elucidation of Miller's theory see *For Your Own Good* 58–63.

[34]Miller 146.

[35]Fiddler, *Rewriting Reality* 3.

[36]Much has been made of the author's own troubled relationship with her mother, which, in the eyes of many critics, forms the background for Jelinek's negative maternal figures. Sigrid Löffler stresses, for example, attempts by the writer's mother to reinforce in her daughter a sense of superiority, writing that Elfriede Jelinek "was raised with an awareness of her exceptional talent and exclusivity, and was convinced of the value and uniqueness of her own perceptions." An intense pressure to excel, as well as the death of Jelinek's father in an insane asylum, led to the author's nervous breakdown at the age of eighteen. It was Jelinek's mother who nursed her back to health during this period, refusing to let her daughter out of her sight even after Elfriede was well enough to venture out alone. Löffler writes: "Accompanied by her mother, [Jelinek] finally ventured out of her terraced house on the edge of Vienna's inner city; with her mother's help she learned once again how to ride streetcars, and how to be with people." "Spezialistin für den Haß," *Die Zeit* (4. Nov. 1983).

[37]The narrator emphasizes the compulsion both Rainer and Anna feel to be the best. If, in reality, they are no more gifted or experienced than others, still they must "pretend" (153).

[38]Elfriede Jelinek, interview with Riki Winter, *Elfriede Jelinek,* ed. Kurt Bartsch and Günther Höfler (Vienna and Graz: Literaturverlag Droschl, 1991) 15. Simone de Beauvoir makes a similar observation in the late 1940s,

writing in her seminal work *The Second Sex* that "the pleasure of feeling absolutely superior — which men feel in regard to women — can be enjoyed by woman only in regard to her children, especially her daughters." De Beauvoir likewise characterizes the mother's "masochistic devotion" to her children, the compensation for her own emptiness, as a form of domination. *The Second Sex* [1949], trans. H. M. Parshley (New York: Vintage Books, 1989) 514–19.

[39]Elfriede Jelinek, "Wahrscheinlich wäre ich ein Lustmörder," interview with Georg Biron, *Die Zeit* (29. September 1984) 47.

[40]The narrator makes a point of saying that, because she is a girl, Anna, the "Lieblingskind," receives special treatment from her mother. Rainer, by contrast, "is more his father's child" (22).

[41]The twins' out of body experiences, their ability to hover over the scene of their own abuse, is strikingly similar to the "constriction" experienced by trauma survivors, who report watching their suffering from a safe and elevated distance. Judith Herman, *Trauma and Recovery: The Aftermath of Violence — From Domestic Abuse to Political Terror* (New York: Basic Books, 1992) 42–47.

[42]Irene Diamond and Lee Quinby, introduction, *Feminism and Foucault: Reflections on Resistance*, ed. Irene Diamond and Lee Quinby (Boston: Northeastern UP, 1988) x.

[43]Alan Sheridan, *Michel Foucault: The Will to Truth* (New York: Tavistock Publications, 1980) 217.

[44]Michel Foucault, interview with J. J. Bouchier, quoted in Sheridan 217.

[45]Foucault, *Power/Knowledge* 39.

[46]Rainer's narcissism is again exposed when he learns of Hans' attempts to improve himself through reading: "Rainer says that Hans should not read; he should just listen to him, Rainer. *He* is the intellectual, not Hans . . . Defend your own little world, Hans. Don't try to be more than you are, because there is already someone here who is better than you: Me." (68).

[47]This scene, which takes place during Rainer and his father's drive in the country (148), once again illustrates the convergence of sexuality and violence in Jelinek's novel. Herr Witkowski's hand, now occupied with the production of sexual gratification, is described as the same hand that, with similar agility, murdered hundreds of his wartime enemies.

[48]Rainer's summation of man's physical properties — "Flesh doesn't take long to stink once it's been killed and left out in the fresh air" (181) — equates human mortality with that of animals; in this case those recently slaughtered. The young Witkowski's words also conjure up images of his father's victims, murdered and left behind to rot.

[49]Elfriede Jelinek, interview with Josef-Hermann Sauter, *Weimarer Beiträge* 6 (1981) 109.

[50]Lorenz 113.

[51]Rainer finds his sister's behavior "revolutionär" (55).

[52]Hoffmeister 117. Although Elfriede Jelinek refers to the familial environment of her childhood as one of "schizophrenic relationships," she takes issue with those critics who claim that her traumatic upbringing has negatively affected both her psychological stability and her artistic talent. (Perhaps the most caustic of such criticisms comes from Brigitte Lehmann, who describes Jelinek's depiction of society as "nobly neurotic, narcissistic, egocentric [and] depressive." "Oh Kälte, oh Schutz vor ihr: Ein Gespräch mit Elfriede Jelinek," *Lesezirkel* 15, 1985). The author has, in fact, been very candid about her difficult family history, but in contrast to many critics, feels these experiences have increased her depth and sensitivity as a writer. In Jelinek's opinion, "such chaotic relationships in one's childhood [make] people productive. . . . There can be very successful people who come from harmonious backgrounds, but they will not be artists." Interview with Donna Hoffmeister 109.

[53]While Georg Schmid concedes that Anna's silences often fall under the category of "Sprachraub" (robbed of speech), whereby speech is superceded by "rage, disgust, horror and hopelessness," he likewise sees in Anna's silences a form of resistance and in her repeated vomiting a refusal to propagate the repressive ideologies of her time. In his words, Anna's purges are "still better than the suggested regurgitation of stereotypes." Georg Schmid, "Das Schwerverbrechen der Fünfzigerjahre," *Gegen den schönen Schein: Texte zu Elfriede Jelinek*, ed. Christa Gurtler (Frankfurt: Verlag Neue Kritik, 1990) 44–45.

[54]Lorenz 113.

[55]In the case of the clothes salesman from Linz, Anna "bites, scratches and slaps" the head of her victim and then (based on her reading of Bataille) takes revenge on his penis: "at least [I should] damage it, so that he can't use it for a while" (211–12).

[56]Anna's behavior during these episodes is in many ways comparable to that of the now famous "Christiana F." of Berlin, whose physical abuse at the hands of her father led to her to recreate this exploitation by provoking other men — teachers, boyfriends, and police officers — into becoming the sexually-abusive or punitive authority figure she so often experienced at home. In her discussion of this case, Alice Miller explains that although Christiana initially relegated her fundamental hatred for her father to her unconscious, "directing her hostility against surrogate male authority figures," her rage is later "turned against herself in the form of addiction." With notable parallels to Jelinek's Anna, Christiana "does to herself what her father had done to her earlier: she systematically destroys her self-respect, . . . condemns herself to speechlessness . . . and isolation, and in the end ruins body as well as soul." Miller 113.

[57]Miller 241.

[58]Michael Zeller, "Haß auf den Nazi-Vater," *Frankfurter Allgemeine Zeitung* (4. Juni 1980).

[59]Lorenz 112–13.

[60]Lorenz 114. In Lorenz's opinion, Frau Sepp's Marxist class-consciousness, sustained in the face of a worker's movement that is no longer politically viable, reflects Elfriede Jelinek's "own ideological predicament." Lorenz describes Austria's Communist Party, of which Jelinek is a member, as an "anachronism on the political scene," and considers Frau Sepp's illusory political designs a reflection of the author's loss of faith in existing socialist societies. Jelinek has expressed her disenchantment with socialist politics in numerous interviews, such as the following statement to Georg Biron: "Although I am a Marxist, I cannot muster a sense of revolutionary optimism. I don't believe in the historically formed power of the working class. For that reason I seem suspect, even to many of my friends." "Wahrscheinlich wäre ich ein Lustmörder" 47.

[61]Frau Sepp's denunciation of Austria's *Kleinbürger* as the class which "cheered Hitler the loudest" echoes Elfriede Jelinek's own comments in the epigraph to this chapter, in which the author characterizes her country's petit-bourgeoisie as the sector most responsible for fascism.

[62]Jelinek, interview with Riki Winter 12–13.

[63]Hiltrud Gnüg, "Zum Schaden den Spott," *Neue Zürcher Zeitung* (21. Aug. 1980).

[64]Lorenz 114.

[65]In defining the behavior of Anna and Rainer in *Die Ausgesperrten* as "analogues of power born of impotence," locating in the siblings' artistic, criminal, and sado-masochistic pursuits an attempt at freedom outside the established order, Frank Young highlights an issue central to Jelinek's depiction of postwar Austrian society. "Elfriede Jelinek — Profile of an Austrian Feminist," *Continental, Latin-American and Francophone Women Writers: Selected Papers from the Wichita State University Conference on Foreign Literature, 1984–1985*, eds. Eunice Myers and Ginette Adamson (London: UP of America, 1987) 102.

[66]Miller 265.

[67]Zeller, "Haß auf den Nazi-Vater."

[68]Schmid 52–53.

[69]Jelinek, interview with Donna Hoffmeister 115.

[70]Hoffmeister 97.

[71]Jelinek, interview with Donna Hoffmeister 114–15.

[72]Fiddler, *Rewriting Reality* 93.

[73]Hoffmeister 97.

[74]Lorenz 116.

[75]Heinz Sichrovsky, "Die Ausgesperrten," *Arbeiter Zeitung* (17 Nov. 1979) 8–9.

[76]Jelinek, interview with Donna Hoffmeister 107. Jelinek explains in her interview with Sigrid Berka that she became aware of the documentary literature on Wunderer just prior to her completion of the novel, and that she then incorporated some of this information into her description of Rainer's murders. The teenagers' participation in a gang, Jelinek adds, was her own invention. "Ein Gespräch mit Elfriede Jelinek," *Modern Austrian Literature* 24.2 (1993) 147–48.

[77]Fiddler, *Rewriting Reality* 97.

[78]Jelinek, interview with Georg Biron 47.

[79]Jelinek, interview with Riki Winter 15.

[80]Jelinek, interview with Georg Biron 47. Jelinek elaborates further upon this concept of "super-realism" in her statements to Josef-Hermann Sauter: "In my opinion, it is legitimate for an author to depict negative circumstances, and to use the exaggeration of negativity to awaken spontaneous emotions that lead to insight: this is horrible, this must be changed, such brutality must not be allowed to continue." *Weimarer Beiträge* 115.

[81]Quoted in Tobe Levin, "Introducing Elfriede Jelinek: Double Agent of Feminist Aesthetics," *Women's Studies International Forum* 9. 4 (1986) 438.

[82]Herman 4.

[83]Elfriede Jelinek states in her interview with Georg Biron that, of all her novels, *Die Ausgesperrten* sold the fewest copies. "Wahrscheinlich wäre ich ein Lüstmörder" 48.

[84]Levin 436.

[85]Fiddler, *Rewriting Reality* 27. Fiddler notes that the vehement attacks levied against Elfriede Jelinek are not limited to those of professional journalists. "Ordinary members of the public," she writes, "have expressed their disgust at this 'distasteful' author in letters to newspapers and magazines." She concludes further in her article "Demythologizing the Austrian 'Heimat'" that it was not the author's focus on such issues as femininist pornography and female masochism that instigated public criticism of her works. In Fiddler's opinion, Jelinek's notoriety is primarily the result of her "bold deprecation of her own mother country." *From High Priests to Desecrators* 25.

[86]Lamb-Faffelberger 192.

[87]Hoffmeister 111.

[88]Münchner Literaturarbeitskreis, "Gespräch mit Elfriede Jelinek," *mamas pfirsiche — frauen und literatur*, 9–10 (1978) 181.

[89]Gnüg, "Zum Schaden den Spott."

[90]Hoffmeister 108.

[91]Münchner Literaturarbeitskreis, "Gespräch mit Elfriede Jelinek" 179–80.

[92]As Jelinek states in her interview with Margarete Lamb-Faffelberger: "I don't believe that what I feel is hatred. It is simply very exaggerated, excessively satirical analysis. I would say that 'Haßgesang' applies more to Thomas Bernhard than it does to me, because I actually take sides in my texts, quite passionately in fact, which no one seems to notice." *Valie Export und Elfriede Jelinek im Spiegel der Presse* 186.

[93]Fiddler, "Demythologizing the Austrian Heimat" 36.

[94]Herman 2–3.

Re-experiencing the Horror:
Elisabeth Reichart's *Februarschatten*

> There are many who think, "Yeah, okay. We were
> partly to blame." But they feel absolutely no connec-
> tion to what really happened. There is, so to speak, no
> historical consciousness.[1]

> This issue of guilt actually stems from the following
> questions: To what extent were individuals guilty?
> What kind of power did individuals have? How did they
> respond to this power — whether it be great or small
> — and what have been the consequences? . . . Hilde
> also understood this, even as a child; that she could
> choose, that she could decide. I am a firm believer in
> individual responsibility.[2]

ELFRIEDE JELINEK, IN A 1985 INTERVIEW, states with conviction
that Austria has largely repressed its National Socialist past. The
author admits that such denial is also evident in Germany; but she argues that Austria's tendency to see itself solely as the victim of Hitler's
regime, rather than as a country of collaborators and perpetrators,
makes an acknowledgment of personal or national culpability all the
more unlikely. The myth that Austria had been annexed to Germany in
1938 without its political consent led Austria to regard its special status
as exculpatory and fostered the belief that the Third Reich and the
Holocaust were "uniquely German" dilemmas.[3] Jelinek goes on to say
that, in contrast to present-day Germany, there are few in Austria who
are willing to challenge this misguided and self-serving view of history.
In her words, Austria remains a country where complacent, provincial
attitudes triumph, and where the truth about Austro-fascism is most
often relegated to silence.[4]

Literary scholars have noted that, in general, postwar Austrian literature reveals a similar reluctance to grapple with the issues of the
Third Reich. Unlike their counterparts in East and West Germany,
where "several generations of writers have turned their attention to the
Nazi past and the war,"[5] relatively few postwar Austrian writers have

addressed their country's role during the Hitler years or examined the social and psychological implications of Nazism in the years that followed.[6] For many, it was not until Kurt Waldheim's candidacy for president that the question of Austrian guilt became a recognized theme.[7] Despite this pervasive avoidance of the past, however, some Austrian writers have rejected their country's call to silence and have exposed through their writing both the horrors of the Third Reich and the repercussions "rippling through Austria"[8] in the wake of Austro-fascism.[9] Central to the vision of these young writers (many of whom were born after the war)[10] is the belief that Austrians were not simply the victims of Hitlerian aggression, but rather were facilitators of Nazi criminality through widespread participation and compliance. With these writers came a "sustained and vigorous investigation of Austrian complicity" comparable to the literary efforts of West Germans.[11] Perhaps not surprisingly, their work has met with suspicion and derision, and has led to charges that these younger writers "soil the nest"[12] of their own homeland. For those authors intent on unmasking Austria's past, such polemics can only be regarded as proof that there is something to hide.[13]

With the publication of her first novel *Februarschatten* (February Shadows)[14] in 1984, Elisabeth Reichart entered Austria's literary scene as a novelist committed to examining Austria's complicity in National Socialism. Like others of her generation, Reichart contends that Austria has failed in its obligation to own up to the past and attributes her decision to write about the Nazi era to "a sense of personal responsibility and duty."[15] Central to this feeling of personal and professional obligation is a desire to end Austria's collective amnesia. Reichart openly rejects her country's "so-called victim status," and defines her work as a necessary disruption of the "absolute silence that reigned over Austria's crimes."[16] In addition to this ethical motivation, Reichart shares with other writers of her generation a need to examine her own individual identity against the backdrop of her national history.[17] Just as an understanding of the past is crucial for an assessment of the present,[18] so too must the attitudes and behavior of former generations be seen to shape Austria's postwar youth. Reichart has stated that her investigation of her country's secrets exposes the experiences and values into which she was born and from which she can never fully escape. In this sense, Reichart concludes, "my writing is always tied to my biography."[19]

In keeping with this vision of historical responsibility and personal examination, Reichart chose as the basis for her first novel an event that occurred "within playing distance" of her Upper Austrian village of

Steyregg.[20] Although the author had lived for years in Austria's Mill District, it was not until she reached adulthood that her grandmother revealed its bloody history. On February 2, 1945, Reichart learned, local citizens hunted down and murdered almost 500 escaped Russian prisoners from the nearby concentration camp in Mauthausen. The prisoners were killed with whatever instruments the villagers could find — threshers, garden tools, knives, hay forks. The participants were both men and women, young and old. And as history would bear out, few members of the rural community chose to intervene. Those who helped the Russian fugitives "were the rare exceptions in an overall pattern of timidity, fear and frenzied brutality."[21] The massacre would come to be known as the "Mühlviertler Hasenjagd" (Mill District Rabbit Hunt), a name that implies a macabre sporting event "which some, at least, seemed to have enjoyed."[22]

Reichart attributes her impetus for writing *Februarschatten* to her painful yet belated awareness of this event. Her discovery of the Mühlviertel manhunt solidified her commitment to breaking Austria's silence. Referring to her grandmother's story as a "Schockerlebnis" (moment of shock), the author considers it the starting point for her resistance, through literature, to all forms of repression and forgetting.[23] Equally important was Reichart's need to understand how people from her own region of Austria, ordinary citizens far removed from mainstream politics,[24] could so easily have become criminals. She explains:

> The "Rabbit Hunt" occurred in the region where I grew up. Those who participated in it were people I could have met on the street. When I learned of the event — at the time I was no longer a child — I wanted to know what kind of people those were, people who attacked other defenseless persons with pitchforks.[25]

Reichart's shock over the actions of unpolitical Austrian civilians[26] and her frustration over the silence which shrouded their crimes in mystery led her to examine the murderous events of February 2, 1945 through the eyes of a fictional Austrian woman who experienced the massacre firsthand. The author's choice of a female protagonist is instructive. In rejecting her country's claim to victimhood, Reichart likewise rejects the notion that Austrian women were simply bystanders to the events taking place around them. *Februarschatten* reveals that the lure of National Socialism enticed Austrians young and old, men and women, and depicts the crimes committed during Hitler's Reich not as the inevitable outcome of a totalitarian regime, but as actions originating in moments of individual choice. Despite Hitler's glorification of traditional "feminine" virtues and historians' attempts to present women as the "timeless backdrop against which Nazi men made history,"[27] *Februar-schatten* suggests that the experiences of women resist such easy categorization. Reichart's novel parallels more recent claims that women both supported and resisted National Socialism and were the victims of Nazi aggression as well as the perpetrators of Nazi violence. *Februarschatten* serves, in effect, as a literary reminder that "women, no less than men, destroyed ethical vision, debased humane traditions, and rendered decent people helpless."[28]

Central to Reichart's project in the novel is not only how her female protagonist took part in the Mill District manhunt but why. The author states in several interviews that her primary interest in history involves its effect on everyday individuals, especially women.[29] According to Reichart, society has long neglected the experiences of women during wartime. She considers it her goal to give voice to the women "whose stories have largely been excluded from public dialogue."[30] In writing of history as lived and experienced by women, Reichart makes clear that women, like men, are products of the society in which they live and gives special attention to the ways in which political and social forces shape women's "thought, language, expectations, roles, and interpersonal relationships."[31] *Februarschatten* depicts a landscape where personal, familial, and national concerns are inextricably intertwined and highlights the narrator's struggle between the societal dictates of her time and her own desire for self-determination. Similarly, the novel juxtaposes the narrator's personal and political allegiances with the culturally endorsed atmosphere of coercion and conformity that surrounds her, an atmosphere which ultimately gives way to hatred, persecution, and violence.[32]

Hilde, the narrator-protagonist of *Februarschatten*, is a woman embroiled in a psychic crisis. Her childhood spent under National Socialism has shattered her sense of security and self-esteem and has placed her in a world she no longer trusts. Hilde exhibits the behavior of a trauma survivor. Despite the many years which separate her from her youth, she remains haunted by events from the past, events which have destroyed her "fundamental assumptions about the safety of the world [and] the positive value of the self."[33] Hilde is likewise convinced she is alone in her suffering. No one, she feels, can understand her anguish, her depression, and her rage. For decades, she has lived a life in the company of others but has remained painfully alone.

The negative psychological impact of Hilde's childhood experiences is compounded by the fact that she is incapable of communicating these experiences to others. The atrocities she witnessed as a young girl are so horrific, so overwhelming, that her only means of psychic survival is to deny all memories of the event; in effect, to pretend the devastation never occurred.[34] Hilde's denial of the past can be viewed as a lifesaving defense, an attempt at self-protection without which she would be too paralyzed to go on living. At the same time, it is this very dismissal of the past, and the resulting absence of her testimony, that blocks the healing of Hilde's wounds — a recovery predicated upon the acknowledgment of personal responsibility. Judith Herman, in her analysis of trauma and its manifestations, highlights this "unspeakable" aspect of traumatic events and underscores the paradoxical necessity of truth-telling for the healing process.

> The conflict between the will to deny horrible events and the will to proclaim them aloud is the central dialectic of psychological trauma. People who have survived atrocities often tell their stories in a highly emotional, contradictory, and fragmented manner which undermines their credibility and thereby serves the twin imperatives of truth-telling and secrecy. When the truth is finally recognized, survivors can begin their recovery. But far too often secrecy prevails, and the story of the traumatic event surfaces not as a verbal narrative but as a symptom.[35]

In Reichart's *Februarschatten*, this struggle between truth-telling and secrecy, revelation and silence, is complicated by the narrator's conviction that she is at once a victim of cruel and unjust circumstances and an agent of injustices perpetrated against others. Hilde is from the opening pages of the novel a woman consumed with guilt. Her repeated references to this ubiquitous and poisonous *Schuld* suggest a deep sense of shame regarding her earlier fascination with National Socialism, a fascination which would lead her to betray her brother Hannes. But Hilde also feels that she is the one betrayed. Beginning with her experiences under Nazism, Hilde has come to view life as a series of betrayals — by her parents, her country, her husband, and now her daughter. Hilde's tortured *Weltanschauung* is a worldview shaped by self-loathing, anger, paranoia, and distrust, and compels her simultaneously toward confession and concealment. On the one hand, she craves giving voice to her decades-old story of confusion, guilt, and complicity. On the other, she harbors an obstinate desire for self-protection and revenge. What the reader discovers in the course of Reichart's narrative is that, victim or perpetrator, all barriers to truth-telling must ultimately be overcome. As Judith Herman reminds us, the reality of the traumatic event does not simply disappear. It will either be shaped into language as a public, healing narrative or will erupt in private night-mares of what has been left unexpressed.

Terry Eagleton points out that in many literary texts, what is not said can be as instructive as what is. These "subtexts," Eagleton proposes, elucidate the intriguing "blindnesses" of a text, and encourage the reader to ponder what the work "does not say and *how* it does not say it." In his view, "what seems absent, marginal, or ambivalent about it may provide a central clue to its meanings."[36] Eagleton attributes these gaps and evasions to unconscious processes at work in the mind of the author. But his insights apply also to the silences of the fictional char-acters themselves. The oppositional forces of silence and narration in *Februarschatten* can perhaps best be understood in terms of a complex ambiguity between language and its absence. As Ernestine Schlant has observed, linguistic expression is no guarantor of a complete and un-adulterated truth. Just as "silence is constituted by the absence of words," and hides unspoken assumptions or ideologies, so too can lan-guage become the "cover and cover-up for a silence that . . . becomes audible only through words."[37] The fact that neither language nor si-lence is always what it seems is further amplified by the operation of two distinct kinds of silence. The first results from too much knowl-edge; the second from a refusal to become aware. It is this second si-lence, Schlant proposes, that allows the repression of memory and guilt.[38]

The secrets unveiled in *Februarschatten*, articulated almost exclu-sively through Hilde's inner monologue, represent a complicated and often confusing combination of factual details, truthful confessions, defensive denials, self-imposed silences, willful distortions, and inade-quate recall. The halting, breathless sentences of Reichart's narrative mirror the difficulties embedded in Hilde's efforts to both bear witness to her trauma and to hide it from private and public awareness. It has been suggested that Hilde's broken sentences expose her "reluctance to remember and the pain remembering causes her."[39]

At the same time, these compulsive, fragmented utterances — in both form and content — provide clues concerning Hilde's past and present experiences and eventually serve to reveal the inextricable bond between them. Christa Wolf, in her afterword to *Februarschatten*, as-serts quite rightly that the reader is made a participant in this conflict between language, truth-telling, and silence. Writing from Drispeth in 1984, Wolf recounts how Reichart's *Februarschatten* "gripped my at-tention," and yet confesses that reading the novel "was a commitment that required much effort. "I felt," Wolf writes, "as if I were partici-

pating in an excavation project." According to Wolf, the reader participates "in the convulsions of a woman who needs to cough up something terrible." And, like Hilde, what she eventually discovers is
"terrifying."[40]

Reichart's depiction of Hilde's youth and adulthood reveal that her
crisis of language is nothing new. As the novel opens, Hilde recalls the
death of her husband Anton and the sudden imposition of a future devoid of male strength and authority. Tellingly, Hilde's reaction to
Anton's death is described not simply as an emotional dilemma, but as
a linguistic one. Hilde feels it is her "duty" to hear the nurse's pronouncement that her husband is dead, and she resents the quiet, self-
composed voice that delivers the news. "This matter-of-fact calmness,"
Hilde insists, "had nothing to do with the word. This word demanded
screams. It demanded rage" (5). Hilde does not scream. Nor does she
cry. The narrator's inhibitions regarding the expression of her grief
hints at the paralysis, both emotional and linguistic, that grips her in
the wake of Anton's death. For Hilde, the loss of Anton signals the loss
of her own identity. Convinced by her in-laws that she is "nothing
without Anton," Hilde desperately attempts to resuscitate Anton's
presence by addressing him in her thoughts, recalling their years as
husband and wife, and faithfully visiting his grave. Hilde views her marriage to Anton as her salvation. She refers to her husband as her
Maßstab (standard) and as the "big strong man"(86) on whom she
pinned her hopes. Hilde likewise credits Anton with her rescue from an
abusive, impoverished family, as well as for her escape from the suffocating, provincial town of her youth. What Hilde cannot bring herself
to say, and what emerges as the actual "subtext" of her marriage, is that
this long-awaited liberation would soon become a prison.

There is considerable irony in the fact that Anton's most beloved
feature is his voice. Hilde greatly admires its soft, gentle quality and
contrasts it favorably to the overbearing and shrill "victors' voices" (13)
that dominated the Austria of her youth. Anton's voice will, however,
prove victorious over Hilde's. Because of her husband's soft-
spokenness, Hilde finds it difficult, if not impossible, to "accommodate
one's own voice to his."

> I practiced speaking softly.
> You had enough to worry about.
> My voice should not be an additional burden. (15)

> She had finally learned to be quiet.
> She had learned it for Anton. (23)

Hilde's fear that she has inherited the "loud words" of her family, combined with her gratitude towards Anton for taking her away, leads her to assume a marital identity based upon subservience, self-abnegation, and silence. Fearful that she will fall out of favor, Hilde continually cooks new meals for Anton, keeps their home spotless, tends the garden with ever greater diligence, and nurses him when he is sick. Despite Anton's gentleness, he subtly colludes in his wife's self-denial and self-censorship. He scrutinizes her behavior at social events, supervises her consumption of wine, and abruptly falls into silence whenever she enters the room. Hilde accepts this lonely lifestyle without questioning. Anton's education and social status provide her with the public recognition and respect she lacked as a child; his reliance upon her domesticity makes her feel needed. In sum, Hilde "seeks to compensate for her negative self-image through identification with patriarchal authority" and is easily convinced that "her own self-effacement was not too great a sacrifice."[41]

Hilde's conscious suppression of her voice, and her almost total submission to Anton's authority, not only nullifies her desires and aspirations, but thwarts her ability to speak about the past. Although Hilde overhears Anton's discussions with their daughter regarding the war, she does not take part in them. She leaves all answers to her husband. It is apparent from Anton's responses to Erika's inquiries that neither his social stature nor his uncontested access to language compels him to tell the truth. Anton's statements are evasive, even false. There is no mention of his attendance at *Hitlerjugend* rallies, nor of his tour of active duty. His one defense against being a Nazi is his current membership in Austria's Socialist Party. Faced with Erika's unrelenting questions, Anton's rhetoric proves both empty and ineffectual. And, much to Hilde's surprise, her husband ultimately looks ridiculous.

> The past pushed its way into the present again through the questions of their daughter. Having repressed everything made no difference. The father's wrinkled brow made no difference. Presenting the years as harmless made no difference. Between the wrinkles and the claims of innocence the daughter's questions crept in. Erika's questions. . . . That was the only time that the daughter had laughed at the father. (21–22)

With Anton's death, Hilde is robbed of her husband's "shield of authority," the protective presence that sheltered her from the loneliness and poverty of her youth. She has no visitors from the local community. She receives no social invitations. In the words of one critic, Hilde "has to give up her borrowed identity and immediately falls back into isolation, inferiority, and vulnerability, falls back into the past where the February shadows have been lurking."[42] Just as importantly, Anton's death forces Hilde to abdicate her role as passive and silent partner. She can no longer rely on Anton to evade Erika's interrogations and is forced into a reckoning with the past that demands she bear witness.

Despite Hilde's unwillingness to blame her husband for her silence, her fragmented and halting reflections reveal that Anton was, in fact, an obstacle to her vital act of testimony. The reader learns that Anton's patriarchal presence was also instrumental in the development of their daughter Erika. According to Hilde, her husband wanted a son and foisted upon Erika a masculine identity "as if [his] wish had been fulfilled" (29). Erika is forced to play games that girls do not play. She wears pants while the other girls wear dresses. And, always obedient to her father's will, Erika "followed his orders" and suppressed her tears: "A boy does not cry" (33). It becomes increasingly obvious in the course of Hilde's disclosures that her husband's chauvinistic actions produce an unexpected twist. Anton's imposition of a masculine model on his daughter Erika allows her to enter territory traditionally dominated by men. It also encourages her to discard her mother's submissive, silent role. Erika is educated, inquisitive, and determined. She actively participates in Communist Party politics and voices her concerns through open protest. Erika is, in short, the antithesis of the values forced upon her mother. Her father's attempts to shape her in his own image make Erika strong, independent, and articulate. In opposition to her father's wishes, Erika will be instrumental in breaking her mother's silence. She will reject — both for herself and for Hilde — society's mandate to forget.

Hilde's return to the trauma of her youth ultimately demands that she sever herself from the life she had with Anton. Her journey with Erika to the village where she grew up is accompanied by the feeling that she is not simply remembering her childhood but reliving it. In the inn where she and Erika are staying, Hilde concludes:

> So I am still the daughter of Schalk.
> So I am still one of the people from the house.
> It doesn't exist. The time in between.
> Anton never existed.
> Only the house and the village existed.
> And I have returned. (91)

Hilde's sensation that time has stood still, that her adult years are inconsequential when compared to the past, parallels her immersion in a childhood which exposes the horrors behind her silence. Hilde's journey reveals that the traumatic events of her childhood are not contained within a single February night, but rather encompass the daily acts of violence, cruelty, and abuse endemic to an entire community. In the course of Hilde's recollections, "we become shockingly aware of the interdependence between the familial violation of Hilde's self and the institutionalized crime against innocent people in the Third Reich, the dehumanization of her *Lebenswelt* (environment) [and] the savage extinction of human beings in concentration camps like Mauthausen."[43] Significantly, what arises from Hilde's individual confrontation with the Nazi past is a picture of Austrian society that exceeds the life of one individual. "Private memories function here to warn us about the underside of civilization."[44]

The associative and disjointed images that erupt into Hilde's awareness bear witness to the renewed immediacy of her experiences as well as to the difficulty of expressing these experiences within the confines of language. Hilde has largely heeded her country's call to silence. Raised in a culture whose motto is "forget it," Hilde seeks to banish all memories of her traumatic childhood. She provides few extensive accounts of formative persons and events and frequently poses questions for which she has no answers. Hilde resists Erika's documentation of her life story and claims not to know "this woman who is dealt with in broken off sentences." For Hilde, "she is a phantom of the daughter's imagination" (74). The narrator is fearful not only of the past, but of what she has become. Hilde defends herself against her daughter's "egotistic" inquiry by convincing herself that there is really nothing to say.

> A book about my life.
> What is there to write about it?
> No one would want such a sad life placed before his eyes.
> Everyone would want to forget such a sad life. . . .
> Hilde preferred to read stories about people who had actually
>   experienced something. (27)

Hilde resents Erika's unfettered access to language. Unlike Hilde, who learned as a young girl to keep silent, Erika "never stops asking questions"[45] and has the luxury of putting her thoughts down on paper. Hilde resists her daughter's inquiry and keeps most of her experiences and observations safely hidden behind a wall of silence. At the same time, the compulsive, torrential nature of her inner monologue annuls her contention that her life is not worth retelling. The problem, we discover, is not that Hilde's memories should be suppressed, but that she does not feel entitled or empowered to express them. Judith Herman maintains that trauma is rarely met by silence alone; she insists that all attempts to disavow overwhelming events are joined by an urge to "proclaim them aloud."[46] Hilde's memories, rendered in the form of truncated and jumbled sentences, confirm both the intensity of her pain and the gradual dismantlement of denial through the powerful reclamation of language.

Hilde's troubled relationship to language precedes the critical date of February 2, 1945. The deprivations of her childhood (an alcoholic father, an emotionally distant mother, a poverty-stricken neighborhood), together with the contempt Hilde receives from more affluent villagers, convince her that she exists on the margins of a society that has rejected her. Hilde's repeated use of such words and phrases as *ausgeschlossen* (excluded), *im Stich gelassen* (abandoned), and *übersehen* (overlooked) point to a childhood spent in isolation, a childhood where both resentment and desire remained fundamentally unverbalized.[47] Hilde's exclusion from positive forms of discourse is absolute. She is forbidden to go to dances and speak with boys her own age. She is sent by her father to beg for cider "in a voice made small" (66). She is beaten for expressing her love of nursing, and fends off her father's blows with "her head pulled in" (72). The severity of Hilde's alienation from language is perhaps most powerfully exposed in her account of the invading Russian army.[48] Betrayed by her mother, who does nothing to protect her, Hilde silently ascends the stairs to her room. She says nothing as she passes the screaming women around her. And she utters not a word when the soldier approaches her bed. We are told that when the Russians leave "there was talking again in the house." For Hilde, however, "it remained quiet" (64).

As Hilde's story unfolds, it becomes apparent that her crippled relationship to language is not wholly attributable to her victimization. Her story begins, in fact, with a declaration of guilt. According to Hilde's inner thoughts, she has betrayed the two most important people in her life: her husband Anton and her brother Hannes. She believes that she not only let them down, but directly contributed to their deaths. This sense of culpability leaves her no peace. "*Guilty* then. *Guilty* now. . . . All the *guilt* has been in me for a long time" (6–7). In the case of Anton, Hilde situates her guilt in a lack of action. She accuses herself of passively and silently awaiting Anton's death, for failing to provide him with adequate encouragement and comfort.

> I am *guilty*.
> I left you alone.
> I went away from Hannes.
> That began earlier, much earlier.
> You were afraid of being alone.
> Your room was cold. Was white.
> White. White and cold like that February morning. (7)

The deaths of Anton and Hannes are linked for Hilde "by the common factor of her guilty behavior."[49] Just as her family neglected her, Hilde feels she has neglected those who deserved her loyalty and support. But as the mystery surrounding Hannes' death unfolds, there arises a crucial distinction between Hilde's wordless acceptance of her husband's illness and her physical and verbal agency in the case of her brother. Hilde's sudden return to February 1945 reveals that the corrupt environment of her childhood, a community permeated by poverty and violence as well as by a spirit of "*Obrigkeitsdenken* (blind trust in authority) and *Untertanengeist* (submissiveness),"[50] severely impaired both mature self-awareness and sound moral judgment. Like the citizens of her village, Hilde's actions reveal that the population's submission to authority expressed itself not only in self-abnegation, but in the creation of willing, enthusiastic agents of murderous aggression.

It is no doubt significant that Hilde's descent into the past is accompanied by a scream. Prior to this point, Hilde has no such outlet for her inner anguish. She is unable to voice her sadness regarding Anton, her resentment at her daughter's freedom, or her anger over her neighbors' self-righteousness. What Hilde makes clear, however, is that this suppression of her emotions has added to her pain. "No tears. Wanting to scream. Wanting to scream one word: No! Not being able to scream" (7). Hilde's outburst, which occurs relatively late in the novel, marks a turn from private torment toward public confession and heralds the ascendancy of truth-telling over secrecy. It is Hilde's first step along the continuum between silence and language and arises unmediated, uncensored, and unformed. Hilde's scream also signifies her guilt. She is horrified by the outcome of that fateful February night, but also by her participation in it. Hilde's testimony, her conversion of unspoken memories to speech, will serve to indict the inhabitants of her village in mass murder. At the same time, it will expose Hilde's own moral cowardice and the decisions made by individual citizens to abandon justice and compassion.

The one person who defies complicity in the murderous "Rabbit Hunt" and actively seeks to save a life is Hilde's brother Hannes. Convinced that moral responsibility touches each individual present, Hannes urges Hilde to help him hide an injured Russian escapee. Hannes passionately argues that "everyone who does nothing to stop this manhunt makes himself guilty" (104), rejecting the notion that such actions are justified on behalf of the German Reich. Hilde's confusion in the face of her brother's defiance rests in the conflict between two opposing loyalties — Germany and Hannes. In deciding her course of action, Hilde will weigh her isolation and loneliness against her inclusion in a cause that openly seeks her help. Just as importantly, she will ultimately be made to choose between speech and silence.

> Silent. Struggling.
> Between Germany and Hannes.
> Germany or Hannes. Germany or Hannes
> The *warmth* of Hannes. Or the *warmth* of Germany.
> On the way home she decided for Germany. (107)

The decision referred to in this passage is Hilde's betrayal of her brother's confidence. Although Hilde never states this explicitly, her words suggest that she discloses the whereabouts of the Russian fugitive, a decision that leads to the soldier's murder and to her brother's death by hanging. Hilde's struggle to identify the proper recipient for her secret is instructive. In seeking to answer the question "To whom should she tell it?" (107), Hilde eliminates her father because he is drunk and her mother because she ignores her. Left then with no one to tell, Hilde becomes convinced that her mother represents the maternal arms of Germany and will reward her with the recognition she so craves. The tragic irony of Hilde's action is that her desire to be needed, inseparable from her desperate desire to be heard, results in the loss of the one person with whom Hilde can openly communicate. Her relationship with Hannes is not simply one of warmth but of words. Hilde describes Hannes as "my *only* brother. Among all my brothers" (6) and recalls how as children they would spend hours "under one blanket" (54) studying and talking. The bond between brother and sister is severely weakened by Hilde's attraction to Pesendorfer's Nazi rhetoric: "Hannes was no longer her Hannes. Hannes did not understand. Pushed her away" (103). The murder of the Russian fugitive effectively terminates their companionship and solidarity. After the soldier's corpse is left lying in the courtyard, Hannes avoids Hilde altogether. He refuses to share the same bed and turns away from her in silence. Hilde's response to Hannes' anger reveals her adoption of the village's destructive yet self-protective ethos. The only words she is capable of uttering are "forget it" (110).

Upon hearing that Hannes is dead, Hilde succumbs to silence and begins her lifelong imprisonment behind the walls of secrecy and denial. Hilde's rejection of language and her concomitant turn inward is joined by her parents' retreat into forgetfulness and the absence of any discussion about their son's tragic death. This same suppression of recent events is seen among the villagers. The members of the rural community absolve themselves of guilt by wordlessly removing the blood from their houses and by quietly attending a mass for purification. "The pure Mary. The pure people. The pure village. The pure house. Everything pure" (106).[51] Hannes' death coincides with the emergence of the shadows referred to in the title. These shadows, a ubiquitous presence in Reichart's novel, symbolize Hilde's guilty conscience.[52] They relentlessly pursue her in the years following the massacre and underscore her inability to free herself from her traumatic past. It is only in speaking of her story, in voicing her role as both victim and accomplice, that Hilde begins to break free of the events that plague her. In the words of one critic, Hilde's testimony enables her to "take control of her past and possibly her present life as well."[53]

Pierre Janet has written that in order for trauma survivors to make sense of their experiences they must first accommodate the traumatic incident into their current concept of self and into the ever-emerging text of their personal life histories. The path to such integration is language, the conversion of traumatic memory into narrative memory. Traumatic memories, Janet proposes, occur sporadically as involuntary, solitary reminders of what one has suffered. Narrative memory is a social act and involves the open communication of one's suffering to others. It is only through the linguistic articulation of trauma, Janet concludes, that the survivor renews the connections essential to recovery.[54] This same necessity of private awareness and public testimony is central to Reichart's project in *Februarschatten*. Hilde does not accomplish her reckoning with the past alone. It is Erika who persuades Hilde to revisit the village of her childhood. It is Erika who asks the questions which break her mother's silence. And it is Erika who validates her mother's experience by putting her story down on paper. Erika functions, in other words, not only as the catalyst for her mother's confession, but as the necessary witness to, and receiver of, her testimony. Erika serves as her mother's companion on the journey into Hilde's tainted past and participates with her in the reliving and re-experiencing of painful events. Erika also becomes part of her mother's struggle "to go beyond the event and not be submerged and lost in it."[55] The importance of Erika's involvement in her mother's excavation and recovery is confirmed by Hilde's statement that she cannot find peace "until the shadows become her truth" (8). Erika's project requires that Hilde return, both physically and emotionally, to the site of her traumatic childhood. The completion of Erika's book signals Hilde's triumph over secrecy, denial, and the "stolid investment in her own victimisation."[56] And it begins her process of truth-telling and healing. Hilde's arduous acknowledgment of her role as both victim and accomplice is, to borrow from Shoshana Felman, a first step away "from the shock of being stricken" and exemplifies the "vital, critical necessity of moving on."[57]

In the final pages of *Februarschatten*, the traumatic events of Hilde's youth have become, literally and metaphorically, a more fully integrated chapter in her ongoing history. Her assertive, indeed aggressive, behavior at the novel's end suggests that Hilde begins to take charge not only of the past, but of the future. It is Hilde, not Erika, who initiates their departure from her childhood village, and it is Hilde who symbolically takes control by occupying the driver's seat. In the words of Juliet Wigmore, Hilde "is able to leave the past behind her from a position of strength, instead of only being manipulated by it. . . . Having thus recognized that she is responsible for her own fears, she can begin to counter them."[58] This is not to say that Hilde's self-examination and testimony are complete. Her lingering anger and resentment towards her daughter expose a continued desire to seek asylum in forgetfulness, as well as a willingness to escape full responsibility for her actions by transferring the burden or "shadows" of the past onto Erika. Hilde's emotional relief in the final moments of the novel is combined with a "malicious pleasure at the sight of her daughter's shock."[59]

> Sleep. Sleep.
> Waiting for the shadows. Waiting for the Februarschatten.
> They have caught up with me. Too many shadows for me. . . .
> The daughter is standing again in her place in front of the window.
> With her shoulders hunched forward. . . .
> "Let's leave at last!"
> The daughter's eyes.
> Shadow eyes. (113–14)

Hilde's failure to complete her private and public reckoning with the past underscores Reichart's contention that her country is in no way free from the specter of National Socialism nor from its duty to acknowledge and mourn Austria's complicity. In a 1994 interview, for example, the author charges her compatriots with a continued "absence of historical consciousness." Although many Austrians now confess that their country acted wrongly during the Hitler years, there exists, in Reichart's opinion, "no connection to reality," no acknowledgment of the concrete human costs.[60] Reichart does not limit Austria's need for awareness and responsibility to those who experienced the war firsthand. The final scene of *Februarschatten* shows Hilde and Erika together, confirming that each generation, including those born only after the war, must confront the past anew. Erika not only facilitates and accompanies Hilde's disclosures, she also bears the burden of her story.

In making the contents of Hilde's personal life public, Elisabeth Reichart challenges the prevalent exclusion of women from historical accounts of war. Her commitment to documenting women's experiences during the Third Reich thematizes the ways in which women both supported and resisted National Socialism and exposes the political and societal mechanisms that shaped and guided their choices. The testimony enacted in *Februarschatten* operates, therefore, on two levels: within the world of the fiction and in society at large. In uncovering her complicity in her village's crimes and in re-examining her own status as victim, Hilde bears witness to the bloody events of February 1945 and "acknowledges her own part in creating her present situation."[61] Just as importantly, Reichart gives voice to the unspoken traumas of women in general and bears witness to those experiences — both past and present — too often shrouded in silence. Reichart's attempt in the novel to unveil her country's secrets, "to put an end to the common strategies of negation, repression, and disavowal,"[62] has little to do with reproach or blame. Her *Erinnerungsarbeit* or work of remembering sets out to show that every individual bears personal responsibility for his or her acts"[63] and seeks to understand rather than condemn. In many respects, the goal of the author and her fictional heroine become one: to end the struggle between "competing and opposing words."[64] To remember and to forget.

Notes

[1]Linda DeMeritt and Peter Ensberg, "'Für mich ist die Sprache auch ein Schatz': Interview mit Elisabeth Reichart," *Modern Austrian Literature* 29.1 (1996) 5.

[2]Elisabeth Reichart, personal commentary to *February Shadows* (9. July 1988). Quoted in Maria-Regina Kecht, "Faschistische Familienidyllen: Schatten der Vergangenheit in Henisch, Schwaiger und Reichart," *Austrian Writers and the Anschluss: Understanding the Past — Overcoming the Past*, ed. Donald G. Daviau (Riverside, CA: Ariadne Press, 1991) 336.

[3]Ernestine Schlant, *The Language of Silence: West German Literature and the Holocaust* (New York: Routledge, 1999) 5.

[4]Jacqueline Vansant, "Gespräch mit Elfriede Jelinek," *Deutsche Bücher* 15.19 (1985) 5.

[5]Juliet Wigmore, "'Vergangenheitsbewältigung' in Austria: The Personal and The Political in Erika Mitterer's *Alle Unsere Spiele* and Elisabeth Reichart's *Februarschatten*," *German Life and Letters* 44.5 (October 1991) 477.

[6]Maria-Regina Kecht, "Resisting Silence: Brigitte Schwaiger and Elisabeth Reichart Attempt to Confront the Past," in *Gender, Patriarchy and Fascism: The Response of Women Writers*, ed. Elaine Martin (Detroit: Wayne State UP, 1993) 244.

[7]For a discussion of Waldheim's bid for the Austrian Presidency and the controversy surrounding his complicity in Nazi war crimes see Robert Edwin Herzstein, *Waldheim: The Missing Years* (New York: Arbor House/William Morrow, 1988).

[8]Kecht 244.

[9]There are numerous studies by historians and literary scholars on National Socialism within a specifically Austrian context. Among the best are: Bruce Pauley, *From Prejudice to Persecution: A History of Austrian Anti-Semitism* (Chapel Hill: U of North Carolina P, 1992); Pauley, *Hitler and the Forgotten Nazis: A History of Austrian National Socialism* (Chapel Hill: U of North Carolina P, 1981); *Conquering the Past: Austrian Nazism Yesterday and Today*, ed. F. Parkinson (Detroit: Wayne State UP, 1989); *Das grosse Tabu: Österreichs Umgang mit seiner Vergangenheit*, ed. Anton Pelinka and Erika Weinzierl (Vienna: Verlag der Österreichische Staatsdruckerei) 1987.

[10]Examples of recent women writers who take up the issue of Austria's complicity in National Socialism include Marie-Thérèse Kerschbaumer, Elfriede Jelinek, Waltraud Anna Mitgutsch, and Elisabeth Reichart. Contemporary

male novelists who thematize the Nazi era in Austria are Andreas Okopenko, Franz Rieger, Peter Henish, Erick Hackl, and Gerald Szyszkowitz.

[11] Schlant 5.

[12] Allyson Fiedler, in her essay "Demythologizing the Austrian 'Heimat,'" points out that the pejorative term *Nestbeschmutzung* ("soiling the nest") is not uncommon in Austria and refers to those male and female writers who undermine the popular concept of the Austrian people as "peace-loving, simple, sociable and carefree folk, who spend their time enjoying the good things in life." Writers frequently accused of "soiling the nest" include Elfriede Jelinek, Thomas Bernhard, Wolfgang Bauer, and Peter Turrini. "Demythologizing the Austrian 'Heimat': Elfriede Jelinek as 'Nestbeschmutzer,'" *From High Priests to Desecrators: Contemporary Austrian Writers*, eds. Ricarda Schmidt and Moray McGowan (Sheffield, England: Sheffield Academic Press, 1993) 25–26.

[13] For an insightful, detailed discussion of the importance of the Nazi past for a new generation of Austrian writers see Klaus Zeyringer, *Innerlichkeit und Öffentlichkeit: Österreichische Literatur der achtziger Jahre* (Tübingen: Francke, 1992).

[14] Elisabeth Reichart, *Februarschatten*. Vienna 1984. Page references refer to the Aufbau Taschenbuch edition, Berlin 1997. All translations from the original are my own.

[15] Christiana Schwieghofer, "Wir haben uns selber betrogen: Steyregg, Wien, Tokio, und retour: Annäherung an die Dichterin Elisabeth Reichart," *Die Presse* (June 16–17, 1990). Quoted in Linda DeMeritt, "The Possibilities and Limitations of Language: Elisabeth Reichart's *Fotze*," *Out from the Shadows: Essays on Contemporary Austrian Women Writers and Filmmakers*, ed. Margarete Lamb-Faffelberger (Riverside, CA: Ariadne Press, 1997) 128.

[16] DeMeritt and Ensberg 4.

[17] Nadine Hauer, in her article "NS-Trauma und kein Ende," suggests that the social-psychological predicament of Austria's younger generations arises from the knowledge that their parents' collusion in Nazism existed under the pretense of "normality," an agreed upon agenda for social relations which, through socialization or moral cowardice, could easily be repeated. It is precisely this fear of replicating their parents' behavior, Hauer concludes, that allows the postwar "taboo" regarding the Third Reich to continue and which establishes dangerous parallels between the silence of the *Mittäter* and that of their children. Nadine Hauer, "NS-Trauma und kein Ende," *Das grosse Tabu: Österreichs Umgang mit seiner Vergangenheit*, eds. Anton Pelinka and Erika Weinzierl (Vienna: Verlag der Österreichische Staatsdruckerei, 1987) 33.

[18] Kecht 245.

[19] DeMeritt and Ensberg 7.

[20]Linda DeMeritt, "In Search of a Personal Voice," *Austria Kultur* 5.5 (1995) 1.

[21]Gordon J. Horwitz, *In the Shadow of Death: Living Outside the Gates of Mauthausen* (New York and Toronto: Free Press, 1990) 142.

[22]Jennifer E. Michaels, "Breaking the Silence: Elisabeth Reichart's Protest Against the Denial of the Nazi Past in Austria," *German Studies Review* 19.1 (1996) 15.

[23]DeMeritt and Ensberg 5–7.

[24]Donna L. Hoffmeister, "Female Consciousness and the Holocaust," commentary to *February Shadows*, trans. Donna L. Hoffmeister (Riverside, CA: Ariadne Press, 1989) 154.

[25]Roscher 131.

[26]Michaels 15.

[27]Claudia Koonz, *Mothers in the Fatherland. Women, the Family and Nazi Politics* (New York: St. Martin's Press, 1987) 3.

[28]Koonz 17.

[29]See, for example, the author's interview with Achim Roscher, "Elisabeth Reichart im Gespräch," *Neue deutsche Literatur* 35. 9 (1987) 129.

[30]DeMeritt, "The Possibilities and Limitations of Language" 128. Elisabeth Reichart's interest in women's wartime activities is already evident in her doctoral dissertation, "Heute ist morgen: Fragen an den kommunistischen organisierten Widerstand im Salzkammergut." Central to Reichart's study of the Austrian resistance are the following questions: "Where is women's history? What is women's history?" Cited in Michaels, "Breaking the Silence" 13.

[31]DeMeritt, "In Search of a Personal Voice" 2.

[32]Marianne Krumrey draws similar attention to this convergence between the personal and the historical. In her review of *February Shadows*, Krumrey writes that Elisabeth Reichart's novel "reveals the full tragedy of a human being who, although powerless, is bound to history by her guilt. . . . The goal of the novel is not to condemn. What it achieves, however, is a powerful exploration of the dialectical relationship between an individual and history." Marianne Krumrey, "Quälende Erinnerung," *Neue deutsche Literatur* 35.9 (1987) 185.

[33]Judith Herman, *Trauma and Recovery: The Aftermath of Violence from Domestic Abuse to Political Terror* (New York: Basic Books, 1992) 51.

[34]I am borrowing here from Alexander and Margarete Mitscherlich's application of Freud's distinction between denial (a defense mechanism "related to disturbing perceptions of external reality") and repression (which refers to the "unpleasure-producing perception of one's own instinctual impulses"). As

trauma necessarily entails the experience of shocking or painful events within the physical environment, it is therefore correct to speak of the survivor's psychic disavowal of such events as evidence of denial rather than of repression. Alexander and Margarete Mitscherlich, *Die Unfähigkeit zu trauern: Grundlagen kollektiven Verhaltens* (Munich: R. Pier & Co. Verlag, 1967) 39.

[35]Herman 1.

[36]Terry Eagleton, *Literary Theory: An Introduction* (Minneapolis: U of Minnesota P, 1975) 178. I am grateful to Ernestine Schlant for illuminating the applicability of Eagleton's statements for the German postwar novel.

[37]Schlant 7.

[38]Hamida Bosmajian, *Metaphors of Evil: Contemporary German Literature and the Shadow of Nazism* (Iowa City: U of Iowa P, 1979) 17.

[39]Michaels 15.

[40]Christa Wolf, "Struktur von Erinnerung," afterword to *Februarschatten*, 117.

[41]Kecht 258.

[42]Kecht 258–59.

[43]Kecht 259.

[44]Hoffmeister 154. For a provocative rethinking of the binary opposition between the individual and society, see Dominick LaCapra, *Representing the Holocaust: History, Theory, Trauma* (Ithaca: Cornell UP, 1994). LaCapra posits that the strict separation between individual and collective behavior should give way to an understanding of the confluence between personal and societal norms. In his view, "what happens to the individual may not be purely individual, for it may be bound up with larger societal, political, and cultural processes that often go unperceived." 171.

[45]Michaels 16.

[46]Herman 51. Shoshana Felman reaches a similar conclusion in her study of traumatic events, and emphasizes not only the mechanics of silence, but "the liberation of the testimony from the bondage of the secret." Shoshona Felman and Dori Laub, *Testimony: Crises of Witnessing in Literature, Psychoanalysis, and History* (New York: Routledge, Chapman and Hall, 1992) xix.

[47]Elisabeth Reichart's contention that the family is the microcosm of a hegemonic, authoritarian society is cogently expressed in her 1994 interview with Linda DeMeritt. "For me the family is for 90 to 99 percent of humanity a prison. There are certainly exceptions, but I do not know a single person who was allowed to develop their own freedom and individuality, their own thoughts and feelings. And if they had been raised that way, they would again have been forced into it." "Für mich ist die Sprache auch ein Schatz" 10.

[48]The author states in her 1987 interview with Achim Roscher that the postwar presence of Russian troops in the area of the Mühlviertel allowed local citizens to focus on the Soviet "occupation" of Austria and ignore the reasons they were there in the first place. "By the 1950s the Soviets were no longer considered liberators, but occupation forces. *Why* they were here, the people had conveniently forgotten." "Im Gespräch mit Elisabeth Reichart" 131.

[49]Wigmore, "'Vergangenheitsbewältigung' in Austria" 483.

[50]Kecht 261.

[51]Elisabeth Reichart makes a point of indicting the local priest in the villagers' murderous rampage. Echoing the work of historians and eyewitnesses, which provides convincing proof of widespread complicity among religious leaders, Reichart writes that "even the pastor had decided for Germany. Had encouraged them to continue the search. To search further. Until the last criminal had been found. Until this blemish had been washed away from the German earth. Until the German soil had been purified again" (107).

[52]Kecht 252.

[53]Wigmore, "'Vergangenheitsbewältigung' in Austria" 485.

[54]Pierre Janet, *Psychological Healing* [1919] vol.1, trans. E. Paul and C. Paul (New York: Macmillan, 1925) 663. Janet elaborates on this distinction between traumatic and narrative memory by saying that

> The person . . . must . . . know how to associate the happening with the other events of his life, how to put it in its place in that life-history which each one of us is perpetually building up and which for each of us is an essential element of his personality. A situation has not been been satisfactorily liquidated, has not been fully assimilated, until we have achieved, not merely through our movements, but also an inward reaction through the words we address to ourselves, through the organization of the recital of the event to others and to ourselves, and through the putting of this recital in its place as one of the chapters in our personal history.

[55]Felman and Laub 76. Dori Laub insists that the presence of a willing listener is essential to the process of bearing witness. According to Laub, "it is the encounter and the coming together between the survivor and the listener, which makes possible something like a repossession of the act of witnessing. This joint responsibility is the source of the reemerging truth." "An Event Without A Witness: Truth, Testimony and Survival," in *Testimony: Crises of Witnessing in Literature, Psychoanalysis, and History* 86.

[56]Hoffmeister 150.

[57]Felman and Laub 28.

[58]Wigmore, "'Vergangenheitsbewältigung' in Austria" 486.

[59]Kecht 254.

[60]DeMeritt and Ensberg 5.

[61]Juliet Wigmore, "'Auch Schweigen kann Verrat sein.' Coming to Terms with Women's History: Elisabeth Reichart's *Februarschatten* and *Komm über den See*," *From High Priests to Desecrators* 122.

[62]Kecht 246.

[63]Kecht 246.

[64]DeMeritt, "The Possibilities and Limitations of Language" 128.

Conclusion

A S RECENT EVENTS BEAR OUT, the many years that separate us from the period of National Socialism, the Second World War, and the Holocaust have done little to diminish its impact. Whether it be the much debated wreath-laying ceremony at Bitburg, the dispute among German historians concerning the uniqueness of the Holocaust, the candidacy of Kurt Waldheim for the Austrian presidency, recent commemorations of the Second World War, or the public reception of *Schindler's List*, the controversies surrounding each of these episodes has its origins in the catastrophic events of the Third Reich and are powerful testimony to a dilemma as yet unresolved.

The pervasive presence of the Third Reich within the postwar cultural sphere is perhaps nowhere more apparent than in Germany and Austria, the two countries that formed the cornerstones of Hitler's Reich. An investigation of the German and Austrian literary scene reveals that the political and academic controversies of recent years crystallize around issues long raised by the countries' major writers. As Judith Ryan reminds us, viewed from the vantage point of literary history, such debates seem "remarkably belated."[1] For over a quarter-century, German-speaking novelists have given the lie to the notion that the collapse of Nazism represented a *Stunde Null* (ground zero), the promise of a fresh start unencumbered by the sins of the past. From a variety of perspectives and through a multiplicity of techniques contemporary writers have engaged in an ongoing confrontation with the issues of complicity, guilt, and atonement. How is cultural identity to be defined after the murderous nationalism of the Third Reich? Is it meaningful to speak of collective guilt or were the crimes committed under National Socialism the product of individual acts of barbarism and acquiescence? Should writers employ the term *Vergangenheits-bewältigung* — with its implication of mastery or resolution — to describe their own projects of remembrance and mourning? And are those too young to have supported Hitler obliged to inherit the burden of earlier generations?

Contemporary novelists' focus on the family, as both the breeding ground of fascism and the site of its most profound repercussions, has produced a body of literature characterized by a rigorous engagement with the cultural legacy of the Third Reich. Despite the popularly-held view that literature offers a respite from history's harsh realities, writers from both Germany and Austria have persistently given voice to what has been silenced, repressed, or forgotten about their countries' murderous past.[2] It is their unwillingness to escape the truths of National Socialism that has subjected the dark sides of history to greater illumination. Recent literary depictions of the family during and after Hitler have in common a "personalization" of fascism. Moving beyond traditional notions of sociopolitical phenomena, contemporary writers portray fascism as a psychological and emotional experience that has profoundly affected familial relationships, as well as attitudes toward postwar parental authority. Some authors speak from the vantage point of their own childhood. Others use the present as a springboard for reflection and analysis. For each, the painful (and often submerged) content of the past is subjected to a rigorous process of remembering and finally is "brought to the surface."[3] These stories expose the denial and shame exhibited by parents complicit in the Third Reich, the anger and disappointment of sons and daughters, and the inability of the so-called *Spätgeborene* (later generations) to elude the burden of a corrupt heritage.

Dominick LaCapra, focusing on the far-reaching impact of Nazi genocide, proposes that the Holocaust exceeds the confines of history and affects "everyone who comes into contact with it: perpetrator, collaborator, bystander, resister, those born later."[4] In similar fashion, Shoshana Felman summarizes the events of the Second World War as an era which cannot be "encapsulated in the past." It is a history, she writes, "which is essentially not over," a history whose traumatic consequences "are still actively evolving."[5] What contemporary German-speaking writers have achieved is a vision of the family in which all such observations converge. By fusing the personal and the political, they offer convincing evidence that the painful history of the Third Reich is neither behind us nor outside us, and that no one can afford the luxury of remaining neutral.

Notes

[1]Judith Ryan, "Postoccupation Movements in West Germany," *Legacies and Ambiguities: Postwar Fiction and Culture in West Germany and Japan*, eds. Ernestine Schlant and J. Thomas Rimer (Baltimore and London: The Johns Hopkins UP, 1991) 204.

[2]Maria-Regina Kecht, "Faschistische Familienidyllen: Schatten der Vergangenheit in Henisch, Schwaiger und Reichart," *Austrian Writers and the Anschluss: Understanding the Past — Overcoming the Past*, ed. Donald G. Daviau (Riverside, CA: Ariadne Press, 1991) 313–15.

[3]Kecht 315.

[4]Dominick LaCapra, *History and Memory After Auschwitz* (Ithaca: Cornell UP, 1998) 9.

[5]Shoshana Felman and Dori Laub. *Testimony: Crises of Witnessing in Literature, Psychoanalysis, and History*. (New York: Routledge, Chapman and Hall, Inc., 1992) xiv.

Works Cited

Primary Texts

Bernhard, Thomas. *Auslöschung*. Frankfurt am Main: Suhrkamp Verlag, 1986.

Jelinek, Elfriede. *Die Ausgesperrten*. Reinbek bei Hamburg: Rowohlt Verlag, 1980.

Reichart, Elisabeth. *Februarschatten*. Vienna: Österreichische Staatsdruckerei, 1984.

Schneider, Peter. *Vati*. Darmstadt: Luchterhand Verlag, 1987.

Wolf, Christa. *Kindheitsmuster*. Berlin and Weimar: Aufbau Verlag, 1976.

Critical Literature

Introduction

Bahktin, Mikhail. *The Dialogic Imagination*. Trans. Caryl Emerson and Michael Holquist. Austin: U of Texas P, 1981.

Bar-On, Dan. *Legacy of Silence: Encounters with Children of the Third Reich*. Cambridge: Harvard UP, 1989.

Daemmerich, Horst and Diether Haenicke, Eds. *The Challenge of German Literature*. Detroit: Wayne State UP, 1971.

Demetz, Peter. *After the Fires: Recent Writing in the Germanies, Austria and Switzerland*. New York: Harcourt Brace Jovanovich, 1986.

———. *Postwar German Literature: A Critical Introduction*. New York: Schocken Books, 1972.

Fries, Marilyn. "Problems of Narrating the *Heimat*: Christa Wolf and Johannes Bobrowski." *Cross Currents* 9 (1990): 219–30.

Hinderer, Walter. "The Challenge of the Past: Turning Points in the Intellectual and Literary Reflections of West Germany, 1945–1985," *Legacies and Ambiguities: Postwar Fiction and Culture in West Germany and Japan.* Eds. Ernestine Schlant and J. Thomas Rimer. Baltimore: The Johns Hopkins UP, 1991: 81–98.

Kaes, Anton. *From Hitler to Heimat: The Return of History as Film.* Cambridge: Harvard UP, 1989.

Kecht, Maria-Regina. "Faschistische Familienidyllen: Schatten der Vergangenheit in Henisch, Schwaiger und Reichart." *Austrian Writers and the Anschluss: Understanding the Past — Overcoming the Past.* Ed. Donald G. Daviau. Riverside, CA: Ariadne Press, 1991: 313–37.

Mahlendorf, Ursula. "Confronting the Fascist Past and Coming to Terms with It." *World Literature Today* 55. 4 (1991): 553–650.

Ryan, Judith. "Postoccupation Literary Movements and Developments in West Germany," *Legacies and Ambiguities: Postwar Fiction and Culture in West Germany and Japan.* Eds. Ernestine Schlant and J. Thomas Rimer. Baltimore: The Johns Hopkins UP, 1991: 189–206.

———. *The Uncompleted Past: Postwar German Novels and the Third Reich.* Detroit: Wayne State UP, 1983.

Schlant, Ernestine. *The Language of Silence: West German Literature and the Holocaust.* New York: Routledge, 1999.

Schneider, Michael. *Den Kopf verkehrt aufgesetzt oder die melancholische Linke: Aspekte des Kulturzerfalls in den siebziger Jahren.* Darmstadt: Luchterhand Verlag, 1981.

Sichrovsky, Peter. *Schuldig geboren: Kinder aus Nazifamilien.* Cologne: Kiepenheuer & Witsch, 1987.

Tachibana, Reiko. *Narrative as Counter-Memory: A Half-Century of Postwar Writing in Germany and Japan.* Albany: State U of New York P, 1998.

Westernhagen, Dörte von. *Die Kinder der Täter.* Munich: Kösel, 1987.

Wolf, Christa. "Struktur von Erinnerung." Afterword to *Februarschatten.* Berlin: Aufbau Taschenbuch Verlag, 1997: 117–19.

Christa Wolf

Birmele, Jutta. "Christa Wolf: A Quest for Heimat." *Der Begriff 'Heimat' in der deutschsprachigen Literatur.* Ed. H. W. Seliger. München: iudicium verlag, 1987: 71–80.

Böll, Heinrich. "Wo habt ihr bloß gelebt?" *Christa Wolf: Materialienbuch.* Ed. Klaus Sauer. Darmstadt: Hermann Luchterhand Verlag, 1990: 7–15.

Caruth, Cathy. Introduction. *American Imago* 48.1 (1991): 1–12.

———. "Unclaimed Experience: Trauma and the Possibility of History." *Yale French Studies* 79 (1991): 181–92.

Dollenmayer, David. "Generational Patterns in Christa Wolf's *Kindheitsmuster.*" *German Life and Letters* 39 (1986): 229–34.

Foucault, Michel. *Discipline and Punish: The Birth of the Prison.* Trans. Alan Sheridan. New York: Vintage Books, 1979.

Gättens, Marie-Luise. "Language, Gender, and Fascism: Reconstructing Histories in *Three Guineas, Der Mann auf der Kanzel,* and *Kindheitsmuster.*" *Gender, Patriarchy and Fascism in the Third Reich: The Response of Women Writers.* Ed. Elaine Martin. Detroit: Wayne State UP, 1993: 32–64.

Hirsch, Marianne. *The Mother/Daughter Plot: Narrative, Psychoanalysis, Feminism.* Indianapolis: Indiana UP, 1989.

Juers, Evelyn. "Who's Afraid of Christa Wolf?" *The Cambridge Quarterly* 21 (1992): 213–21.

Kaufmann, Hans. "Subjektive Authentizität: Gespräch mit Hans Kaufmann." *Die Dimension des Autors.* Darmstadt: Hermann Luchterhand Verlag, 1987: 55–75.

Krystal, Henry. "Integration and Self-Healing in Post Traumatic States: A Ten Year Retrospective." *American Imago* 48.1 (1991): 93–118.

Lifton, Robert Jay. "Interview with Cathy Caruth." *American Imago* 48.1 (1991): 153–75.

Love, Myra. *Christa Wolf: Literature and the Conscience of History.* New York: Peter Lang Publishing, 1991.

Mahlendorf, Ursula. "Confronting the Fascist Past and Coming to Terms with It." *World Literature Today* 55 (1981): 553–650.

Martin, Elaine. "Women Right/(Re)Write the Nazi Past: An Introduction." *Gender, Patriarchy and Fascism in the Third Reich. The Response of Women Writers.* Ed. Elaine Martin. Detroit: Wayne State UP, 1993: 11–31.

Meyer-Gosau, Francke. "Culture Is What You Experience: An Interview with Christa Wolf." Trans. Jeanette Clausen. *New German Critique* 27 (1982): 89–100.

Mitscherlich, Alexander and Margarete. *Die Unfähigkeit zu trauern: Grundlagen kollektiven Verhaltens.* München: R. Piper & Co. Verlag, 1967.

———. "The Authors' Forward to the American Edition." *The Inability to Mourn.* Trans. Beverly Placzek. New York: Grove Press, 1975: xv–xxi.

Mitscherlich, Margarete. "Die Frage der Selbstdarstellung: Überlegungen zu den Autobiographien von Helene Deutsch, Margaret Mead und Christa Wolf." *Neue Rundschau 91* (1980): 291–316.

Øhrgaard, Per. "Ein Foto mit Hut: Bemerkungen zu Christa Wolf: *Kindheitsmuster.*" *Orbis Litterarum* 42 (1987): 375–87.

Pickerodt, Gerhart. "Christa Wolfs Roman *Kindheitsmuster.* Ein Beitrag zur 'Vergangenheitsbewältigung?'"*Exil: Wirkung und Wertung. Ausgewählte Beiträge zum fünften Symposium über deutsche und österreichische Exilliteratur.* Eds. Donald Daviau and Ludwig Fischer. Columbia, SC: Camden House, 1985: 293–308.

Roshnowski, Stanislaw. "Der Roman als Form des historischen Bewußtseins: *Kindheitsmuster* von Christa Wolf und *Der Aufenthalt* von Hermann Kant." *Literatur im Wandel: Entwicklungen in europäischen sozialistischen Ländern 1944/5 bis 1980.* Berlin: Aufbau Verlag, 1986: 430–47.

Ryan, Judith. *The Uncompleted Past: Postwar German Novels and the Third Reich.* Detroit: Wayne State UP, 1983.

Schneider, Michael. "Fathers and Sons, Retrospectively: The Damaged Relationship between Two Generations." Trans. Jamie Owen Daniel. *New German Critique* 31 (1983): 3–51.

Wolf, Christa. *Fortgesetzer Versuch: Aufsätze, Gespräche, Essays.* Leipzig: Reclam, 1980.

———. "Erfahrungsmuster: Diskussion zu *Kindheitsmuster.*" *Die Dimension des Autors: Essays und Aufsätze, Reden und Gespräche, 1959–1985.* Ed. Angela Drescher. Darmstadt: Hermann Luchterhand Verlag, 1987: 806–43.

———. "Lesen und Schreiben." *Die Dimension des Autors: Essays und Aufsätze, Reden und Gespräche, 1959–1985.* Ed. Angela Drescher. Darmstadt: Hermann Luchterhand Verlag, 1987: 463–503.

Thomas Bernhard

Bernhard, Thomas. *Der Stimmenimitator.* Frankfurt am Main: Suhrkamp, 1978.

———. *Die Ursache. Eine Andeutung.* Salzburg: Residenz Verl, 1975.

Craft, Robert. "Comedian of Horror." *The New York Review of Books* (27 Sept 1990): 40–48.

Dierick, A. P. "Thomas Bernhard's Austria: Neurosis, Symbol or Expedient?" *Modern Austrian Literature* 12.1 (1979): 73–93.

Dowden, Stephen. *Understanding Thomas Bernhard.* Columbia, SC: U of South Carolina P, 1991.

Fetz, Gerard. "Thomas Bernhard and the Modern Novel." *The Modern German Novel*. New York: Berg Publishers Ltd., 1987: 89–108.

Fraund, Thomas. *Bewegung, Korrektur, Utopie: Studien zum Verhältnis von Melancholie und Aesthetik im Erzählwerk Thomas Bernhards*. Frankfurt am Main: Peter Lang, 1986.

Helms-Derfert, Hermann. *Die Last der Geschichte. Interpretationen zur Prosa von Thomas Bernhard*. Vienna and Weimar: Böhlau Verlag, 1997.

Hofmann, Kurt. "Eine katholische Existenz." *Aus Gesprächen mit Thomas Bernhard*. Vienna: Löcker Verlag, 1988: 51–60.

Höller, Hans. "Menschen, Geschichte(n), Orte und Landschaften." *Antiautobiographie. Thomas Bernhard's Auslöschung*. Eds. Hans Höller and Irene Heidelberger-Leonard. Frankfurt am Main: Suhrkamp, 1995: 217–34.

Holz, Arnim. "Morgen Salzburg." *Von einer Katastrophe in die andere: 13 Gespräche mit Thomas Bernhard*. Ed. Sepp Dreissinger. Weitra: Bibliothek der Provinz, 1992: 35–48.

Honegger, Gitta. "Bernhard's Last Novel." *Partisan Review* 63 (1996) 528–31.

Jung, Werner. "Die Anstrengung des Erinnerns." *Neue Deutsche Hefte* 35.1 (1988): 96–104.

Klug, Christian. "Interaktion und Identität. Zum Motiv der Willensschwäche in Thomas Bernhard's *Auslöschung*." *Modern Austrian Literature* 23.3/4 (1990): 17–37.

Kohut, Heinz. *Narzißmus. Eine Theorie der psychoanalytischen Behandlung narzißtischer Persönlichkeitsstörungen*. Frankfurt am Main: Suhrkamp, 1976.

Konzett, Matthias. "*Publikumsbeschimpfung*: Thomas Bernhard's Provocations of the Austrian Public Sphere." *The German Quarterly* 68.3 (1995): 251–70.

Lopate, Phillip. "On Not Reading Thomas Bernhard." *Pequod: A Journal of Contemporary Literature and Literary Criticism* (1992): 72–83.

Martin, Charles. *The Nihilism of Thomas Bernhard*. Amsterdam: Rodopi, 1995.

Mittermayer, Manfred. *Thomas Bernhard*. Stuttgart and Vienna: J. B. Metzler Verlag, 1995.

Motola, Gabriel. "Thomas Bernhard's Austria." *Pequod: A Journal of Contemporary Literature and Literary Criticism* 33 (1992): 54–62.

Rambures, Jean-Louis. "Alle Menschen sind Monster, sobald sie ihren Panzer lüften." *Von einer Katastrophe in die andere. 13 Gespräche mit Thomas Bernhard.* Ed. Sepp Dreissinger. Weitra: Bibliothek der Provinz, 1992: 104–13.

Stephens, Michael. "Homage to Thomas Bernhard." *Pequod: A Journal of Contemporary Literature and Literary Criticism* 33 (1992): 84–91.

Thorpe, Kathleen. "Reading the Photograph in Thomas Bernhard's Novel *Auslöschung.*" *Modern Austrian Literature* 21. 3/4 (1988): 39–50.

Weinzierl, Ulrich. "Bernhard als Erzieher. Thomas Bernhard's *Auslöschung.*" *German Quarterly* 63 (1990): 455–61.

Peter Schneider

Adorno, Theodor. *Noten zur Literatur III.* Frankfurt am Main: Suhrkamp, 1965.

———. *Prismen: Kulturkritik und Gesellschaft.* Frankfurt am Main: Suhrkamp Verlag, 1955.

Arendt, Hannah. *Eichmann in Jerusalem: A Report on the Banality of Evil.* New York: Penguin Books, 1963.

Bar-On, Dan. *Legacy of Silence: Encounters with Children of the Third Reich.* Cambridge: Harvard UP, 1989.

Burgess, Gordon. "'Was da ist, das ist [nicht] mein': The Case of Peter Schneider." *Literature on the Threshold: The German Novel in the 1980s.* Eds. Arthur Williams, Stuart Parkes, and Roland Smith. New York: Berg Publishers, 1990: 107–21.

Byhan, Inge. "So entkam mein Vater." *Bunte Illustrierte* (June 1985): 16–33.

———. "Von Reue keine Spur." *Bunte Illustrierte* (July 1985): 108–17.

———. "Keiner fragte nach seinen Taten." *Bunte Illustrierte* (July 1985): 16–34, 108.

Hochhuth, Rolf. *Der Stellvertreter.* Reinbek bei Hamburg: Rowohlt, 1963.

Kreis, Gabriele. "Ach Vati, deine Substantive." *Konkret* 6 (1987): 66f.

Levin, Ira. *The Boys From Brazil.* New York: Dell, 1977.

Lifton, Robert Jay. *The Nazi Doctors: Medical Killing and the Psychology of Genocide.* New York: Basic Books, 1986.

Mitscherlich, Alexander and Margarete. *Die Unfähigkeit zu trauern: Grundlagen kollektiven Verhaltens.* Munich: R. Piper & Co. Verlag, 1967.

Mitscherlich, Margarete. *Erinnerungsarbeit: Zur Psychoanalyse der Unfähigkeit zu trauern.* Frankfurt: S. Fischer Verlag, 1987.

Nagel, Wolfgang. "Zu Besuch bei einem Ungeheuer." *Die Zeit* (April 1987).

Nyiszli, Miklos. *Auschwitz: A Doctor's Eyewitness Account.* Trans. Tibere Kremer and Richard Seaver. New York: Fawcett, 1960.

Posner, Gerald and John Ware. *Mengele: The Complete Story.* New York: McGraw Hill, 1986.

Riordan, Colin. Editor's Introduction. *Vati: German Texts Edition.* Manchester: Manchester UP, 1993.

———. Interview with Peter Schneider (24 June 1990). Quoted in *Vati: German Texts Edition.* Ed. Colin Riordan. Manchester: Manchester UP, 1993: 1–31.

Ryan, Judith. "Postoccupation Literary Movements and Developments in West Germany." *Legacies and Ambiguities: Postwar Fiction and Culture in West Germany and Japan.* Eds. Ernestine Schlant and J. Thomas Rimer. Baltimore: The Johns Hopkins UP, 1991: 189–206.

Schlant, Ernestine. Introduction. *Legacies and Ambiguities: Postwar Fiction and Culture in West Germany and Japan.* Eds. Ernestine Schlant and J. Thomas Rimer. Baltimore: The Johns Hopkins UP, 1991: 1–31.

Schneider, Michael. *Den Kopf verkehrt aufgesetzt oder die melancholische Linke: Aspekte des Kulturzerfalls in den siebziger Jahren.* Darmstadt: Luchterhand Verlag, 1981.

Schneider, Peter. *Deutsche Ängste: Sieben Essays.* Darmstadt: Luchterhand Verlag, 1988.

———. "Postwar German Strategies in Coming to Terms with the Past." *Legacies and Ambiguities: Postwar Fiction and Culture in West Germany and Japan.* Eds. Ernestine Schlant and J. Thomas Rimer. Baltimore: The Johns Hopkins UP, 1991: 279–88.

Schönfeld, Gerda-Marie. "So eine Nachbarschaft." *Der Spiegel* (9 March 1987): 216–19.

Sichrovsky, Peter. *Schuldig geboren: Kinder aus Nazifamilien.* Cologne: Kiepenheuer & Witsch, 1987.

Wittstock, Uwe. "Vatis Tod." *Frankfurter Allgemeine Zeitung* (11 April 1987).

Elfriede Jelinek

Bachmann, Ingeborg. *Wir müssen wahre Sätze finden.* München: R. Piper & Co. Verlag, 1983.

Bar-On, Dan. *Legacy of Silence: Encounters with Children of the Third Reich.* Cambridge: Harvard UP, 1989.

Berka, Sigrid. "Ein Gespräch mit Elfriede Jelinek." *Modern Austrian Literature* 24.2 (1993): 127–55.

Biron, Georg. "'Wahrscheinlich wäre ich ein Lustmörder': Ein Gespräch mit Elfriede Jelinek." *Die Zeit* (29 Sept. 1984).

Bronfen, Elisabeth. *Over Her Dead Body: Death, Femininity and the Aesthetic.* New York: Routledge, 1992.

Day, Gary. "Looking at Women: Notes Toward a Theory of Porn." *Perspectives on Pornography: Sexuality in Film and Literature.* Eds. Gary Day and Clive Bloom. New York: St. Martin's Press, 1988: 83–100.

de Beauvoir, Simone. *The Second Sex* [1949]. Trans. H. M. Parshley. New York: Vintage Books, 1989.

Diamond, Irene, and Lee Quinby. Introduction. *Feminism and Foucault: Reflections on Resistance.* Eds. Irene Diamond and Lee Quinby. Boston: Northeastern UP, 1988: ix–xx.

Fiddler, Allyson. "Demythologizing the Austrian 'Heimat': Elfriede Jelinek as 'Nestbeschmutzer.'" *From High Priests to Desecrators: Contemporary Austrian Writers.* Eds. Ricarda Schmidt and Moray McGowan. Sheffield: Sheffield Academic Press, 1993: 25–44.

———. *Rewriting Reality: An Introduction to Elfriede Jelinek.* Oxford: Berg Publishers Limited, 1994.

Foucault, Michel. *Discipline and Punish: The Birth of the Prison.* New York: Vintage Press, 1979.

———. *Power/Knowledge: Selected Interviews and Other Writings, 1972–77.* Ed. Colin Gordon. New York: Pantheon Books, 1980.

Gnüg, Hiltrud. "Zum Schaden den Spott." *Neue Zürcher Zeitung* (21 Aug. 1980).

Hall, Stuart. *Introducing Fascism.* New York: Totem Books, 1994.

Herman, Judith. *Trauma and Recovery: The Aftermath of Violence — From Domestic Abuse to Political Terror.* New York: Basic Books, 1992.

Hoffmeister, Donna. "Access Routes into Postmodernism: Interviews with Innerhofer, Jelinek, Rosei and Wolfgruber." *Modern Austrian Literature* 20. 2 (1987): 97–130.

Kappeler, Susan. *The Pornography of Representation.* Minneapolis: The U of Minnesota P, 1986.

Lamb-Faffelberger, Margarete. *Valie Export und Elfriede Jelinek im Spiegel der Presse: Zur Rezeption der feministischen Avantgarde Österreichs.* New York: Peter Lang, 1992.

Lehmann, Brigitte. "Oh Kälte, oh Schutz vor ihr: Ein Gespräch mit Elfriede Jelinek." *Lesezirkel* 15 (1985): 3.

Levin, Tobe. "Introducing Elfriede Jelinek: Double Agent of Feminist Aesthetics." *Women's Studies International Forum* 9. 4 (1986): 435–42.

Löffler, Sigrid. "Spezialistin für den Haß." *Die Zeit* (4 Nov. 1983).

Lorenz, Dagmar. "Elfriede Jelinek's Political Feminism: *Die Ausgesperrten.*" *Modern Austrian Literature* 23. 3/4 (1990): 111–19.

Miller, Alice. *For Your Own Good: Hidden Cruelty in Child-rearing and the Roots of Violence.* Trans. Hildegarde and Hunter Hannum. New York: The Noonday Press, 1990.

Münchner Literaturarbeitskreis "Gespräch mit Elfriede Jelinek." *mamas pfirsiche — frauen und literatur* 9–10 (1978): 171–81.

Sauter, Josef-Hermann. "Interviews mit Barbara Frischmuth, Elfriede Jelinek, Michael Scharang." *Weimarer Beiträge* 6 (1981): 99–128.

Schmid, Georg. "Das Schwerverbrechen der Fünfzigerjahre." *Gegen den schönen Schein: Texte zu Elfriede Jelinek.* Ed. Christa Gurtler. Frankfurt: Verlag Neue Kritik, 1990: 44–55.

Schmitz-Burgard, Sylvia. "Body Language as Expressions of Repression: Lethal Reverberations of War in *Die Ausgesperrten.*" *Elfriede Jelinek: Framed by Language.* Eds. Jorun B. Johns and Katherine Arens. Riverside, CA: Ariadne Press, 1994: 194–228.

Sheridan, Alan. *Michel Foucault: The Will to Truth.* New York: Tavistock Publications, 1980.

Sichrovsky, Heinz. "Die Ausgesperrten." *Arbeiter Zeitung* (17 Nov. 1979).

Sontag, Susan. "Fascinating Fascism." *A Susan Sontag Reader.* New York: Farrar, Straus and Giroux, 1982: 305–25.

Suleiman, Susan. Interview with *Harvard Gazette* (5 Oct. 1990).

Theweleit, Klaus. *Male Fantasies: Women, Floods, Bodies, History.* Trans. Stephen Conway. Minneapolis: U of Minnesota P, 1987.

Vansant, Jaqueline. *Against the Horizon: Feminism and Postwar Austrian Women Writers.* New York: Greenwood Press, 1988.

———. "Gespräch mit Elfriede Jelinek." *Deutsche Bücher* 15.1 (1985): 1–9.

———. "Challenging Austria's Victim Status: National Socialism and Austrian Personal Narratives." *The German Quarterly* 67.1 (1994): 38–57

Winter, Riki. "Gespräch mit Elfriede Jelinek." *Elfriede Jelinek.* Eds. Kurt Bartsch and Günther Höfler. Vienna and Graz: Literaturverlag Droschl, 1991: 9–19.

Young, Frank. "Elfriede Jelinek: Profile of an Austrian Feminist." *Continental, Latin-American and Francophone Women Writers: Selected Papers from the Wichita State University Conference on Foreign Literature, 1984–1985.* Ed. Eunice Myers and Ginette Adamson. London: UP of America, 1987: 97–105.

Zeller, Michael. "Haß auf den Nazi-Vater." *Frankfurter Allgemeine Zeitung* (4 June 1980).

Elisabeth Reichart

Bosmajian, Hamida. *Metaphors of Evil: Contemporary German Literature and the Shadow of Nazism.* Iowa City: U of Iowa P, 1979.

DeMeritt, Linda. "In Search of a Personal Voice." *Austria Kultur* 5.5 (1995): 1–4. Online. Available: www.aci.org/SearchPersonal/1617.html.

———. "The Possibilities and Limitations of Language: Elisabeth Reichart's Fotze." *Out from the Shadows: Essays on Contemporary Austrian Women Writers and Filmmakers.* Ed. Margarete Lamb-Faffelberger. Riverside, CA: Ariadne Press, 1997: 128–42.

DeMeritt, Linda, and Peter Ensberg. "'Für mich ist die Sprache auch ein Schatz': Interview mit Elisabeth Reichart." *Modern Austrian Literature* 29.1 (1996): 1–22.

Eagleton, Terry. *Literary Theory: An Introduction.* Minneapolis: U of Minnesota P, 1975.

Felman, Shoshana and Dori Laub. *Testimony: Crises of Witnessing in Literature, Psychoanalysis, and History.* New York: Routledge, Chapman and Hall, 1992.

Fiddler, Allyson. "Demythologizing the Austrian 'Heimat': Elfriede Jelinek as 'Nestbeschmutzer.'" *From High Priests to Desecrators: Contemporary Austrian Writers.* Eds. Ricarda Schmidt and Moray McGowan. Sheffield: Sheffield Academic Press, 1993: 25–44.

Hauer, Nadine. "NS-Trauma und kein Ende." *Das grosse Tabu: Österreichs Umgang mit seiner Vergangenheit.* Eds. Anton Pelinka and Erika Weinzierl. Vienna: Verlag der Österreichischen Staatsdruckerei, 1987: 28–41.

Herman, Judith. *Trauma and Recovery: The Aftermath of Violence from Domestic Abuse to Political Terror.* New York: Basic Books, 1992.

Herzstein, Robert Edwin. *Waldheim: The Missing Years.* New York: Arbor House/William Morrow, 1988.

Hoffmeister, Donna L. "Female Consciousness and the Holocaust." Commentary to *February Shadows.* Trans. Donna L. Hoffmeister. Riverside, CA: Ariadne Press, 1989: 147–62.

Horwitz, Gordon J. *In the Shadow of Death: Living Outside the Gates of Mauthausen.* New York and Toronto: Free Press, 1990.

Janet, Pierre. *Psychological Healing* [1919] vol.1. Trans. E. Paul and C. Paul. New York: Macmillan, 1925.

Jelinek, Elfriede. "Gespräch mit Elfriede Jelinek." Jacqueline Vansant. *Deutsche Bücher* 15 (1985): 1–9.

Kecht, Maria-Regina. "Faschistische Familienidyllen: Schatten der Vergangenheit in Henisch, Schwaiger und Reichart." *Austrian Writers and the Anschluss: Understanding the Past — Overcoming the Past.* Ed. Donald G. Daviau. Riverside, CA: Ariadne Press, 1991: 313–37.

———. "Resisting Silence: Brigitte Schwaiger and Elisabeth Reichart Attempt to Confront the Past," in *Gender, Patriarchy and Fascism: The Response of Women Writers.* Ed. Elaine Martin. Detroit: Wayne State UP, 1993: 244–73.

Koonz, Claudia. *Mothers in the Fatherland. Women, the Family and Nazi Politics.* New York: St. Martin's Press, 1987.

Krumrey, Marianne. "Quälende Erinnerung." *Neue deutsche Literatur* 35.9 (1987): 184–86.

LaCapra, Dominick. *Representing the Holocaust: History, Theory, Trauma.* Ithaca: Cornell UP, 1994.

Michaels, Jennifer E. "Breaking the Silence: Elisabeth Reichart's Protest Against the Denial of the Nazi Past in Austria." *German Studies Review* 19.1 (1996): 9–27.

Mitscherlich, Alexander and Margarete. *Die Unfähigkeit zu trauern: Grundlagen kollektiven Verhaltens.* Munich: R. Piper & Co. Verlag, 1967.

Parkinson, F., ed. *Conquering the Past: Austrian Nazism Yesterday and Today.* Detroit: Wayne State UP, 1989.

Pauley, Bruce. *From Prejudice to Persecution: A History of Austrian Anti-Semitism.* Chapel Hill: U of North Carolina P, 1992.

———. *Hitler and the Forgotten Nazis: A History of Austrian National Socialism.* Chapel Hill: U of North Carolina P, 1981.

Pelinka, Anton, and Erika Weinzierl, Eds. *Das grosse Tabu: Österreichs Umgang mit seiner Vergangenheit.* Vienna: Verlag der Österreichische Staatsdruckerei, 1987.

Reichart, Elisabeth. "Heute ist morgen: Fragen an den kommunistischen organisierten Widerstand im Salzkammergut." Doctoral dissertation, Universität Salzburg, 1983.

Roscher, Achim. "Elisabeth Reichart im Gespräch." *Neue deutsche Literatur* 35.9 (1987): 129–32.

Schlant, Ernestine. *The Language of Silence: West German Literature and the Holocaust.* New York: Routledge, 1999.

Schwieghofer, Christiana. "Wir haben uns selber betrogen: Steyregg, Wien, Tokio, und retour: Annäherung an die Dichterin Elisabeth Reichart." *Die Presse* (16–17 June 1990).

Wigmore, Juliet. "'Auch Schweigen kann Verrat sein.' Coming to Terms with Women's History: Elisabeth Reichart's *Februarschatten and Komm über den See.*" *From High Priests to Desecrators: Contemporary Austrian Writers.* Eds. Ricarda Schmidt and Moray McGowan. Sheffield: Sheffield Academic Press, 1993: 119–34.

———. "'Vergangenheitsbewältigung' in Austria: The Personal and The Political in Erika Mitterer's *Alle Unsere Spiele* and Elisabeth Reichart's *Februarschatten.*" *German Life and Letters* 44.5 (1991): 477–87.

Wolf, Christa. "Struktur von Erinnerung." Afterword to *Februarschatten.* Berlin: Aufbau Taschenbuch Verlag, 1997: 117–19.

Zeyringer, Klaus. *Innerlichkeit und Öffentlichkeit: Österreichische Literatur der achtziger Jahre.* Tübingen: Francke, 1992.

Conclusion

Felman, Shoshana, and Dori Laub. *Testimony: Crises of Witnessing in Literature, Psychoanalysis, and History.* New York: Routledge, Chapman and Hall, 1992.

Kecht, Maria-Regina. "Faschistische Familienidyllen: Schatten der Vergangenheit in Henisch, Schwaiger und Reichart." *Austrian Writers and the Anschluss: Understanding the Past — Overcoming the Past.* Ed. Donald G. Daviau. Riverside, CA: Ariadne Press, 1991: 313–37.

LaCapra, Dominick. *History and Memory After Auschwitz.* Ithaca: Cornell UP, 1998.

Ryan, Judith. "Postoccupation Movements in West Germany." *Legacies and Ambiguities: Postwar Fiction and Culture in West Germany and Japan.* Eds. Ernestine Schlant and J. Thomas Rimer. Baltimore and London: The Johns Hopkins UP, 1991: 189–206.

Index